NTC's
Dictionary
of
German
False
Cognates

NTC's
Dictionary
of
German
False
Cognates

Geoff Parkes · Alan Cornell

Printed on recyclable paper

NTC Publishing Group
Lincolnwood, Illinois USA

ACKNOWLEDGMENTS

Special thanks are due to Anetta Gänsler-Parkes, who has given invaluable help throughout the project, and to Manuela von Papen, Chris Perkins, and Barbara Pollitzer-Seidlhofer, who have also offered continued support and many helpful suggestions. Other useful contributions have been made by Franz Fries, Gabriele Hübner, and Susi Marek. Finally, we would like to thank students, past and present, of the following institutions; by confronting us with problem words—both intentionally and unintentionally—over many years, they have played an enormous part in determining the subject matter for this book:

Southampton English Language Centre; the Universities of Bonn, Vienna, Zürich, Stuttgart, Braunschweig, Göttingen, Erlangen, Heidelberg; the Pädagogische Hochschule Weingarten; Plymouth Business School.

1996 Printing

Published by National Textbook Company, a division of NTC Publishing Group.
©1992 by NTC Publishing Group, 4255 West Touhy Avenue,
Lincolnwood (Chicago), Illinois 60646-1975 U.S.A.

6 7 8 9 BC 9 8 7 6 5 4 3 2

LIST OF ABBREVIATIONS USED

A	Austrian usage	Fr.	French
adj.	adjective	geol.	geology
adv.	adverb	geom.	geometry
agr.	agriculture	gramm.	grammar
AmE	American English	hist.	historical
anat.	anatomy	hort.	horticultural
arch.	archaic	hum.	humorous
astron.	astronomy	inform.	informal
biol.	biology	intrans.	intransitive
bot.	botany	jdm., jdn.	jemandem, jemanden
BrE	British English	jur.	jurisprudence
chem.	chemistry	masc.	masculine
coll.	colloquial	math.	mathematics
conj.	conjunction	med.	medicine
comm.	commercial	mil.	military
cul.	culinary	mus.	music
D	German usage	naut.	nautical
eccl.	ecclesiastical	neut.	neuter
econ.	economics	pej.	pejorative
elec.	electrical	phys.	physics
esp.	especially	pl.	plural
fig.	figurative	prep.	preposition
fin.	financial	print.	printing
form.	formal	refl.	reflexive
rel.	religion	Sw.	Swiss usage
sex.	sexual	tech.	technical
sl.	slang	theat.	theatrical
s.o.	someone	trans.	transitive
s.t.	something	zool.	zoology

INTRODUCTION

False cognates or "false friends" have long been a familiar problem in language learning and, in some cases, the cause of humorous or embarrassing mistakes. The most notorious are usually the simplest—those cases in which two words look and sound similar but have quite different meanings. Thus someone who is *genial* need not be "genial." A German who says *Ich komme eventuell* may not come "eventually" or indeed at all. And a *Präservativ* is certainly not an additive to prevent food spoiling! Yet just a brief perusal of this volume will reveal that such straightforward cases are in a minority: much more often we are dealing with pairs of words whose meanings overlap in some, but not all, respects. Here the issues are more complex, but just as important, and a study of such partial false cognates will sharpen students' precision in the use of vocabulary as well as help them to avoid mistakes that, at worst, may seriously hamper effective communication.

In theory it would be possible to establish strict criteria for the definition of false cognates: such criteria would lay down precise limits for the degree of formal and/or phonetic similarity necessary to categorize a pair of words as false cognates. But there is no real point in adopting this approach, and in this dictionary we have been more flexible. Thus the reader will find, alongside pairs identical in form or very similar in sound, more divergent pairs which have seemed to us to be interesting and worthy of inclusion. We have even included a few—for example, *selbstbewußt* and *Unternehmer*—where one part of the word bears no resemblance to the corresponding English word. It seemed to us wrong to omit these when our experience has showed us how often they lead to misunderstandings.

It would be impossible to produce a totally definitive dictionary of false cognates, if only because of the lack of generally agreed criteria for defining them and the way in which linguistic change leads to the emergence of new false cognates and the disappearance of old ones (thus "sympathetic" and *sympathisch* are closer together now than a few decades ago). This volume aims at a very wide coverage of the phenomenon and the reader will thus find total and partial false cognates, simple pairs that cause problems for the beginning learner, and also items that are encountered relatively infrequently and are of more interest to the advanced student.

Why list false cognates in a dictionary? Such a work can of course be used as a work of reference, but we feel it is especially useful as a volume that can be worked through systematically or browsed through with profit. One reason for studying false cognates is the aspect of prevention: find out about them before they find you out. Yet there is another aspect, not always recognized. It is generally accepted that vocabulary can be learnt more easily if it is linked to some mnemonic element. Ironically, the very difficulty of false cognates, the "trap" they represent, can help the learner to remember their true meanings having once grasped the source of possible confusion. For example, once the fact that *Schellfisch* and "shellfish" do not mean the same thing is lodged in our minds, this will give the German word greater prominence and, however odd this may seem, make it easier to remember the true meaning of that word—"haddock."

Some general comments about the entries are necessary. On the whole we have not included very technical or specialist usages of German words, in particular those of the sort that the average, educated German-speaking layperson does not know. We have been brief in our treatment of the German translation of the English half of each pair: it is not the task of this volume to replace a comprehensive English–German dictionary, and users should consult one of these if they require further details. We have also included a number of so-called pseudo-anglicisms, i.e., German words formed on the analogy of English and felt by most Germans to be English, but which are not in fact English (e.g., *Dressman, Happy-End, Twen*).

Finally, a large number of false cognates involve German words that are loanwords (*Fremdwörter*) and belong to that rather elevated style level Duden calls *Bildungssprache*—the language of the "educated speaker." In our research we have sometimes found disagreement among native speakers over what these words mean precisely or exactly how they should be used. In such cases we try to represent what seems to be the consensus viewpoint, or to mention the most important divergent opinions if there is no consensus. The authors would of course be pleased to hear from any readers with suggestions for modifications, amendments, and additions.

ABC Can be used as in English to express "the ABC of gardening," etc.; but it also has a military sense: *der ABC-Alarm/ABC-Waffen* atomic, biological, and chemical warning/weapons.

Abort, der Normally "miscarriage," but it is occasionally used to mean "abortion" too. There is a homonym, with usage restricted mainly to South Germany, meaning "lavatory" or "toilet."
Abortion = *die Abtreibung* (more common than *der Abort*)
To abort (intrans., of mother) = *eine Fehlgeburt haben*
(trans., to perform an abortion) = *eine Schwangerschaft abbrechen*

Abrakadabra, das Can be used for the conjurer's magic word, "abracadabra," but also means "nonsense."

absolvieren To take, do, complete—usually a course or an exam. *Tom hat gerade einen Computerkurs absolviert.* Tom has just taken (BrE done) a course on computers.
To absolve someone from sins/from blame = *jdn. von Sünden lossprechen/von Schuld freisprechen*

Achse, die Means both "axis" and "axle."
auf Achse sein to be out and about, to be on the move.
Ax(e) = *die Axt, das Beil*

Achsel, die Shoulder. *Ich konnte nur hilflos zuschauen und mit den Achseln zucken.* All I could do was look on helplessly and shrug my shoulders.
Axle = *die Achse*

Acker, der Field (usually a farmer's field under cultivation). *Geh nicht über diesen Acker! Der Bauer hat den gerade mit Kartoffeln bepflanzt!* Don't walk over that field! The farmer has just sown potatoes there!
Acre = *der Morgen*

adäquat Suitable, fitting. *Die Strafe war dem Delikt des Studenten adäquat.* The punishment was suitable for the student's offense.
Adequate = *genug, ausreichend*

adrett Neat. *Die Krankenschwestern sahen in ihren neuen Uniformen sehr adrett aus.* The nurses looked very neat in their new uniforms.
Adroit = *gewandt, geschickt*

Advokat, der (Sw, A) Lawyer. In Germany the word is regarded as old-fashioned or pejorative. In Germany, the current word is *Rechtsanwalt* or *Rechtsberater.*
Advocate (supporter) = *der Verfechter.* an advocate of social reform *ein Verfechter von Sozialreform*

Affäre, die   Affair (all meanings), i.e., usually a true cognate. Note, however, one important idiomatic exception: *sich aus der Affäre ziehen* to extricate oneself. *Der Politiker konnte sich ganz gut aus der Affäre ziehen.* The politician managed to extricate himself from the incident pretty well.

Affekt, der   Emotion, heat of the moment. *Er hat den Mord im Affekt begangen.* He committed the murder in the heat of the moment.
Effect = *die Wirkung, der Effekt*
To affect = *beeinflussen, betreffen*
To effect = *verwirklichen, bewirken*

Afrikaner(in), der (die)   African (black).
Afrika(a)ner (white inhabitant of South Africa, native speaker of Afrikaans) = *der (die) Afrika(a)nder(in)*

After, der   Anus.
After (prep.) = *nach*
  (conj.) = *nachdem*

Agende, die   Diary, pocket notebook: (eccl.) liturgy.
Agenda (form.) = *die Tagesordnung*
  (inform.) = *das Programm*

Aggregat, das   Aggregate (geol.); also "unit," "(electricity) generator," "set of machines." The word in isolation is somewhat vague, and needs to be seen in a specific context for the meaning to become clear. *Die Schokoladenfabrik hat gerade ein neues Aggregat angeschafft.* The chocolate factory has just acquired a new generator.

agil   Physically agile, but also "sharp," "quick-witted."

Agonie, die   Death throes, death struggle. *Der Patient liegt schon in der Agonie.* The patient is already in his death throes.
Agony (great pain) = *die Qual, große Schmerzen*

Akademiker(in), der (die)   Can have the general meaning of an academic, or bookworm, but more often refers specifically to a university graduate.

Akkord, der   This is used to refer to the method of paying someone per unit produced; "piecework." *Diese Töpfer arbeiten im Akkord; sie verdienen 10 Mark pro Tasse.* These potters are paid per unit/are on piecework; they earn 10 Marks per cup.
Accord (agreement) = *Übereinstimmung*
Of its own accord = *von selbst*

akkreditieren   **1.** To accredit.   **2.** (fin.) To give someone credit (BrE facilities). *Meine Bank hat mich in Höhe von 10.000 Dollar akkreditiert.* My bank has given me credit up to 10,000 dollars.
To accredit something to someone = *jdm. etwas zuschreiben* The discovery of Uranus is accredited to William Herschel. *Die Entdeckung von Uranus wird William Herschel zugeschrieben.*

akkurat Meticulous, precise; neat, tidy. *Er hat die neuen Pläne sehr akkurat ausgearbeitet.* He has worked out the new plans meticulously. *Sie hat eine sehr akkurate Schrift.* She has very neat handwriting.
Accurate = *genau*

akquirieren **1.** (old) To acquire. **2.** (comm.) to solicit (s.o.'s business), to try to get customers, (BrE) to canvass. *Herr Schmidt akquiriert für Zentralheizung.* Mr. Schmidt is trying to get customers to buy central heating.
To acquire = *erwerben, anschaffen*

Akquisition, die (comm.) Soliciting, trying to get customers, (BrE) canvassing.
Acquisition = *die Erwerbung, die Anschaffung*

Akt, der **1.** Act (general, or theater) **2.** Naked person, nude (art, photography) *In unserem Kunstkurs haben wir einen Akt gezeichnet.* In our art course, we drew a nude. **3.** Sexual intercourse.
Act = *die Tat, der Akt*

Akte, die File, record. *Der neue Personalchef möchte Einsicht in alle Akten nehmen.* The new personnel officer wants to have a look at all the files.
Act = *die Tat, der Akt*

Akteur, der **1.** Participant, protagonist. *Die Akteure im Börsenskandal haben alles dementiert.* The protagonists in the stock exchange scandal have denied everything. **2.** Actor.
Actor = *der (die) Schauspieler(in)* (This is far more common than *der Akteur.*)

Aktion, die **1.** (D) Can mean "action," but more often means "campaign," "drive"; also "operation" (mil., police). *Die "Aktion Sorgenkind" hat dieses Jahr schon fünf Millionen Mark gesammelt.* The Save-the-Children Campaign has collected five million marks so far this year. **2.** In Swiss German, *Aktion* frequently refers to a "special offer" in the shops. *Aktion! Alle Strumpfhosen stark reduziert!* Special offer! All tights drastically reduced!
Action = *die Handlung, die Tat, die Aktion*

Aktiva (und Passiva) (pl.) Assets (and liabilities).
Active = *aktiv*

aktivieren Usually means "to activate," but also (comm.) "to enter on the assets side."

Aktualität, die Current relevance, relevance today, topicality. *Aktualitäten* Current events.
Actuality = *die Wirklichkeit*

aktuell This has many translations, depending on context, but it *never* means "actual." The word generally refers to objects or events that are important now, fashionable now, or are of current relevance. *die ak-*

tuelle Lage the current/present situation; *ein aktuelles Thema* a topical issue; *ein aktuelles Kleid* a fashionable dress; *ein aktueller Bericht* an up-to-date report.

Actual = *eigentlich, tatsächlich*

Alarm, der   Means both "alarm" and "alert." *die Alarmanlage* (burglar) alarm. *der Fliegeralarm* Air-raid warning. *der blinde Alarm* False alarm. *alarmbereit* On the alert. *Die nächsten Krankenhäuser halten sich alarmbereit.* The nearest hospitals are on the alert/are standing by.

alarmieren   "To alarm" and "to alert." *Sobald ich sein verdächtiges Verhalten bemerkt hatte, alarmierte ich die Polizei.* As soon as I had noticed his suspicious behavior, I alerted the police. *All dieses Gerede über chemische Waffen hat mich sehr alarmiert.* All this talk about chemical weapons greatly alarmed me.

Alb, der   Elf.

die Alb (D) The hills of Swabia (southwest Germany).

Alps = *die Alpen*

Albtraum, der.   SEE **ALPTRAUM.**

Album, das   Double album (i.e., two long-playing records).

Single album = *die LP*

alert (adj.)   Lively, vivacious.

Alert = *aufmerksam, aufgeweckt*

Alibi, das   Alibi. But *Alibi-* in combinations normally means "token ————." *Bei dieser Prüfungskommission kam ich mir sowohl wie die Alibifrau als auch die Alibinegerin vor.* On that board of examiners, I seemed to be both the token female and the token black.

Alkoholika (pl.)   Alcoholic drinks.

An alcoholic (person) = *der (die) Alkoholiker(in)*

All, das   (Outer) space; the universe.

All = *alle* (+ pl.); *ganz* (+ noun); *sämtliche* (+ pl. noun)

alle   **1.** Used predicatively, this often means that something is used up, finished: there's none left. *Ach nein! Der Rotwein ist alle!* Oh no! There's no red wine left. *Komm—mach das Eis alle!* Come on—finish off the ice cream!   **2.** It is also a colloquial word for "exhausted," "pooped." *Du siehst ganz alle aus!* You look absolutely pooped!

Allee, die   Avenue.

Alley = *die Gasse*

Bowling alley = *die Kegelbahn*

Allüren, die   Airs (BrE airs and graces). *Sie hat in der letzten Zeit wegen ihrer Allüren viele Freunde verloren.* She's lost a lot of friends recently by putting on airs (and graces).

When this behavior is observed among the famous, e.g., film stars, it is often referred to in German with the word *Staralüren*. This can be translated either by "airs (and graces)" again, or by a relevant idiom.

Seit ihrem ersten Film, hat diese Schauspielerin Starallüren. Ever since her first film, this actress has been putting on airs/has thought she's a hot property.

Allure = *die Lockung, der Reiz*

Alm, die   Alpine pasture.

Alms = *die Almosen*

Alms house = *das Armenhaus*

Alp, der   Mythological demon, said to cause nightmares by sitting on a sleeping person's chest. SEE **ALB.**

Alps = *die Alpen*

Alptraum, der   Not, as it seems at first sight, a dream about the Alps, but a nightmare. SEE **ALB.**

A dream about the Alps = *ein Traum von den Alpen*

also   1. So, therefore.   2. (interjection) "Well, well!" "Well, I never!" "There you are !" "You see!" etc. *Also! Du hast dich doch entschieden, mitzukommen!* Well, well! So you've decided to join us after all!

Also = *auch*

Alt-   In compound nouns this usually retains the meaning of "old." *der Altbau* Old building. *die Alttradition* Old tradition. In some compounds, however, "old" is not a possible translation—notably in *das Altbier* A specially brewed dark beer. *altbekannt* Well-known. *altchristlich* Early Christian.

In several combinations, *Alt-* contains the idea of something that has either outlived its usefulness or that needs to be recycled: *das Altmaterial* Scrap. *das Altmetall* Scrap metal. *das Altpapier* waste paper.

Alt, der   (mus.) Alto; contralto. *Sie hat einen schönen Alt.* She has a nice contralto voice. *Der Altsänger* Alto singer. *das Altsaxophon* Alto saxophone. *die Altflöte* Alto flute.

altern   To age, grow old. Of wine it can also mean "to mature." *vorzeitig altern* to become prematurely aged

To alter (trans.) = *ändern, abändern, verändern*

(intrans.) = *sich (ver)ändern*

am anderen Tag   1. This usually means "the next day" or "the following day." *Er ist am Montag angekommen, und am anderen Tag hat er uns das Geld gegeben.* He arrived on Monday and gave us the money the following day.   2. Less often, in contrastive sentences, it can mean "on the other day." *Wir werden die Vorstellungsgespräche am 22. und am 27. Mai führen. An dem einen Tage sehen wir die Klempner und am anderen Tag die Anstreicher.* We're going to hold the interviews on the 22nd and 27th of May. On one day we're seeing plumbers and on the other day decorators.

The other day (i.e., recently) = *vor kurzem, neulich*

ambulant As an outpatient. *Er wurde ambulant behandelt.* He was treated as an outpatient. *ambulante Patienten* Outpatients.

Ambulanz, die 1. The outpatients' department of a hospital. *Nach dem Unfall wurden seine Wunden in der Ambulanz versorgt.* After the accident, his wounds were treated in the outpatients' department. **2.** Ambulance.

analphabetisch Not, as one might think, the opposite of "alphabetical," but "illiterate."

Unalphabetical = *nicht alphabetisch, nicht in alphabetischer Reihenfolge*

Angel, die Can mean a "fishing pole," BrE "fishing-rod"; also the "hinge" of a door. *Nach Komplimenten angeln/fischen* To fish for compliments.

Angel = *der Engel*

Anger, der An old word for a pasture or meadow, and in dialect can be a village square, BrE village green.

Anger = *Wut, der Zorn*

Angina, die In conversation this usually describes nothing more serious than a very sore throat, or tonsillitis! *Ich gehe heute nicht in die Vorlesungen: ich habe eine furchtbare Angina.* I'm not going to lectures today: I have a very sore throat.

Angina (heart condition) = *die Angina pectoris*

Angst, die Fear. *Angst haben* To be afraid. *Ich habe Angst vor Schlangen.* I'm afraid of snakes. In German, the use extends from mild fear right through to paranoia. (*Platzangst* = both claustrophobia and agoraphobia.) In English, especially in literary and theatrical commentaries, the use of "angst" tends to be restricted to the more serious end of that scale, and refers more specifically to tension and/or a threatening atmosphere. In such cases, the German *Angst* is not normally a good translation.

There's usually a lot of angst in a Kafka novel = *Bei einem Roman von Kafka herrscht normalerweise eine bedrohliche Atmosphäre.*

ängstlich Can mean either "anxious" (see below) or "timid." Note that the German *ängstlich* is reserved for descriptions of character or temperament, and is thus much narrower in its usage than the English "anxious." For this reason, "anxious" has various German translations, depending on meaning. *Rehe sind ängstliche Tiere.* Deer are timid animals.

She's anxious by disposition = *Sie ist ein ängstlicher Typ.*

I'm anxious about the children, where on earth are they? = *Ich mache mir Sorgen um die Kinder: wo sind sie bloß geblieben?*

He's anxious to succeed in his new job = *Ihm liegt viel daran, daß er in seinem neuen Job Erfolg hat.*

animieren Can mean "to animate" (a film), but usually means "to prompt," "to encourage," "to stimulate." *Sein faszinierender Vortrag über Wölfe in der Arktis hat mich dazu animiert, eine Reise nach Nord-kanada zu buchen.* His fascinating lecture about wolves in the Arctic prompted me to plan a trip to Northern Canada.

Annonce, die Advertisement, usually of the two- or three-line type in a newspaper. *Wenn wir unseren Fernseher verkaufen wollen, müssen wir eine Annonce in die Zeitung setzen.* If we want to sell our television, we have to put an advertisement in the newspaper.

Announcement (formal/general) = *die Bekanntgabe, die Bekannt-machung*

(over loudspeaker) = *die Durchsage*

(of forthcoming attraction, e.g., a visiting lecturer) = *die Ankündigung*

annoncieren Usually "to advertise." SEE **ANNONCE.** Can occasionally mean "to announce," e.g., a forthcoming marriage or engagement.

Antibabypille, die The (contraceptive) pill. It certainly does not imply that the adults in question are in general anti-baby in outlook!

antik Nothing to do with antics, but "ancient." *der antike Mensch* ancient man. Can also mean "antique" (adj.).

Antics = *die Eskapaden*

(when negative) *die Mätzchen*

Antike, die Antiquity, the ancient world.

Antique = *die Antiquität*

Antiquar(in), der (die) Occasionally does mean an "antiquary," i.e., an expert on, or a dealer in, antiques, ancient sculptures or paintings, etc. Far more often it just means "second-hand bookseller"; the books could be only two or three years old. *Antiquarisch* Second-hand. *Ich habe das Buch antiquarisch gekauft.* I bought the book second-hand.

Antiquariat, das Bookshop selling either genuinely ancient books, or, more probably, any second-hand books. SEE **ANTIQUAR(IN).**

Antiquität, die Not the name for a past period, but the object from a past period: an antique. *Er sammelt Antiquitäten.* He collects antiques.

Antiquity = *das Altertum, die Antike*

apart Refers to the unusual character of something/someone, not to physical separation: "distinctive," "unusual," "striking." *Schauen Sie ihre Kleidung an: sie ist wirklich eine aparte Frau!* Just look at the way she's dressed: she really is a striking woman!

Apart (short distance away) = *zur Seite, beiseite*

Separated (e.g., in a failed marriage) = *getrennt*

Apart from = *abgesehen von*

Apartment, das   Small apartment with only one or two rooms; BrE small flat, one- or two-room flat. SEE **APPARTEMENT**.

Apartment = *die Wohnung*

Apparat, der   Can mean "apparatus," but is usually an appliance, set, gadget, or some specific sort of machinery or equipment. *Sie haben eine neue Stereoanlage gekauft! Was für ein schöner Apparat!* You've bought a new stereo! What a beautiful piece of equipment! *Der Fotoapparat* camera.

Apparatus (e.g., for gymnastics) = *das Gerät*

Appartement, das   Usually used in the same way as DAS **APARTMENT** (Q.V.), but can also refer to a suite of rooms, e.g., in a hotel.

Apartment = *die Wohnung*

Appell, der   Is occasionally used to mean "appeal," e.g., to make an appeal for the hostages' release, though in such cases the verb *appellieren* is nearly always preferred. It usually denotes a military roll call. *Hodgkins ist zum Appell nicht angetreten.* Hodgkins failed to show up for roll call.

Appeal (for charity, for sympathy, to reason, to common sense) = *der Appell, der Aufruf*

(attraction) = *die Attraktion*

To appeal (raise an objection, esp. in court) = *Einspruch erheben*

Approbation, die   Certificate, license to practice. *jdm. die Approbation entziehen* To take away someone's license to practice; to strike someone off. *Dem Doktor Schwarzohr wurde im vorigen Jahr die Approbation entzogen.* Dr. Schwarzohr was struck off (the list of medical practitioners) last year.

Approbation = *die Zustimmung, die Billigung*

(of critics) *der Beifall*

Après-Ski, das   In most cases this is not a false cognate. In German, as in English, it refers to the social gatherings and general merriment after a day on the slopes. In some parts of Germany, however, the word is also used for the clothing worn after skiing; and in Swiss German it can also mean a walk taken after skiing.

Arche, die   Not an "arch" but an "ark," as in "Noah's Ark" (*die Arche Noah*).

Arch = *der Bogen*

Argument, das   This does mean "argument," in the sense of a fact or reason used to support one's point of view. *Hier ist eine Liste von Argumenten für und gegen die Abtreibung.* Here is a list of arguments for and against abortion. It does not, however, mean "argument" in the sense of a quarrel, fight, or BrE row.

Argument (quarrel) = *die Auseinandersetzung*

Armatur, die Fitting, instruments. Most commonly heard in the compound *das Armaturenbrett* the "dashboard" on a car.

Armature (elec.) = *der Anker*

Armband, das Bracelet; watch strap. *die Armbanduhr* Wristwatch.

Armband (e.g., black armband worn at funerals) = *die Armbinde*

Aroma, das Can be used just as in English to mean "aroma," but also means "flavor." *Komm! Wir essen ein Eis! Welches Aroma ißt du am liebsten?* Come on! Let's have an ice cream! What flavor do you like best?

Aroma = *der Duft, das Aroma*

arrangieren, sich Often used in bargaining or haggling contexts, meaning "to come to terms with," "to reach an agreement," "to agree on terms with someone," "to make a deal with someone." *Wir haben uns mit dem Hotelchef bezüglich der Zimmer arrangiert und haben dann einen Sonderpreis bekommen.* We made a deal on the rooms with the hotel manager and got a special price. The simple verb *arrangieren* is used in the same way as the English "to arrange."

Arrest, der Not only "arrest" but also various other types of detention, especially military or educational. *"Sie sind unter Arrest," sagte der Polizist.* "You're under arrest," said the policeman. *Dieser Politiker steht seit zwei Wochen unter Hausarrest.* This politician has been under house arrest for two weeks. *Als Kind wurde Heino oft von seinen Eltern mit Arrest bestraft.* As a child, Heino was often grounded by his parents as a punishment. *Der Soldat ist mit Hausarrest bestraft worden.* The soldier has been punished by being confined to barracks.

Arrest = *die Festnahme, die Verhaftung, der Arrest*

Arsen, das Arsenic.

Arson = *die Brandstiftung*

Art, die **1.** Usually means "kind," "sort," "type." *Welche Käseart bevorzugst du?* What sort of cheese do you prefer? *Diese Art von Film gefällt mir überhaupt nicht.* I don't like this type of film at all. **2.** Can also mean "manner," "style," or "way." *Sie meinte, ich würde den Bettler beschimpfen, aber das ist nicht meine Art.* She thought I was going to swear at the beggar, but that's not my style.

Art (fine art: drawing, painting, etc.) = *die Kunst*

(skill, special ability) = *das Geschick, die Kunst*

artig Nice, kind, polite, good, well-behaved. It is used mainly for children and animals. *Sei doch artig, Bello! Setz dich!* Be a good dog, Bello! Sit down!

An arty person = *ein Künstlertyp*

Artist(in), der (die) This means "performing artist," or "artiste," especially in the circus.

Artist (painter) = *der (die) Künstler(in)*

As, das Not an "ass," but an "ace" (the card); an "ace" (untouchable serve, e.g., at tennis); or an "expert," as in "an ace baseball player" (*ein Baseballas*). In music, *As* means "A flat."

As (comparison) = *wie*

Ass (donkey) = *der Esel*

Aspekt, der Besides "aspect," this somewhat formal word can also mean "point of view." *Unter diesem Aspekt betrachtet, sieht das Problem erheblich schwieriger aus.* Seen from this point of view, the problem seems considerably more difficult.

Aspect = *der Aspekt, die Seite*

Assessor(in), der (die) A fairly low rank in the German hierarchy of civil servants. A teacher, for example, who has finished training but has not yet been tenured is sometimes described as *ein Assessor.* (This is one stage higher than *ein Referendar.*) There is no single translation for this, but "junior ———" (in our example, "junior teacher") probably gets nearest.

Assessor (for insurance claims) = *der Schätzer*

      (university examiner) = *der (die) Prüfer(in)*

      (tax inspector) = *der (die) Finanzbeamte(-tin)*

Assistent(in), der (die) This normally means an assistant teacher, i.e., a student of foreign languages who goes abroad for a year to practice the language being studied, while teaching his/her mother tongue at a school. It is also one rank of "junior professor" at university.

Assistant (general) = *der (Mit)helfer*

      (shop assistant) = *der (die) Verkäufer(in)*

Asyl, das This sometimes refers to a building providing shelter, but it is no longer used to mean a mental asylum. More often nowadays it refers to abstract forms of shelter, notably political asylum. *Drei Turner aus diesem Land haben uns um Asyl gebeten.* Three gymnasts from that country have asked us for political asylum. *das Obdachlosenasyl* Hostel for the homeless.

(Mental) asylum = *die Irrenanstalt.* It is important to note that this German expression, like its English counterpart, carries very negative connotations. *Die (Nerven)heilanstalt* (mental home) and *die psychiatrische Klinik* (mental hospital) are perhaps more worth learning.

Athlet(in), der (die) Usually means "athlete," i.e., a sportsman, just as in English. It can also, however, mean a "he-man": someone who looks muscular and strong, but who in fact might not be athletic, in the sporting sense, at all. *Am Samstag ist Lulu bei unserer Party mit einem echten Athleten aufgetaucht: zwei Meter groß und Muskeln so breit!* Lulu turned up at our party on Saturday with a real he-man: six feet six tall and muscles out to here!

Athlete (general, all sports) = *der (die) Athlet(in)*
(track and field) = *der (die) Leichtathlet(in)*

Attacke, die   Usually means "attack," but can also be a "cavalry charge."

Attack = *der Angriff, die Attacke*

attackieren   To attack, but also "to make a cavalry charge."

To attack = *angreifen, attackieren*

Attest, das   Certificate, esp., doctor's certificate, medical excuse, BrE sick-note. *Fritz gab dem Sportlehrer sein Attest und verließ die Sporthalle.* Fritz gave the athletic teacher his medical excuse and left the gymnasium.

attestieren   To certify; to provide someone with a certificate or medical excuse/BrE sick-note. SEE **ATTEST.** *Ehe Sie drei Tage frei nehmen, Herr Müller, müssen Sie Ihre Krankheit von einem Arzt attestieren lassen.* Before you take three days off, Mr. Müller, you'll have to get a medical excuse from a doctor.

To attest to something (someone's honesty, truthfulness, etc.) = *etwas bestätigen/bescheinigen*
(the authenticity of signatures, documents, photocopies) = *beglaubigen*

Auditorium, das   Lecture-hall. *Das Audimax* (short for *das Auditorium Maximum*) the main lecture-hall at a university.

Auditorium (in a theater or cinema) = *der Zuschauerraum*

ausländisch   Foreign; from overseas, from abroad. *Für ausländische Waren muß eine Sondergebühr entrichtet werden.* A special duty must be levied on foreign goods.

Outlandish (clothes, appearance) = *sonderbar, wunderlich*
(behavior) = *befremdend*

Autograph, das   An author's original manuscript. (This is also, in fact, a little-known meaning of the English word "autograph.")

Autograph (famous person's signature) = *das Autogramm*

Automat, der   Vending-machine, e.g., for chocolates, cigarettes. *der Spielautomat* Slot-machine; fruit-machine, (BrE) one-armed bandit.

Automat = *das Automatenrestaurant*

Automaton (robot) = *der Roboter*

Autoskooter.   SEE **SKOOTER.**

Autostop(p), der   Can mean "autostop," i.e., the automatic shut-off mechanism on cassette decks, etc. It is also, however, the word for "hitchhiking." *Autostop(p) machen, per Autostop(p) fahren* To hitchhike. *Wir sind von Paris nach Rom per Autostop gefahren.* We hitchhiked from Paris to Rome.

avisieren   Means "to advise," but only in the sense of "to send notification of," "to notify."

To advise (to offer advice, help) = *raten, beraten*

B

Backe, die   Refers to either of two parts of the body, but not in the areas one might think: "cheek" or "buttock."

Back (part of body) = *der Rücken*

(of book, piece of paper, etc.) = *der Hinterteil, die Rückseite*

(of chair) = *die Rückenlehne*

Bad, das   Bath; bathroom, i.e., room containing a bathtub, though not necessarily a toilet as well; swim. *Ein Bad nehmen* can mean either "to take a swim" or "to take a bath," so the context is all-important. Town names beginning with the word "Bad" are spas, or health resorts, often with numerous clinics. Such clinics usually offer medicinal baths, and many have swimming pools too: a double reason for calling the towns "Bad-something"! A few examples of such towns are: *Baden-Baden, Bad Kreuznach, Bad Waldsee, Bad Dürrheim, Bad Homburg.*

baden   To take/have a bath; to take/have a swim; to bathe someone/to give someone a bath, esp., a child; to clean a wound, BrE to bathe a wound. *Ich schwitze fürchterlich: ich muß unbedingt baden.* I'm sweating terribly: I simply have to take a bath. *Das Wetter ist so schön! Wollen wir heute nachmittag baden gehen?* The weather's so lovely! Shall we go swimming this afternoon? *Barbara hat gerade ihre Tochter Maria gebadet, weil sie so schmutzig war.* Barbara has just given her daughter Maria a bath because she was so dirty.

To bathe (clean a wound) = *säubern, baden*

(swim) = *schwimmen, baden*

Bagage, die   **1.** The meaning "baggage" is somewhat dated now; more often it means "riff-raff," "low types." *Er hat gestern abend wieder die ganze Bagage vom Gasthaus mitgebracht.* Last night he brought all the riff-raff from the pub with him again.   **2.** In Swiss German, it can also mean "trouble," "difficulty."

Baggage = *das Gepäck*

Bagatelle, die   While English has two widespread meanings of this word, German has only one: "trivial thing," "trifling matter," "matter of no importance."

Bagatelle (toy-sized pinball game) = *das Tivoli*

(trifling matter) = *die Bagatelle, die Nebensächlichkeit*

Ballaststoffe (pl.)   Nothing to do with ballast, but "roughage" in one's diet.

Ballast = *der Ballast*

Ballon, der   Balloon, but also "carboy," "demijohn" (chem.).

Band, der   Volume, i.e., one in a series of books. *Band 2* Volume 2. *Ein gewaltiger Band* a huge book. *Das spricht Bände über ihn.* That speaks volumes about him.

Band (mus.) = *die Band, die Kapelle*

Band, das   Has a vast number of meanings. Only the most important are listed here.   **1.** Ribbon (worn in hair, round a hat, etc.).   **2.** Tape (for recording)—referred to either as *Band* or *Tonband. etwas auf Tonband aufnehmen* to record something (from another machine, e.g., another tape-recorder); *etwas auf Tonband sprechen* to record something (by speaking into a microphone).   **3.** *das Fließband* = conveyor belt, production line, assembly line. *etwas am laufenden Band herstellen* To produce something nonstop. *etwas am laufenden Band tun* To keep on doing something.   **4.** Ligament. *der Bänderriß* Torn ligaments. *die Bänderzerrung* Pulled ligaments. *Der Fußballspieler mußte wegen eines schweren Bänderrisses seine Karriere aufgeben.* Because of seriously torn ligaments, the football player had to give up his career.   **5.** (radio) Wavelength, frequency, band.

Band (mus.) = *die Band, die Kapelle*

Bandage, die   Means "bandage" when used literally to describe what one puts around wounds, but used figuratively it denotes various kinds of toughness. *Das sind harte Bandagen.* That's really tough (luck). *Der Lehrer hat den Schüler mit harten Bandagen angefaßt.* The teacher got quite tough/strict with the pupil. *ohne Bandagen* With the gloves off.

Bande, die (coll.)   Gang, crew, bunch. In sport it can also mean "cushion" (billiards), "fence" (riding), or "crash-barrier" (ice-skating). *Wir spielen ohne Bande* (indoor soccer). We'll play off the walls.

Band (mus.) = *die Band, die Kapelle*

bang(e) (adj.)   Scared, frightened. SEE **BANGE**.

Bange, die   Normally found in the phrase *Bange haben* = to be afraid, to be worried. *Ich habe keine Bange vor der Prüfung morgen.* I'm not worried about the test tomorrow. *Nur keine Bange!* Don't worry!

Bang (noise) = *der Knall* There was a bang. *Es hat geknallt.*

The gun went bang = *Die Pistole hat peng gemacht.*

The balloon went bang = *Der Ballon ist geplatzt.*

bangen   To be afraid. *Er bangt um seine Karriere.* He's worried about his career.

To bang = *knallen, peng machen*

Bank, die   **1.** Bank (financial institution; pl. = *die Banken*).   **2.** Bench (e.g., in a park; pl. = *die Bänke*).

Bank (of river) = *das Ufer*

Bankett, das   also *die Bankette.* Usually the shoulder, or BrE verge(s), at the side of a road. *Bankette nicht befahrbar* Soft shoulder/Soft verges. It can also mean "banquet," though *das Festessen* is perhaps the more common word for this.

Bann, der   **1.** Spell. *Er steht im Bann der Schauspielerin.* He's under the actress's spell.   **2.** In church history it also means "excommunication." *Sie haben den Priester in den Bann getan.* They excommunicated the priest.

Ban = *das Verbot; ein Alkoholverbot* a ban on alcohol.

bannen   **1.** To bewitch, captivate, enthrall. *Er wurde von ihren grünen Augen gebannt.* He was bewitched by her green eyes. *wie gebannt* Fascinated, spellbound.   **2.** To exorcise, drive out. *böse Geister bannen* To exorcise evil spirits.   **3.** To avert. *eine Gefahr bannen* To avert a danger

To ban = *verbieten*

Baracke, die   Hut, shack, especially in slum areas. *Das Barackenlager* often means a refugee camp.

Barracks (mil.) = *die Kaserne*

Bark, die (naut.)   Bark (BrE barque), i.e., a large sailing ship with three or more masts. SEE **BARKE.**

Bark (of tree) = *die Rinde, die Borke*

Barke, die (naut.)   Skiff, i.e., a small boat, powered either by oars, sail, or motor. SEE **BARK.**

Bark (of tree) = *die Rinde, die Borke*

Barkeeper, der   Pseudo-anglicism meaning "bartender" (BrE "barman" or "barmaid").

Barmixer, der   Pseudo-anglicism meaning "bartender," "cocktail mixer."

Mixer (soft drink added to whiskey, gin, etc.): There is no single word in German to describe soft drinks, cherries, etc., which are often added to spirits or wines to make long drinks or cocktails. Such things are referred to in a general way as *die anderen Zutaten.* SEE **MIXER.**

Basis-   Although *Basis* on its own usually means "basis," it rarely retains this meaning in compound nouns. *die Basisarbeit* The groundwork. *die Basisgruppe* Action group (usually radical). In politics and labor unions, *die Basis* means "the grass roots supporters," "the rank and file."

Bastard, der   This is nothing like as strong as its English equivalent, and does not really count as a swearword in German. It means "hybrid," "cross," "half-breed," (BrE) "half-caste."

Bastard (literally) = *ein uneheliches Kind*
       (as swearword) = *der Scheißkerl*

Batterie, die   This usually means "battery," but has a second, unrelated meaning. *Die (Misch)batterie* in the shower-room means the "regulator," or "mixer," controlling the flow of hot and cold water through the faucets.

Beefsteak, das This does not usually refer to a beefsteak in the American or British sense, but means "hamburger" or "minute steak."
Beefsteak = *das Steak*

Beet, das In gardening, this means "bed" or "patch." *das Blumenbeet* flower bed
Beet = *die Rübe, die Bete*
BrE Beetroot = *die rote Bete, die rote Rübe*
Sugar beet = *die Zuckerrübe*

Beginnen, das Enterprise, scheme, plan.
Beginning = *der Beginn, der Anfang*

Beige, die This often means "heap" or "pile," especially in South Germany, Switzerland, and Austria. The German adjective *beige*, with a small "b," denoting a color, is not a false cognate.

bekommen 1. To get, receive. *Gestern habe ich eine Postkarte aus Australien bekommen.* I got a postcard from Australia yesterday. 2. (in restaurant) To have. *Ich bekomme zwei Würstchen, bitte.* I'll have two sausages, please. 3. (a child) To have, expect. *Frau Lobitz bekommt nächsten Monat Zwillinge.* Mrs. Lobitz is expecting twins next month. 4. In the context of debts and digestive problems, there is no single-word translation for *bekommen:* the English equivalent takes on a different structure. *Ich bekomme 15 Mark von dir für das Wörterbuch.* You owe me 15 Marks for the dictionary. *Spirituosen bekommen mir nicht: ich kriege sofort Magenschmerzen.* Spirits don't agree with me: I get stomach pains right away.
To become = *werden*

Benzin, das (and in a few dialects **der**) Gas(oline); (BrE) petrol.
Benzine = *das Leichtbenzin*

beraten To advise. *Er wurde schlecht beraten.* He was given bad advice.
To berate (scold) = *auszanken, schelten*

Berliner, der Not only an inhabitant of Berlin, but also a doughnut—the solid, round type with jam in the middle. *die Berliner Weiße* A light, fizzy beer with a dash of raspberry juice or woodruff—a surprisingly delicious mixture!

besiegen To beat, defeat, conquer.
To besiege (in battle) = *belagern*
(fig., e.g., with requests, offers, etc.) = *überschütten*
(to pester) = *bestürmen*

beten To pray, say one's prayers.
To bet = *wetten*

Beule, die Can mean a "boil," or a "bump" on one's body (e.g., after one knocks one's head); but it also means a "dent," e.g., in a car after an accident.
Boil (med.) = *der Furunkel, die Beule*

bewahren   To protect, keep, preserve. *Im Falle einer Notlandung, müssen Sie Ruhe bewahren.* In the event of an emergency landing, you must keep calm. *aufbewahren*   **1.** (food) To keep.   **2.** (papers, documents, valuables) To look after, to take good care of. *Du solltest diese Medaille sorgfältig aufbewahren.* You should take good care of this medal.

To beware of someone/something = *sich vor jdm./etwas hüten*

bewähren, sich   To prove oneself/itself; to prove one's worth; to prove worthwhile. *Smith hat sich schon in seinem neuen Job bewährt.* Smith has already proved his worth in his new job.

To beware of someone/something = *sich vor jdm./etwas hüten*

Biene, die   Not a "bean," but a "bee."

Bean = *die Bohne*

Bienenstich, der   The culinary meaning crops up more often than the literal meaning of "bee sting." It is a long, thin cake with icing and almonds on top and is filled with custard or vanilla sauce.

Bier, das   This means the drink "beer," and has nothing to do with funerals. *das ist nicht dein Bier!* That's none of your business! *der Bierbauch* A pot-belly. *eine Bierleiche* A drunk.

Bier = *die Bahre*

Biest, das   Not used in quite the same way as "beast," even figuratively. It means a "(little) wretch" or "brat" (of a child); or a "cow," a "bitch" (of a woman). *Ihr Sohn ist vielleicht ein Biest!* Her son really is a little brat!

Beast = *das Tier*

bigott   Over-pious, over-devout.

Bigoted = *intolerant, eifernd*

Bilanz, die   While this can mean "balance" or "balance sheet," it is often used in the phrase *Bilanz ziehen* to mean "to take stock of something." *Bevor wir unsere Geschäfte weiter ausdehnen, sollten wir erst einmal Bilanz ziehen.* Before we expand our business, we should take stock of the situation.

Balance (bodily) = *das Gleichgewicht*
(contrast or change from one's usual activity) = *der Ausgleich*
(scales) = *die Waage*
(harmony) = *die Ausgewogenheit*

bilanzieren   **1.** To balance.   **2.** (fig.) To assess, BrE to weigh up. *Wie kann man den Erfolg dieses Projekts bilanzieren?* How can the success of this venture be assessed?

To balance (weigh up) = *abwägen*
(neutralize, compensate for) = *ausgleichen*
(cause to balance) = *balancieren*
(intrans., be in equilibrium) = *balancieren*

bilden **1.** To educate. *Ein gebildeter Mensch.* An educated person. **2.** To form. *Es gelang den kleineren Parteien nicht, eine neue Regierung zu bilden.* The smaller parties didn't succeed in forming a new government. **3.** To set up. *Um die Durchführbarkeit unserer Baupläne beurteilen zu können, müssen wir eine Expertenkommission bilden.* To judge the viability of our building plans, we have to set up a committee of experts.
To build = *bauen, konstruieren*

Bildung, die Education; formation; setting up. SEE BILDEN. *In seiner Freizeit macht er viel für seine Bildung:* He does a lot in his spare time for his education. *Die Bildung einer Tochtergesellschaft im Ausland ist mit Schwierigkeiten verbunden.* The formation of a subsidiary abroad involves quite a few difficulties. *eine Bildungsreise* An educational trip. *eine Bildungslücke* A gap in one's education.
Building = *das Gebäude, der Bau, die Konstruktion*

Billet(t), das This is still frequently used in Swiss German to mean "ticket."
Billet (mil.) = *das Quartier, die Unterkunft*

Billiarde, die A quadrillion, i.e., 10^{15}, or 1,000,000,000,000,000.
Billiards = *das Billard(spiel)*

Billion, die A trillion, i.e. 10^{12}, or 1,000,000,000,000.
Billion (10^9) = *die Milliarde,* i.e., 1,000,000,000

Bindung, die Means "binding" only in the context of ski bindings. Otherwise it is a "relationship," "tie," or "bond." *Seine enge Bindung an seine Schwester war der Grund dafür, daß er nach Hause zurückkehrte.* His close ties with his sister caused him to return home.
Binding = *das Binden*
(of book) = *der Einband*
(sewing) = *das Band*

Biskuit, das or **der** (cul.) Sponge. *der Biskuitkuchen* Sponge (cake) (soft). *der Löffelbiskuit* Sponge finger (brittle).
Biscuit = *das Brötchen*
(BrE, AmE cookie) = *der Keks*
(BrE, color) = *beige*

Blackout, das or **der** This shares the English theatrical sense (lights going out after a joke) and sometimes the medical sense (losing consciousness), but in conversation Germans also use it to denote a mental block: a total—but temporary—lapse of memory. *Bei der Gerichtsverhandlung sagte er aus, daß er kurz vor dem Unfall einen Blackout hatte und sich nicht mehr erinnern konnte, wie es zu dem Unfall kam.* At the trial he stated that he had had a mental block just before the accident, and that he could no longer remember how the accident happened.
To have a blackout (med., = to faint) = *in Ohnmacht fallen*
Blackout (wartime) = *die Verdunklung*

blamabel This means "shameful" rather than "blamable." *Die Nieder-lage des Tabellenführers war deshalb so blamabel, weil das gegnerische Team nur in der zweiten Liga war.* The defeat of the league leaders was so shameful because their opponents were merely a second-division team. Blamable = *schuld, schuldig*

blamieren To embarrass someone, make a fool of someone, show someone up. *Bei der Party gestern hat mich mein Mann ganz schön blamiert: er hat den Gästen alle meine Jugendsünden erzählt.* My husband really embarrassed me at the party yesterday: he told the guests all the guilty secrets of my youth. *sich blamieren* To show oneself up, to make a fool of oneself. *Beim Empfang des Bürgermeisters habe ich mich ganz schön blamiert: ich war der einzige Gast ohne Krawatte.* I really made a fool of myself at the mayor's reception yesterday: I was the only guest without a necktie.

To blame someone (for something) = *jdm. die Schuld (an etwas) geben; jdn. (einer Sache) beschuldigen*

blank Shiny, bright; bare. *Jeden Sonntag wird Tommys neues Fahrrad blank poliert.* Every Sunday Tommy's new bicycle is polished till it shines. *blanke Augen* Bright eyes. *Nach der Party war das Büfett wie blank gefegt.* After the party the cold buffet was stripped bare. *blanker Unsinn* Utter nonsense.

Blank (adj.) = *leer, unausgefüllt, verständnislos*
(in a gun) = *die Platzpatrone*
To draw a blank = *kein Glück haben*
Blank check = *der Blankoscheck*

blau 1. Though this does mean "blue," it has several idiomatic meanings. *ein blauer Fleck* A bruise. *ein blaues Auge* A black eye. *ein blaues Wunder erleben* To experience a nasty shock, usually as a result of laziness, carelessness, apathy, etc. *Wenn du dein Studium nicht ernster nimmst, wirst du demnächst ein blaues Wunder erleben!* If you don't take your studies more seriously, you'll get a nasty shock! 2. (coll.) Drunk. *Wir waren alle blau.* We were all drunk.

blauäugig 1. Blue-eyed. 2. (fig.) Naive, starry-eyed. *Dieses Mädchen ist vielleicht blauäugig!* This girl really is naive!

Blende, die 1. Most commonly, aperture (on a camera). *Welche Blende brauche ich bei diesen Lichtverhältnissen?* What aperture do I need in these light conditions? 2. Sun-visor, shade, blind, screen. With such meanings, *-blende* normally appears as part of a compound noun. *Anstelle von Vorhängen haben wir an unseren Bürofenstern Sonnenblenden.* Instead of curtains, we have (sun)blinds up at our windows.

Blend = *die Mischung*

blenden To blind, dazzle. *Kannst du bitte die Stehlampe umdrehen? Das Licht blendet mich.* Can you turn the lamp round please? The light's blinding me. *blendend weiße Zähne* dazzlingly white teeth.

To blend = *(ver)mischen, mixen, einrühren*

Blender (machine) = *der Mixer, das Mixgerät*

blind Means "blind," but frequently something else in compounds. *der blinde Passagier* Stowaway. *der Blinddarm* Appendix. *der Blindenhund* Guide-dog. *die Blindschleiche* Slow-worm. *die Blindenschrift* Braille. *der blinde Alarm* False alarm. *Ein blindes Huhn findet auch mal ein Korn* Anyone can get lucky sometime or other!

blinken To indicate, signal, or flash (especially of cars); to gleam (of eyes). *Bevor man nach links oder rechts abbiegt, muß man rechtzeitig blinken.* Before you turn left or right, you have to signal in good time.

To blink = *blinzeln, zwinkern*

Blinker, der Turn signal, (BrE) indicator (on a vehicle).

Blinkers (on a horse) = *die Scheuklappen* He has a blinkered attitude toward life. *Er läuft mit Scheuklappen durchs Leben.*

Blitz, der (Flash of) lightning; flash (on a camera). *blitzschnell* as quick as a flash. *wie ein geölter Blitz* like greased lightning.

Blitz (mil.) = *der Blitzangriff, der Blitzkrieg*
　　　　(by air) *der Luftangriff*

blitzen This verb does not refer to bombing, but to lightning. *Es hat gerade geblitzt!* I just saw a flash of lightning!

To blitz (mil.) = *heftig bombardieren*

Block, der Usually means "block," but note *der (Notiz)block* notepad. *ein blockfreies Land* A nonaligned country. *die Blockflöte* (mus.) Recorder.

Two blocks farther on = *zwei Straßen weiter*

Blockhaus, das Can mean "blockhouse," i.e., a wooden fortification with holes for defensive fire, but more often means "log cabin."

blockieren 1. To block. 2. To (form a) blockade. *Die Boote der streikenden Fischer haben die Einfahrt zum Hafen blockiert.* The boats of the striking fishermen have formed a blockade across the harbor. 3. To lock, to jam. *Als ich in die Kurve hineinfuhr, haben die Bremsen blockiert.* As I drove around the bend, my brakes locked.

blubbern 1. To bubble. *Das heisse Öl im Fonduetopf blubberte, als wir den Deckel abnahmen.* The hot oil in the fondue pot was bubbling when we took the lid off. 2. To mumble, mutter. *Der alte Mann im Krankenhaus blubbert den ganzen Tag vor sich hin; keiner kann ihn verstehen.* The old man in the hospital mumbles away all day long; no one can understand him.

To blubber (cry) = *heulen, flennen*

blutig This does mean "bloody" in the context of cuts, fights, operations, etc., but there are a couple of important exceptions. *ein blutiger Anfänger* A complete beginner.
Das ist mein blutiger Ernst. I'm deadly serious.
A bloody beginner (mainly BrE, with "bloody" used as a swearword to show annoyance) = *ein verdammter Anfänger.*

Bohne, die A "bean," not a "bone."
Bone = *der Knochen*
(in fish) *die Gräte*
backbone = *das Rückgrat*

bohren To bore (i.e., to make a hole), but perhaps more often "to drill." *Nicht weit von hier bohren sie nach Öl.* They're drilling for oil not far from here. *in der Nase bohren* To pick one's nose. *Der kleine Maximilian bohrt liebend gerne in der Nase.* Little Maximilian simply loves picking his nose.
To bore someone = *jdn. langweilen* He bores me stiff/to tears. *Er langweilt mich zu Tode.*

Boiler, der Water heater, hot-water tank; BrE immersion heater. *Schaltest du bitte den Boiler an?* Could you turn the hot water on, please?
Boiler = *der Warmwasserbereiter*
(ships, engines) *der (Dampf)kessel*

bombastisch This means "bombastic" with reference to someone's way of talking. Otherwise it means "overdone," "exaggerated," or "ostentatious," especially of furniture, decorations, clothes, or building style. *Das Haus von den Yuppies war sehr bombastisch eingerichtet.* The furnishing in the yuppies' house was terribly overdone.

Bombe, die Bomb; also "ace" (at sport). *die Geldbombe* Night deposit (for posting into banks' letter boxes at night). *die Eisbombe* (cul.) Bombe glacée.

bomben (coll.) To smash or slam, usually in ball games. *Er hat den Ball ins Tor gebombt.* He slammed the ball into the net.
To bomb (e.g., a town) = *bombardieren*

Boot, das Not a "boot," but a "boat."
Boot = *der Stiefel*
(BrE, = trunk of a car) = *der Kofferraum*

Bowle, die This is a summer punch, usually consisting of strawberries, white wine, champagne, and a dash of some spirit such as rum. It is traditional and well-loved at parties, especially garden parties, over much of German-speaking Europe. Occasionally it also refers to the receptacle for this drink, i.e., the punchbowl.
Bowl = *die Schüssel*

Box, die   This rarely means "box," and is normally the loudspeaker of a stereo system. It is thus usually heard in the plural. *Ich muß unbedingt neue Boxen für meine Stereoanlage besorgen.* I simply must get hold of some new loudspeakers for my stereo. *die Boxen* (pl., motor racing) pits.
Box (chocolates, matches) = *die Schachtel*
    (cardboard) = *der Karton, die Kiste*
    (tools) = *der Kasten*
    (savings, collections) = *die Büchse*

boxen   To box, but also "to punch," "to hit," "to push one's way through." *Die Polizei war hinter ihm her; er hat sich durch die Menge geboxt und ist verschwunden.* The police were after him; he pushed his way through the crowd and vanished.

Boy, der   Bellboy or pageboy in a hotel. Compounds ending in *-boy* often do not refer to boys at all. *der Servierboy* A serving trolley in a restaurant. *der Serviceboy* A similar device on wheels, but in a garage, carrying tools.
Boy = *der Junge*

Branche, die   Usually used in business contexts for "field," "department," "area," "trade." *Bitte stellen Sie mir keine Fragen über Chemie; das ist nicht meine Branche.* Please don't ask me any questions about chemistry; that's not my field. *Er hat zwanzig Jahre lang als Goldschmied gearbeitet; dann hat er die Branche gewechselt und ist Schriftsteller geworden.* He worked as a goldsmith for twenty years, then changed his trade and became a writer.
Branch (tree) = *der Zweig*
    (of business, in another town/country) = *die Zweigstelle, die Filiale, die Geschäftsstelle*

Brand, der   **1.** Fire or blaze. *Die Scheune ist gestern abend von Fanatikern in Brand gesetzt worden.* The barn was set on fire by fanatics last night. **2.** (med.) Gangrene.   **3.** (hort.) Blight.   **4.** (coll.) Terrific thirst.
Brand (of goods) = *die Marke*
    (on a horse) = *das Brandzeichen*

branden   To break, crash, beat (waves on seashore). *Das Meer ist die ganze Nacht gegen die Hafenmauer gebrandet.* The sea crashed against the harbor wall all night long.
To brand (animals) = *mit einem Brandzeichen kennzeichnen*
To brand someone a liar = *jdn. als Lügner brandmarken*

Brandung, die   Surf, breakers. *Das Liebespaar saß bei Mondlicht am Strand und lauschte der Brandung.* The lovers sat on the beach in the moonlight listening to the breakers.

braun   Nearly always means the color brown, but that is not the meaning in the context of the Third Reich. Both before and during the Second

World War, *die Braunen* was one expression for "Nazis"—a reference to the brown shirts worn by certain ranks. *Diese Stadt war in der Kriegszeit sehr braun.* There were a lot of Nazis in this town during the war.

Braut, die Not only a bride but a "bride-to-be," i.e., a "fiancée." Also slang for a "regular girlfriend," a "steady."

brav 1. Good, well-behaved; nice, decent, respectable. *Tilly ist schon immer eine brave Katze gewesen.* Tilly has always been a well-behaved cat. *Die Töchter von Frau Grunch sind alle viel zu brav, um in eine Disko zu gehen.* Mrs. Grunch's daughters are all far too respectable to go to a disco. 2. (pejorative) Tame, unadventurous. *Das Kleid, das Gudrun kaufte, war ganz brav: weitgeschnitten, hochgeschlossen, und knöchellang.* The dress that Gudrun bought was pretty unadventurous: loose-fitting, with a high neckline, and down to her ankles.

Brave = *mutig, tapfer*

Bravo As a reaction, this can be a congratulation, just as in English, but it is also used mid-sentence to mean "very well," "with flying colors." *Klaus hat seine Fahrprüfung mit Bravo bestanden.* Klaus passed his driving test with flying colors.

brechen This is the normal word for "to break," but it is also one way of saying "to be sick," "to vomit." (Alternatives are *erbrechen* and *sich erbrechen*.) *Nach dem Abendessen im Fischrestaurant mußte er die ganze Nacht brechen.* After dinner in the fish restaurant, he was up all night vomiting.

Brief, der Letter (sent through the mail).

Brief (instruction given to attorney or company) = *der Auftrag*
  (legal document) = *der Schriftsatz*

Brillant, der Diamond.

Brilliant (adj., of person) = *hervorragend, brillant*
  (of sunshine) = *strahlend*

bringen To bring or to take. German does not distinguish in the same way as English between movement toward the speaker (bring), movement away from the speaker (take), and movement between two distant parties (take). Also, the English "bring" frequently corresponds to the German *mitbringen*. *Tony brachte das Auto in die Werkstatt, aber ich blieb zu Hause.* Tony took the car to the garage but I stayed at home. *Bring mir bitte meine Brille: sie liegt auf dem Tisch.* Please bring me my glasses: they're on the table. *Wenn ich dich am Sonntag besuche, bringe ich dir eine Flasche Wein mit.* When I come and visit you on Sunday, I'll bring a bottle of wine.

Broschüre, die This is indeed a brochure (or booklet) in Germany and Austria, but in Switzerland it is a common expression for "paperback book."

Brot, das Means both bread in general and a loaf of bread. *Guten Morgen. Ich möchte bitte zwei Brote.* Good morning, I'd like two loaves of bread, please. Informally it can also mean "slice of bread" or "open sandwich." *ein belegtes Brot* usually means "an open sandwich," but is occasionally also used for "a closed sandwich." *ein Käsebrot* A cheese sandwich (usually open).

Bruder, der Not only "brother" but also a colloquial word for "guy," "chap," "character." *Er ist vielleicht ein komischer Bruder!* He really is a funny guy. *ein warmer Bruder* A gay guy. *ein zwielichtiger Bruder* A shady character.

Brust, die Breast, or chest. The German word is certainly not confined to females! *Der Gewichtheber aus Australien hatte eine sehr haarige Brust.* The weightlifter from Australia had a very hairy chest. Note also two idiomatic uses: *Wollen wir schnell einen zur Brust nehmen?* Shall we have a quick drink? *Der verlassene Ehemann suchte eine Brust, an der er sich ausweinen konnte.* The abandoned husband was looking for a shoulder to cry on.

buchen **1.** Usually, to book, e.g., a flight or a movie ticket. **2.** (fig.) To post, to chalk up, to register, especially a victory or a success. *Unsere Mannschaft hat in dieser Saison schon zwölf Siege für sich gebucht.* Our team has already chalked up twelve wins this season.

Buchse, die (elec.) Small socket, e.g., on the rear of a stereo. SEE **Box.**

Büchse, die Can, BrE tin. Sometimes "box" in compounds. *eine Büchse Sardinen* a can of sardines. *eine Sammelbüchse* collection box (for charities or in church). SEE **Box.**

Buckel, der Hump; hunchback. *Es ist medizinisch unmöglich, seinen Buckel zu entfernen.* It's medically impossible to remove his hump. *einen Buckel machen* (of cats) to arch its back. *den Buckel runterrutschen* a colloquial idiom telling someone to get lost. *Was?! Das soll ich auch noch machen? Du kannst mir den Buckel runterrutschen!* What?! I'm supposed to do that as well? Get lost! (BrE) Take a running jump!
Buckle (on shoe, belt) = *die Spange, die Schnalle*

buckeln To bow and scrape, to be obsequious/servile, to be a yes-man/yes-woman, to lick someone's boots. *Der neue Angestellte buckelt ständig vor dem Chef.* The new employee is continually licking the boss's boots.
To buckle (belt, etc.) = *zuschnallen*
　　　　　(intrans., of wheel, metal, etc.) = *sich verbiegen*. The wheel buckled under the pressure. *Das Rad verbog sich unter dem Druck.*

Büfett, das (also **Buffet, Büffet**) Can mean "cold buffet," "counter" in a cafe, or (esp. Sw.) "station restaurant," but the most common meaning is "sideboard." *Meine Tante bewahrt ihr Geschirr in einem sehr wert-*

vollen alten Büffet aus Olivenholz auf. My aunt keeps all her china in a very valuable old sideboard made of olive wood.

Buffet (meal laid out on tables for self-service) = *das kalte Büfett*

Bügel, der   Coat hanger; stirrup. *Der Brillenbügel* (on spectacles) BrE side-piece, earpiece.

Bugle = *das Bügelhorn*

Bukett, das   Bouquet, both for flowers and for the aroma of a wine.

Bucket = *der Eimer*

Bulle, der   Not only a male cow, but also slang for a policeman: a "cop." *Pass mal auf! Die Bullen kommen!* Watch out! The cops are coming!

Bunker, der   Besides the English meanings of "bunker," i.e., "sandy obstacle in golf" and "underground shelter in wartime," the German word has two more meanings: **1.** Storage silo for grain.   **2.** (sl.) Prison.

Büro, das   Office. *Die Klimaanlage in unserem Büro funktioniert nicht.* The air-conditioning in our office isn't working.

Bureau (agency) = *das Büro, das Amt, die Behörde*

(furniture) = *die Kommode*, (BrE) *der Sekretär*

Marriage bureau = *das Ehevermittlungsinstitut, das Eheanbahnungs-institut*

bürsten   To brush.

To burst (balloon, appendix, etc.) = *platzen*

(blister, boil, abscess, etc.) = *aufplatzen*

Butt, der   Flounder (fish).

Butt (buttocks) = *der Po*

(object of someone's jokes, anger, etc.) = *die Zielscheibe*

(barrel) = *das Faß*

(of cigarette) = *der Stummel*, (coll.) *die Kippe*

buttern   Literally "to butter," e.g., a slice of toast, or "to add butter" to something when cooking. Figuratively, and informally, it means "to pour money into something," "to invest in an institution, venture, project," etc. *Herr Link hat den Tennisklub, in dem sein Sohn Mitglied ist, jahrelang kräftig gebuttert.* For years Mr. Link poured money into the tennis club where his son is a member.

C

Callboy, der Male prostitute whose clients contact him by telephone.
Callboy (theat.) = *der (die) Gehilfe (-fin) des Inspizienten*
      (in hotel) = *der Hotelboy*

Caravan, der Trailer; mobile home, BrE caravan. Also means "station
wagon" (BrE estate car). *Wenn er nach Kanada fährt, benutzt er seinen
Benz Caravan, um den Wohnwagen zu ziehen.* When he drives to Canada,
he uses his Benz station wagon to tow the trailer.
BrE Caravan (vehicle) = *der Wohnwagen*
(long line of camels, etc., on the move) = *die Karawane*

catchen To (catch-)wrestle. *Big Daddy catcht heute Abend in Las Vegas
gegen Monster Mouth.* Big Daddy is wrestling tonight in Las Vegas against
Monster Mouth.
To catch (ball, fish, etc.) = *fangen*
      (someone doing something naughty/criminal) = *erwischen,
      ertappen*
You might catch a disease/a cold = *Du könntest dir eine Krankheit/
eine Erkältung holen*

Catcher, der (Catch-)wrestler.
Catcher (in sports, e.g., baseball) = *der Fänger*
Rat catcher = *der Rattenfänger*

Chaot(in), der (die) This can be either an anarchist (but note that *der
(die) Anarchist(in)* also exists) or a person who is extremely messy or
disorganized. *Bakunin war ein echter Chaot.* Bakunin was a real anarchist. *Henry, du bist wirklich der schlimmste Chaot, den ich kenne; wann
räumst du dein Arbeitszimmer endlich auf?* Henry, you really are the mess-
iest person I know; when are you finally going to clean up your study?
Note: The adjectives *chaotisch* and "chaotic" are not false cognates.

Charakteristik, die This denotes either the description or the characteristics of s.o./s.t. *Der Makler gab uns die Charakteristik der Wohnung
am Meer.* The agent gave us the (written) description of the seaside apartment.
Characteristic (feature) = *die Eigenschaft, das Merkmal*
      (math.) *die Charakteristik*

Charge, die **1.** (mil.) Rank. *die oberen Chargen* the upper echelons. **2.**
(theat.) Minor role, (small) character part. *Dieser berühmte Schauspieler zieht solche Chargen vor.* This famous actor prefers such small
character parts. **3.** Batch (of goods). *Alle Antibiotika in der ersten
Charge waren verseucht und mußten an den Hersteller zurückgeschickt*

werden. All the antibiotics in the first batch were contaminated and had to be returned to the manufacturer.

Charge (jur.) = *die Anklage*

(horses, soldiers) = *der Angriff*

(fee) = *die Gebühr*

chartern Not only "to charter" but also "to rent or hire." *Für unseren Urlaub auf dem Segelschiff mußten wir eine Crew von sieben Mann chartern.* For our vacation on the sailing boat we had to hire a crew of seven men.

checken Can mean "to check," but is frequently used as an informal word for "to get," "to understand," "to follow." *Jetzt habe ich dir die Anweisungen schon dreimal erklärt und du checkst sie immer noch nicht!* That's the third time I've explained the instructions to you and you still don't understand them!

To check (machines, cars, etc.) = *überprüfen*

(papers, passports) = *kontrollieren*

(words, meanings in book) = *nachschlagen*

Chef, der Boss, chief, leader, head. *Er ist jetzt Chef einer internationalen Firma.* He's now the boss of an international company. *Der Chef der Drogenbande* the leader of the drug gang. *Der Chefarzt* (med.) senior consultant. *Der Chef des C.I.A.* the head of the C.I.A. *Der Chefredakteur* chief editor, editor-in-chief.

Chef (one of several) = *der Koch*

(the one in charge if there are several) = *der Chefkoch*

Chesterkäse, der A pseudo-anglicism meaning "processed cheddar cheese."

Chip, der Misunderstandings can occur here among British speakers (though not among American speakers) in discussions about food, especially with the plural. *Die Chips* chips, (BrE) crisps. *Die Pommes Frites* French fries, (BrE) chips. In connection with gambling, however, esp., roulette, the word "chip" is used in exactly the same way in German, American English, and British English.

Choker, der (also **Choke, der**) The choke on a car.

Choker (tight necklace) = *der enge Halsreif*

Chor, der It looks like "chore" and sounds like "core," but in fact means "choir" or "chorus." *Hans singt in einem New Orleans Chor.* Hans sings in a New Orleans choir. *"Mögen Sie beide Golf?" fragte ich. "Und wie!," sagten die Zwillinge im Chor.* "Do you both like golf?" I asked. "And how!" chorused the twins.

Chore = *leidige Beschäftigung, lästige Routinearbeit*

Christ, der The first meaning is a "Christian." It can also refer to Christ Himself, though this use is somewhat elevated, literary style. The normal, modern expression for "Christ" is *der Christus.*

Christentum, das   The belief, Christianity, and not a collective word for those who believe.

Christendom (the body of believers) = *die Christenheit*

City, die   Downtown, town center, city center. It is important to realize that German speakers use the word to denote the center of both large cities and quite small towns. *Heute abend gehe ich mit meinen Freunden in die City, um den neuen Woody Allen Film anzuschauen.* I'm going downtown tonight to see the new Woody Allen film.

City = *die Großstadt*

clever   More often than not, the German word is used in a negative sense. In such cases, the English word "clever" is not an impossible translation, but there is usually a better one, e.g., "sly," "cunning," "crafty," "shrewd." *Es war sehr clever von dir, schon vor dem Banküberfall einen falschen Paß drucken zu lassen.* It was very crafty of you to have a false passport printed before the bank robbery.

Clever = *schlau, klug, clever*

(with one's hands) = *geschickt*

Clinch, der   Obviously taken from boxing, but in colloquial German its use has been broadened to include arguments, bitter disagreements, political fights, etc. *Die politischen Gegner nahmen sich gestern im Parlament in den Clinch.* The two political opponents really went at each other in parliament yesterday. *sind im Clinch* Are at loggerheads. *Der Finanzminister und der Verteidigungsminister sind momentan im Clinch.* The finance minister and the defense minister are at loggerheads at the moment.

Clique, die   Set, group, gang, crowd; also clique. The point is that the German word less commonly has negative connotations than the English. *Ich freue mich, daß mein Bruder seine Clique zu meiner Party mitbringen wird.* I'm glad that my brother is bringing his crowd to my party.

Clou, der   Real hoot, laugh; highlight, high point, climax, pièce de résistance. *Es wäre wirklich der Clou, wenn meinem Chef beim Sprung in das Schwimmbecken die Badehose platzen würde!* It would be a real hoot if my boss's swimming trunks were to split as he jumped into the swimming-pool! *Der Auftritt des weltberühmten Zauberers war der Clou der Wohltätigkeitsvorstellung.* The appearance of the world-famous conjuror was the highlight of the charity performance. *Das ist doch gerade der Clou.* That's the whole point; that's just it.

Clue (in police investigation) = *die Spur*

(help in guessing) = *der Anhaltspunkt*

(to a puzzle, mystery) = *der Schlüssel*

Cockpit, das This word causes no problems as long as the conversation is about airplanes, but in Swiss German *das Cockpit* is frequently used for the driver's seat in a car—and not necessarily a racing car.

Collier, das or **Kollier, das** Necklace, usually of high quality, and containing precious stones. The word is particularly common in Swiss German.

Collier = *der Bergmann*

Container, der In German this refers only to large containers, e.g., those loaded onto container ships, or filled with grain; those used for larger-than-usual quantities of domestic trash or garden garbage; those used to collect garbage from building-sites, etc. It is not used, as in English, to describe more or less any vessel, from a pill box to a coffin, designed to contain something.

Container (other than very large containers) = *der Behälter, das Gefäß*

Contenance, die Composure. *Als der Gärtner die Herzogin eine dumme Kuh nannte, verlor sie ihre Contenance und gab ihm eine Ohrfeige.* When the gardener called the Duchess a silly cow, she lost her composure and smacked him on the ear.

Countenance = *das Angesicht, das Antlitz*

Couleur, die Kind, sort, shade, hue. Tends to be used mainly in connection with politics, and to describe politicians of different opinions but within one party. *Republikaner jeder Couleur trafen sich beim Kongreß in Wien.* Republicans of every shade met at the congress in Vienna.

Color = *die Farbe*

Coupé, das In Germany this can refer to a car with a sloping back, as in English. In Switzerland it means a compartment in a train.

Coupon, der (also **Kupon, der**) **1.** Usually "coupon," but can also mean "voucher," "ticket," "copy," BrE "counterfoil." *Dieser Coupon berechtigt Sie zum kostenlosen Eintritt in die Ausstellung.* This voucher entitles you to free entrance to the exhibition. *Bewahren Sie den Coupon von diesem Überweisungsschein gut auf.* Take good care of the counterfoil of this transfer form. **2.** (of clothing material) length. *Dieser Dekostoff ist in Coupons bis zu 25 Meter erhältlich.* This fabric is available in lengths up to 25 meters.

Courage, die German *Courage* and English "courage" are equivalent, though the German word *Mut* is much more common. HOWEVER, SEE **ZIVILCOURAGE.**

Couvert, das. SEE **KUVERT.**

Crux, die Trouble, nuisance, problem. *Die Crux bei unserer Urlaubsreise war, daß die Geschäfte in den spanischen Dörfern keine ausländischen Schecks annahmen.* The problem we had during our vacation was that foreign checks weren't accepted in the Spanish villages.

Crux (of the matter, problem) = *der Kern (der Sache, des Problems)*

Cut, der A sort of tuxedo (BrE cutaway): a very formal sort of morning-suit, usually with tails, cut diagonally from the front of the waist to the back of the knees, and worn only on occasions of extreme formality, e.g., a state funeral.

Cut (clothes, hair) = *der Schnitt*

  (wound) = *die Schnittwunde*

  (price reduction) = *die Senkung, die Ermäßigung*

  (salary, budget, working hours, shortened vacations, etc.) = *die Kürzung*

  (film censorship) = *die Streichung*

  (share) = *der (An)teil*

Power cut = *der Stromausfall*

D

Dame, die Lady; old-fashioned for "madam," esp. in restaurants. *"Also, ein Steak für den Herrn. Und für die Dame?"* "So it's a steak for you, sir. And for madam?" It also means the game of checkers (BrE draughts). There is no aristocratic German title that corresponds to the English "Dame"; the English word is usually kept in German sentences.

Damm, der **1.** Dyke, embankment, wall, causeway. *ein Damm an der holländischen Küste* A dyke on the Dutch coast. *ein Angler auf dem Uferdamm* a fisherman on the embankment. *ein Damm zwischen dem Festland und der Insel* a causeway between the mainland and the island. **2.** (anat.) Perineum. **3.** *auf dem Damm* (idiom) normal, his/her usual self, fit, in good shape, etc. *Nach ihrer Krankheit ist sie jetzt wieder auf dem Damm.* She's now back to normal after her illness. *Nach einer durchfeierten Nacht fühlt er sich nicht so recht auf dem Damm.* After celebrating all night, he's not his usual self.

Dam = *der Staudamm*

dämmen (fig.) To curb, check, hold back; also "to dam" (e.g., a river). *Beim Abschied am Flughafen fiel es mir schwer, meine Tränen zu dämmen.* When I said goodbye at the airport, I found it difficult to hold back my tears. *Nachdem ich sechs Monate lang die gleiche Arbeit machen mußte, war meine Begeisterung für die neue Firma gedämmt.* Six months of having to do the same job curbed my enthusiasm for the new company.

To damn = *verdammen, verurteilen*

Daten (pl.) Though it looks like "dates," this nearly always means "data." *Wir haben die Daten aller Mitarbeiter in unserem neuen Computer gespeichert.* We've put the data about all our employees on our new computer. Note that the singular, *das Datum,* can denote both a datum, i.e., a fact, and a calendar date. *der Datenschutz* Data protection, i.e., the right of any individual to be protected against wrongful or illegal use of data stored on him/her in a computer.

Date (fruit) = *die Dattel*

(appointment) = *der Termin, die Verabredung*

(calendar, birthdays, etc.) = *das Datum*

What's the date today? = *Den wievielten haben wir heute?*

I have a date with the boss this afternoon = *Ich bin heute nachmittag mit dem Chef verabredet.*

dealen To push (drugs). *Er dealt mit Heroin und Marijuana.* He pushes heroin and marijuana.

To deal (cards) = *austeilen, geben*

To deal with s.o. (do business with) = *mit jdm. verhandeln*

To deal with s.t. (a matter, a problem) = *sich mit etwas beschäftigen/ befassen*

(be responsible for) = *für etwas zuständig sein*

Dealer, der (Drugs) pusher, trafficker. SEE **DEALEN.**

Dealer (comm.) = *der Händler*

(wholesaler) = *der Großhändler*

(cards) = *der Kartengeber*

Debütant(in), der (die) Novice, beginner. *Auf dem Gebiet der internationalen Finanzen ist er ein absoluter Debütant.* In the world of international finance, he's an absolute beginner. *Die Debütantin* can also mean "deb(utante)," i.e., a young lady of upper-class background beginning the social round.

Decke, die 1. Blanket, cover. *Wieviele Decken möchtest du heute nacht auf deinem Bett?* How many blankets do you want on your bed tonight? 2. Ceiling.

unter einer Decke (idiom) Can have the pejorative meaning of in league with, "in cahoots with." *Der Besitzer des Spielcasinos steckt mit dem Bürgermeister unter einer Decke.* The casino owner is in cahoots with the mayor.

Deck (on ship) = *das Deck*

(of cards) = *das (Karten)spiel*

defekt Not the noun "defect," but an adjective meaning "faulty," "defective." *Wir möchten diesen Fernseher gegen einen anderen umtauschen; dieser ist defekt.* We'd like to exchange this television for another one; this one is faulty.

Defect (in machine) = *der Fehler*
  (physical handicap) = *der Schaden*
  (in character) = *der Charakterfehler*
Defilee, das March-past, parade, procession. In English it is normally translated by a verb, e.g., "to march past," "to file past." *Beim Defilee der Diplomaten vor dem Präsidenten fiel der Botschafter Boliviens durch sein rotes Hemd auf.* As the diplomats filed past the President, the Bolivian ambassador's red shirt made him conspicuous.

Defile (narrow mountain pass) = *der Hohlweg*
Defilement (womanhood; religious) = *die Schändung*
  (religious) = *die Entweihung*
  (of reputation) = *die Beschmutzung*
defilieren To march or file past. SEE DEFILEE.
To defile = *schänden, entweihen, beschmutzen*
definitiv Can mean "definitive(ly)," but far more often means "definite(ly)." *Seine Antwort auf meine Frage war definitiv.* He gave a definite answer to my question. *Sie hat ihre Teilnahme bei unserem Kammermusikabend definitiv bestätigt.* She's definitely confirmed that she's going to take part in our evening of chamber music.
Definitive = *maßgeblich* This is the definitive book on French history. *Dies ist das maßgebliche Buch über die französische Geschichte.*
degradieren To downgrade; (mil.) to demote. *Unser Club Class Flugticket wurde für den Rückflug auf Touristenklasse degradiert.* Our Club Class air ticket was downgraded to Tourist Class for the return flight. *Nach dem Unfall auf dem Schießplatz, in dem zwei Soldaten ums Leben kamen, wurde der Hauptmann zum Leutnant degradiert.* After the accident on the firing range, in which two soldiers died, the captain was demoted to the rank of lieutenant.
To degrade s.o. = *jdn. erniedrigen*
Degradierung, die Downgrading (of airline ticket); (mil.) demotion. SEE DEGRADIEREN.
Degradation (human) = *die Erniedrigung*
  (physics) = *die Degradation*
Degustation, die The Swiss German word for a tasting—usually wine, but occasionally other things, e.g., cheese. *Wir wurden vom Winzer zu einer Degustation eingeladen.* We were invited to a wine-tasting session by the winegrower.
Disgust = *der Abscheu, der Ekel*
degustieren Swiss German for "to taste," nearly always wine. SEE DEGUSTATION.
To disgust = *anwidern, anekeln, abstoßen*

Dekade, die   Can mean "ten days," "ten weeks," "ten months," or "ten years."

Decade = *das Jahrzehnt*, which is more common than *die Dekade*.

Dekan, der   This means "dean," both in the religious sense and with reference to the head of a university's administration.

Deacon = *der Diakon*

Deklination, die   1. (gramm.) Declension.   2. (physics, astron., magnetism) Declination.

Dekorateur(in), der (die)   Window dresser; interior designer. *Henry arbeitet als Dekorateur bei Macy's.* Henry works as a window dresser at Macy's. *Seine Schwester arbeitet als Dekorateurin in einem Architektenbüro.* His sister works as an interior designer in an architect's office.

Decorator (painter and wallpaperer) = *der Maler*

Dekoration, die   1. Window dressing. SEE **DEKORATEUR**.   2. (in restaurant, etc.) Décor. *Die Dekoration in diesem neuen Restaurant gefällt mir überhaupt nicht.* I don't like the décor in that new restaurant at all.   3. (theater) Set. *Das Publikum brach in rauschenden Applaus aus, als es die (Bühnen)dekoration im Theater sah.* The theater audience broke out into spontaneous applause when they saw the set.   4. Decoration, e.g., of church with flowers at a wedding.   5. Decoration, military honors.

Decoration (ornaments, hats, furniture, cakes, etc.) = *die Verzierung*
>(Christmas trees, buildings, streets, e.g., with garlands) = *der Schmuck*
>(painting, wallpapering, etc.) = *das Tapezieren, das Anstreichen*
>(mil. medal, ribbon) = *die Auszeichnung, die Dekoration*

dekorieren   To dress (windows); to decorate (s.o. with military honors; a church with flowers).

To decorate (hats, cakes, ornaments, etc.) = *verzieren*
>(Christmas trees, buildings, streets with garlands, etc.) = *schmücken*
>(paint) = *(an)streichen*
>(wallpaper) = *tapezieren*
>(give military honors to) = *auszeichnen, dekorieren*

dekuvrieren   To expose, uncover, e.g., a scandal, a fraud, an imposter, a spy, a charlatan. *Er gab sich als reicher Bankier aus—bis er als mittelloser Betrüger dekuvriert wurde.* He pretended to be a rich banker—until he was exposed as a penniless imposter.

To discover = *entdecken, herausfinden*

delikat   Normally means "delicious" or "exquisite" in discussions on food. Occasionally means "delicate," i.e., sensitive, in connection with difficult problems, issues, topics, or questions. *Marion bereitet* *lauter delikate Sachen für ihre Gartenpartys vor.* Marion prepares nothing but exquisite food for her garden parties.

Delicate (fragile) = *zerbrechlich, empfindlich*

(health, colors) = *zart*

(tricky, e.g., problem, issue) = *delikat, heikel*

Delikatesse, die Usually means a "delicacy" of some sort, e.g., caviar. Thus it normally refers to things bought in a delicatessen, and not to the shop itself.

Delicatessen (shop) = *das Delicatessengeschäft*

Delikt, das An offense or crime. *Das Schwarzfahren im Bus ist kein Kavaliersdelikt!* Traveling on the bus without paying is no petty offense!

It is interesting to note that an English word "delict" does, in fact, exist with the same meaning as the German word *Delikt*, though the vast majority of English-speaking people have never heard of it.

Dementi, das Denial.

dementieren To deny. *Der Politiker hat alle Gerüchte über eine Affäre mit seiner Sekretärin strengstens dementiert.* The politician has strongly denied all rumors about an affair with his secretary.

Demented (adj.) = *verrückt, wahnsinnig*

demolieren This shares characteristics with the English word "demolish," but is not so drastic. It means "to smash up," "to beat up," "to wreck," or "to vandalize." *Nachdem ich mit dem Auto gegen die Mauer fuhr, war es ziemlich demoliert.* After I drove into the wall, the car was pretty smashed up. *Die Telefonzelle wurde in der Nacht von Unbekannten demoliert.* The telephone box was vandalized during the night; the perpetrators are unknown.

To demolish (buildings) = *abreißen*

(opponent, e.g., at sport) = *vernichten, zunichte machen*

(food) = *verschlingen, vertilgen*

demonstrativ 1. Emphatic(ally), clear(ly); BrE pointed(ly). *Die Schauspielerin hat die Tür demonstrativ zugeschlagen, und hat den Regisseur sich selbst überlassen.* The actress slammed the door emphatically, leaving the director by himself. *Seine Abwesenheit war ein demonstratives Zeichen dafür, daß er gegen unsere Pläne war.* His absence was a clear sign that he was against our plans. 2. (gramm.) Demonstrative (e.g., pronoun).

Demonstrative (feelings) = *offen, ausdrucksvoll*

(proof) = *eindeutig*

Dentist, der This was the name for a dental technician who, because of the nature of his training, had limited powers to practice dentistry. Such types of training have long since been superseded, but the word survives in a pejorative sense, meaning "second-rate dentist," or "quack."

Dentist = *der Zahnarzt*

Dependance, die Usually a branch of a company. Can also mean the annex of a hotel. *Unser Marketingchef ist neulich in die Dependance in München versetzt worden.* Our marketing manager was recently transferred to the Munich branch.

Dependence (on) = *die Abhängigkeit (von)*

Dependency (country) = *das Schutzgebiet, die Kolonie*

deplaziert, deplaciert Not "displaced," but "out of place." *Er kam mir beim Abendempfang völlig deplaziert vor.* At the evening reception, he struck me as being completely out of place.

Displaced person = *der/die Vertriebene*

Displaced water = *das verdrängte Wasser*

Depot, das Vault or depository (usually in a bank). Can also mean "depot" in connection with buses, trucks, etc. *Die Diamanten von Lady Muckpot werden im Depot der Bank aufbewahrt.* Lady Muckpot's diamonds are kept in the bank's vault.

Deputat, das 1. A teacher's teaching load (in hours per week). *Frau Johnson hat dieses Schuljahr nur ein halbes Deputat von 14 Stunden pro Woche, weil sie vor kurzem Zwillinge bekam.* Mrs. Johnson is only teaching 14 hours, half the normal teaching load, this year, as she had twins recently. 2. (agr.) Payment in kind. *ein Deputat Butter erhalten* to receive free butter, as payment in kind.

Deputy = *der Stellvertreter*

Deputy party leader = *der stellvertretende Parteivorsitzende*

Deputy headmaster/vice-chancellor = *der Konrektor*

Deputy sheriff = *der Hilfssheriff*

Derby, das In Germany this refers to the "derby," i.e., a horse race, just as in English. It can also mean "local derby," i.e., a sports contest between two teams from the same area. In Switzerland, however, it means "struggle" or "fight." *Das war gestern vielleicht ein Derby mit dem Zöllner!* That really was some struggle we had yesterday with the customs official!

Derby (hat) = *die Melone*

designieren Not "to design," but "to designate." *Er ist zum Vizepräsidenten designiert worden.* He was designated vice president.

To design = *entwerfen, planen*

Desinteresse, das Complete lack of interest. Much stronger than the English "disinterest."

Disinterest (neutrality) = *die Unparteilichkeit, die Unvoreingenommenheit*

(apathy) = *die Gleichgültigkeit*

desinteressiert   Uninterested, bored.

Disinterested (neutral, not biased) = *unparteiisch, unvoreingenommen*

(apathetic) = *gleichgültig*

Devise, die   Motto, maxim. *Meine Devise lautet: Mit Ehrlichkeit kommt man am weitesten.* My motto is: It always pays to be honest.

Device (gadget, machine) = *das Gerät, die Vorrichtung*

A literary device = *ein literarischer Kunstgriff*

A nuclear device = *ein atomarer Sprengkörper*

BrE A suspicious device = *ein verdächtiger Gegenstand*

Devisen, die (pl.)   Foreign exchange, foreign currency. *Je mehr wir exportieren, desto mehr Devisen verdienen wir.* The more we export, the more foreign exchange we earn.

Device (gadget, machine) = *das Gerät, die Vorrichtung*

A literary device = *ein literarischer Kunstgriff*

A nuclear device = *ein atomarer Sprengkörper*

BrE A suspicious device = *ein verdächtiger Gegenstand*

devot   An old-fashioned word meaning "falsely humble," "obsequious." *Uriah Heep ist wahrscheinlich Dickens bekannteste devote Figur.* Uriah Heep is probably Dickens's most famous obsequious character.

Devoted = *treu, ergeben, eifrig*

dezent   This word is used of clothes, colors, make-up, music, etc., to mean "quiet," "subdued," "unobtrusive," "restrained," "discreet." *Bei der Beerdigung war sie sehr dezent geschminkt.* Her make-up at the burial was very discreet. *Dezente Musik im Restaurant trug zur romantischen Atmosphäre bei.* Subdued music in the restaurant contributed to the romantic atmosphere.

Decent (morally respectable) = *anständig*

(kind) = *liebenswürdig*

(of decent quality) = *von guter Qualität*

(not scantily dressed, not naked) = *salonfähig* Can I come in? Are you decent yet? *Kann ich eintreten? Sind Sie schon salonfähig?*

Dezenz, die   Discreetness, unobtrusiveness, conservativeness. *Die alte Dame kleidet sich mit viel Dezenz.* The old lady dresses very conservatively.

Decency (manners) = *der Anstand*

(clothes) = *die Anständigkeit*

(behavior) = *die Schicklichkeit*

diagonal   This does mean "diagonal," but takes on quite a different meaning in the phrase *diagonal lesen*, which means "to skim through," (BrE to flick through). *Da er als Wissenschaftler so viele Bücher lesen muß, hat er oft nur Zeit, sie diagonal zu lesen.* Since, as a scientist, he has to read so many books, he often has time only to skim through them.

Diagonalreifen, die (pl.) Cross-ply tires on a car.

Diagramm, das Not only "diagram," but also "graph" or "chart." *das Kreisdiagramm* pie chart.

Diäten, die This can be the plural of *die Diät,* in which case it means "diets." The plural also has the totally different meaning of "parliamentary allowance." *Die Parlamentsmitglieder beziehen monatliche Diäten in Höhe von DM 7800.* The members of Parliament draw a monthly allowance of 7800 marks.

dick "Fat" or "thick," depending on the context, and many other meanings in particular combinations. *ein dicker Mann* A fat man; *ein dickes Wörterbuch* A thick dictionary; *dicke Wände* Thick walls; *eine dicke Rechnung* A large bill; *dicke Freunde* Close friends; *ein dickes Gehalt* A high salary; *dickes Lob* High praise; *ein dicker Mercedes* (pej.) A big fat Mercedes.

    Thick (physical, e.g., tree-trunk, book, thigh) = *dick*

          (stupid) = *doof, dumm*

differenziert Can mean "differentiated," but more often means "comprehensive," "detailed," "covering many different aspects." *Seine Ausführungen zum Thema Atomenergie waren sehr differenziert.* His report on the subject of nuclear energy was very comprehensive.

Diktat, das **1.** Dictation, usually in school or secretarial contexts. *Die Schüler schreiben im Deutschunterricht ein Diktat.* The pupils are doing a dictation in the German lesson. **2.** (command) Dictate.

    Dictates (of reason, common sense) = *die Gebote*

          (other meanings) = *das Diktat*

Diner, das (form.) Luncheon, BrE dinner. *Wir wurden vom Bürgermeister zum Diner eingeladen.* We were invited for luncheon by the mayor.

    Diner (person who dines, in restaurant) = *der Gast, die (der) Speisende(r)*

          (place to eat) = *das Eßlokal*

direkt (adj.) **1.** Similar to the English "direct," but somewhat colder and more negative: "blunt." *Sie war sehr direkt, als sie ihren Tischnachbarn auf seinen Mundgeruch hinwies.* She was very blunt about telling her neighbor at the table that he had bad breath. **2.** Clear. *Er gab mir eine direkte Antwort.* He gave me a clear answer.

    Direct (train) = *durchgehend*

          (link, contact, cause, heat) = *unmittelbar, direkt*

    A direct hit = *ein Volltreffer*

Direktion, die The directors'/managers' offices. It can also mean the managers or directors themselves. *Die Direktion der Firma Müller befindet sich im dritten Stock.* The managers' offices of the Müller Company are situated on the third floor. *Die Direktion der Exportfirma hat ihre aus-ländischen Gäste zu einem Cocktailempfang eingeladen.* The managers of the export company invited their foreign guests to a cocktail reception.

Direction = *die Richtung*

A good sense of direction = *ein guter Orientierungssinn*

New directions (in science, literature, etc.) = *neue Wege*

Good direction (of films, plays, etc.) = *gute Regie*

Directions (how to use a machine, etc.) = *die Gebrauchsanweisung, die Gebrauchsanleitung*

Direktor(in), der (die)   Governor/warden (of prison), senior consultant (of hospital), principal (of university), head teacher (of school).

Director (of company) = *der Direktor, der Leiter, das Vorstands-mitglied*

(films) = *der Regisseur*

disponieren   To make plans or arrangements. *Ich muß unseren Urlaub anders disponieren.* I have to make other arrangements for our vacation. *über jdn./etwas disponieren* To have s.o./s.t. at one's disposal. *Herr Kleinwort disponiert über drei Rolls Royce und vier Sekretärinnen.* Mr. Kleinwort has three Rolls Royces and four secretaries at his disposal. *Ich kann über meine Zeit frei disponieren.* My time is my own.

To dispose of s.t./s.o. = *etwas/jdn. loswerden, beseitigen*

Disposition, die   Arrangement, plan. This tends to be used in the plural. *Ich muß meine Dispositionen für den nächsten Monat treffen.* I have to make my arrangements for next month. *zur Disposition* At one's disposal. *Der Chauffeur steht dem Direktor den ganzen Tag zur Disposition.* The chauffeur is at the director's disposal all day long. *Er hat mir sein neues Auto zur Disposition gestellt.* He has put his new car at my disposal.

Disposition (character) = *die Veranlagung*

Distanz, die   Physical distance; mental detachment, aloofness, coldness. *Distanz gewinnen* To give oneself time to judge s.o./s.t. after an emotional upheaval has passed. *Nach unserer Scheidung muß ich erst einmal die nötige Distanz zu meiner Ehe gewinnen, bevor ich eine neue Beziehung eingehe.* After our divorce, I have to gain a certain detachment from my marriage before I enter into a new relationship.

Distance = *der Abstand, die Entfernung, die Distanz*

distanzieren, sich   To dissociate oneself, detach oneself from s.o. or s.t. Also occasionally translated by "to distance oneself" from s.o. *Meine Tante hat sich nach dem Streit um das Testament meines Onkels von uns distanziert.* After the fight over my uncle's will, my aunt has dissociated herself from us.

divers   Various, several (different), miscellaneous. *Ich muß in der Stadt diverse Dinge erledigen.* I have to get various things done in town. *Kannst du bitte diverse Rotweine besorgen?* Can you get hold of several different red wines, please? *Das erste Kapitel behandelt die Grammatik, das zweite die Aussprache, und das dritte diverse andere Sprachprobleme.* The first chapter deals with grammar, the second with pronunciation, and the third with miscellaneous language problems.

Diverse = *verschieden(artig), unterschiedlich*

Dogge, die   Mastiff. *die deutsche Dogge* Great Dane.

Dog = *der Hund*

Doktor, der   **1.** Medical doctor.   **2.** Academic doctor.   **3.** Doctorate (Ph.D.). It is the third of these that can lead to confusion, since it does not even refer to a person, let alone a medical person. *Fritz hat im vorigen Jahr seinen Doktor in Erlangen gemacht.* Fritz completed his doctorate in Erlangen last year.

Doctor (med.) = *der Arzt/die Ärztin, der Doktor*
(when addressing, or referring to, a medical or academic doctor) = *Herr Doktor/Frau Doktor*

Dom, der   Cathedral. *der Kölner Dom* Cologne Cathedral

Dome (top part of cathedral or other building) = *die Kuppel*
(of skull, heaven) = *das Gewölbe*

Doppeldecker, der   In German, this can refer not only to a double-decker bus but also to the old aircraft, a biplane. *Im Museum steht ein Doppeldecker aus dem Jahr 1910.* There's a biplane in the museum dating back to 1910.

Dose, die   Can, BrE tin; box, bowl, dish. *eine Dose Sardinen* a can of sardines; *eine Bierdose* a can of beer; *eine Schmuckdose* a jewelry box; *eine Pillendose* a pillbox; *eine Zuckerdose* a sugar bowl; *eine Butterdose* a butter dish; *eine Steckdose* (elec.) a socket. Note that *die Dosen* is the plural of both *die Dose* and *die Dosis.*

Dose (med.) = *die Dosis*
(flattery, culture, punishment, etc.) = *die Ration*

I can only take my mother-in-law in small doses = *Ich kann meine Schwiegermutter nur für kurze Zeit ertragen*

dösen   Not "to dose," but "to doze." *eindösen* To doze off. *Großvater döst ständig im Sessel ein.* Grandfather is always dozing off in the armchair.

To dose s.o. = *jdm. Arznei geben*

She's dosed up with antibiotics = *Sie ist mit Antibiotika vollgepumpt*

dosieren   To measure out (usually nonmedical); to measure into doses (usually medical); to dispense. *Ich muß die Zutaten genau dosieren; sonst gelingt der Kuchen nicht.* I have to measure out the ingredients exactly; otherwise the cake won't be a success. *Die Krankenschwester dosierte die Medikamente nach Anweisung des Arztes.* The nurse measured out the drugs into doses according to the doctor's instructions.

To doze = *dösen*

dotieren (mit)   To remunerate with, endow with. *Der Nobelpreis war mit 100.000 Dollar dotiert.* The Nobel Prize was endowed with 100,000 dollars. *Er hat eine gut dotierte Stellung.* His position is well remunerated.
To dote on someone/something = *jdn./etwas abgöttisch lieben*

doubeln   To stand in for. *Unbekannte Schauspieler doubeln in unwichtigen Szenen ihre berühmten Kollegen.* Unknown actors stand in for their famous colleagues in unimportant scenes.
To double (math.) = *verdoppeln*
This room doubles as a study and a guestroom = *Dieses Zimmer dient sowohl als Arbeitszimmer als auch als Gästezimmer*

Double, das   Found almost exclusively in film contexts to mean a "stand-in."
Double (math., amounts) = *das Doppelte*
        (lookalike) = *der (die) Doppelgänger(in)*
A double whiskey = *ein doppelter Whisky*

Dozent(in), der (die)   An expression used in universities and other institutions for higher study meaning "(assistant) professor" or "lecturer." *Herr Jakobs ist Dozent an der Universität in der Nachbarstadt.* Mr. Jakobs is a lecturer/(assistant) professor at the university in the neighboring town.
Dozen = *das Dutzend*

dozieren   To lecture. *Frau Schmidt doziert an der Pädagogischen Hochschule.* Mrs. Schmidt lectures at the college of education (BrE also teachers' training college).
To doze = *dösen*

Drachen, der   This does mean "dragon," both the mythical animal breathing fire and a formidable lady, a "battle-ax"; but it also means "kite," as flown from hilltops on windy days. *Im Herbst lassen Kinder gerne ihre Drachen fliegen.* Children like flying their kites in the fall.

Drachenflieger, der   Hang-glider, i.e., both the person practicing the sport and the flying object itself.
Dragonfly = *die Libelle*

drastisch   Not only "drastic" but also "graphic." *Er hat uns sehr drastisch klargemacht, welche Folgen unser Verhalten haben würde.* He painted a very graphic picture of the consequences of our behavior.

Dreß, der   (sport) Outfit (BrE kit)—clothes rather than equipment. *Ulla hat einen neuen schicken Dreß zum Tennisspielen gekauft.* Ulla has bought a smart new tennis outfit.
Dress (one-piece ladies' garment) = *das Kleid*
Casual dress = *die Freizeitkleidung, die legere Kleidung*
Formal dress = *die Gesellschaftskleidung*

dressieren To train, to discipline, to condition. *Der Hund ist darauf dressiert, die Schafe zusammenzutreiben.* The dog is trained to round up the sheep.
To dress (oneself) = *(sich) anziehen, (sich) kleiden*
To dress oneself up = *sich fein machen*
To dress a window = *ein Schaufenster dekorieren*
To dress a salad = *einen Salat anmachen*
To dress a wound = *eine Wunde verbinden*

Dressman, der Pseudo-anglicism meaning "male model."

dribbeln In soccer or basketball, this does mean "to dribble," i.e., to run with the ball at one's feet. It does not, however, also mean "to allow drinks to run down one's chin."
To dribble (liquids) = *sabbern, kleckern*

Drilling, der Triplet. *Sie hat Drillinge.* She has triplets.
Drilling (for oil, gas, etc.) = *die Bohrung*
   (at dentist's) = *das Bohren*
   (exercises, e.g., gramm.) = *die Übung*
   (mil., on parade ground) = *das Exerzieren*

Droge, die (usually pl., **die Drogen**) This word refers only to narcotics, and not to medical aids such as sleeping pills.
Drug (medical) = *das Medikament*

Drogerie, die Shop similar to both drugstore and (BrE) chemist's. You cannot, however, take a doctor's prescription to a *Drogerie*; for this you have to go to an *Apotheke,* i.e., a pharmacy (BrE chemist's).

Drogist, der Person in charge of a drugstore. SEE **DROGERIE.** He or she is not licensed to fill medical prescriptions.
An American druggist works in a shop that may look very similar to a German *Drogerie.* Since he or she can sell (among other things) prescribed antibiotics, however, the American druggist plays a dual role, combining some functions of both the *Drogist* and the *Apotheker.*

dröhnen To roar, to rumble (thunder), to boom (voices or music). *Seine Stimme dröhnte bis in den ersten Stock.* His booming voice was heard as far as the second floor. *mir dröhnt der Kopf* My head is buzzing.
To drone (aircraft) = *brummen*
   (bees) = *summen*
   (monotonous voice) = *eintönig sprechen*

Drops, der or **das** Type of candy: "fruit drop."
Drop (of water) = *der Tropfen*
   (temperature, price, sales, etc.) = *der Rückgang, der Sturz*
There's a sheer drop here = *Hier geht es steil hinunter.*
Dropsy = *die Wassersucht*

dudeln To hum. *Er dudelt den ganzen Tag ein Lied vor sich her.* All day long he's humming some song to himself. *einen dudeln* (mainly South Germany) To have a little drink.

To doodle = *Männchen malen, kritzeln*

dumm Means "dumb" in the sense of "stupid" or "foolish," but not in the sense of "unable to speak." It also has a variety of other meanings in fixed expressions. *Ich habe das dumme Gefühl, daß er nicht kommen wird.* I have a nasty feeling he's not going to show up. *Jetzt wird's mir zu dumm; ich gehe nach Hause.* I've had enough of this; I'm going home. *dummes Zeug reden* To talk nonsense. *sich dumm und dämlich reden* To talk till one is blue in the face.

Dumb (stupid) = *dumm*

    (mute) = *stumm*

Deaf and dumb = *taubstumm* Deaf and dumb language *die Taubstummensprache*

Dutzend- Although *das Dutzend* means "dozen," *Dutzend-* in compounds often does not. Instead, it conveys the idea of "ordinary," "like many others." *die Dutzendwaren* Mass-produced goods; *das Dutzendgesicht* Run-of-the-mill face; *der Dutzendmensch* Nondescript person.

E

Ebbe, die Closely connected with English "ebb," but the German word often refers to the position of the water at the end of the ebbing, i.e., "low tide," rather than the process of ebbing itself. *Bei Ebbe gehen wir gerne am Strand spazieren.* We like walking along the beach at low tide.

At a low ebb (emotionally) = *auf einem Tiefpunkt*

eben **1.** Smooth, even, flat, level. *Die Oberfläche meines neuen Schreibtisches ist nicht sehr eben.* The surface of my new desk is not very smooth. *Holland ist sehr eben.* Holland is very flat. *Dieses Grundstück ist für einen Tennisplatz nicht eben genug.* This piece of land is not level enough for a tennis court. **2.** As a temporal adverb, it means "just." It is important to realize that "just" can mean (1) "recently" (i.e., past reference), in which meaning the German is normally *gerade eben: Der Verteidigungsminister ist gerade eben zurückgetreten.* The defense minister has just resigned. and (2) "briefly," "for a short time" (i.e., present or future reference): *Ich gehe eben zum Arzt.* I'm just stopping by the doctor's. **3.** As a reaction, *eben* normally means "exactly," "precisely," "quite." *John: Er stößt sie ab, weil er Mundgeruch hat. Tim: Ja, eben.* John: He turns her off because he has bad breath. Tim: Yes, exactly.

Even (adj., smooth, level, etc.) = *eben*

(adv.) = *auch, selbst, sogar* Even a beggar has good qualities. *Auch/Selbst/Sogar ein Bettler hat gute Eigenschaften.*

Echo, das Not only "echo" but also "response." *Mein Vortrag über die Zerstörung der Umwelt fand bei den Zuhörern ein lebhaftes Echo.* My lecture about the destruction of the environment met with a lively response from the audience.

Effekt, der Usually means "effect," but can also mean "impression." *Meine Schwiegermutter, die Herzogin, hat auf meine Freunde einen tollen Effekt ausgeübt.* My mother-in-law, the countess, made a big impression on my friends.

Effect = *die (Aus)wirkung, der Effekt*

Effekten, die (pl.) **1.** (econ.) Stocks and shares, bonds. *die Effektenbörse* the stock exchange; *der Effektenmarkt* the stock market; *der Effektenmakler* stockbroker. **2.** (dated) Personal effects, property.

Effects = *die Auswirkungen, die Effekte*

effektiv Effective, but also very often "really," "for sure," "in fact." *Ich kann nicht gehen: ich habe effektiv keine Zeit.* I can't go; I really don't have time. *Ich weiß effektiv, daß er am Raub nicht beteiligt war.* I know for sure that he had no hand in the robbery.

Effective = *wirksam, wirkungsvoll, effektiv*

Effet, der Side spin (in pool or billiards). *Er hat den Ball mit Effet geschossen.* He put side spin on the ball.

Effect = *die Wirkung, der Effekt*

egal **1.** This has many shades of meaning, but normally has to do with indifference. *Es ist mir egal, ob du heute zum Essen kommst oder morgen.* It makes no difference to me whether you come for a meal today or tomorrow. *Es ist dir doch ganz egal, wie ich mich fühle!* You couldn't care less how I feel! **2.** It also means "the same," "identical." *Die beiden Häuser sind egal.* The two houses are identical.

Equal = *gleich, gleich groß*

Egel, der Leech.

Eagle = *der Adler*

Egge, die (agr.) Harrow.

Egg = *das Ei*

eggen (agr.) To harrow.

To egg s.o. on = *jdn. anstacheln*

Einsicht, die **1.** Reason, sense. *Es ist unmöglich, meine verliebte Tochter zur Einsicht zu bringen.* It's impossible to make my love-sick daughter see reason. **2.** Conclusion. *Ich bin zu der Einsicht gekommen, das es für* *mich besser wäre, mein Studium zu beenden.* I came to the conclusion that it would be better to give up my studies. **3.** Knowledge, understanding, insight. *Mein Vater hat auf seiner Reise durch China neue Einsichten in das Leben der Landbevölkerung gewonnen.* During his journey through China, my father gained new insights into the life of the people out in the country. *einsicht nehmen* To take a look at. *Der neue Chef nahm Einsicht in die Akten aller Angestellten.* The new boss took a look at the files of all the employees.

Insight = *das Verständnis, der Einblick, die Einsicht*

Elaborat, das (pej.) Piece of poor writing, literary concoction. *Er tat die neue Goethe-Biographie als übles Elaborat ab.* He dismissed the new biography of Goethe as a pathetic literary concoction.

Elaborate (adj.) = *kunstvoll, ausführlich, kompliziert*

elastisch Has the same idea as "elastic" in English, but is used in a much wider variety of contexts and in more combinations. *ein elastischer Gang:* a springy walk; *ein elastischer Körper:* a supple body; *ein elastischer Stoff:* a stretchy material; *elastisches Metall:* flexible metal.

Elastic band = *das Gummiband*

Elastic stockings = *die Gummistrümpfe*

Element, das **1.** Element. **2.** (elec.) Battery.

Element (general) = *das Element*

     (chem.) = *der Grundstoff*

Elements (basics) = *die Grundbegriffe*

elementar Usually a true cognate, i.e., "elementary," but can also mean "strong" or "violent." *Ein elementarer Haß sprach aus seinen Worten.* His words betrayed a violent hatred.

Elementary = *elementar, einfach, simpel*

Emigrant, der Means "emigrant" in the context of someone leaving a country voluntarily. Otherwise it means "émigré," i.e., someone fleeing a country for political reasons.

eminent "Eminent" when used of people, but "utmost" in connection with importance or significance. *Unser Treffen ist von eminenter Wichtigkeit.* Our meeting is of the utmost importance. *Seine Entdeckung im Labor ist von eminenter Bedeutung.* His discovery in the laboratory is of the utmost significance.

Eminent = *angesehen, berühmt, eminent*

Emission, die **1.** (fin.) Issue/issuing. *Die Emission der Aktien findet am Montag statt.* The shares issue takes place on Monday. **2.** (phys.) Emission. *Die Emission giftiger Gase von Kohlekraftwerken muß in Zukunft stark eingeschränkt werden.* The emission of poisonous gases from coal-fired power stations must be drastically reduced in the future. **3.** (Sw.) Radio or television program or broadcast. *Heute abend findet im Fern-*

sehen eine Emission zum Thema Leihmütter statt. There's a program on television tonight about surrogate mothers.

Emission (light, heat, radiation) = *die Ausstrahlung*
      (fumes, X-rays) = *die Emission*
      (sex.) = *der Samenerguß*
      (heat, sound) = *die Abgabe*
      (gas, liquids, smell) = *das Ausströmen*

emittieren 1. (fin.) To issue shares, bonds, etc. **2.** (phys.) To emit.
To emit (light, heat) = *ausstrahlen*
      (heat, sound, smoke) = *abgeben*
      (gas) = *emittieren*

Ende, das End, but also "outcome," "upshot," "conclusion," "close," "result," "ending"; various other meanings in idioms. *Wir haben unsere Verhandlungen mit der Firma Keil zu einem guten Ende gebracht.* We have brought our negotiations with the Keil company to a satisfactory conclusion. *Es ist noch ein ganzes Ende bis zur Bushaltestelle* (coll.) It's still quite a long way to the bus stop. *Er ist Ende vierzig.* He's in his late forties. *am Ende der Welt* In the middle of nowhere; *letzten Endes* Ultimately, when all is said and done, in the final analysis.

energisch Means "energetic," but also "vigorous" or "strong," especially of denials, campaigns, protests, defenses, etc. *Sie setzt sich energisch für den Schutz des ungeborenen Lebens ein.* She campaigns vigorously for the protection of the unborn.

Engagement, das 1. Commitment or involvement. *Durch sein Engagement für die Behinderten hat er viele Freunde gewonnen.* He has won many friends through his commitment to the disabled. **2.** Engagement, i.e., hiring, e.g., of actors, musicians.
Engagement (to be married) = *die Verlobung*
      (appointment) = *die Verabredung*
      (hiring of musicians, actors, etc.) = *das Engagement*
      (hiring of servants, manual workers, etc.) = *die Einstellung*

engagiert Committed, involved. *Sie ist kommunalpolitisch stark engagiert.* She is deeply involved in local politics.
Engaged (to be married) = *verlobt*
      (toilets, phone) = *besetzt*
      (busy, of persons) = *beschäftigt*

Engländer, der Not only an Englishman, but also an adjustable wrench. *Der Handwerker benötigte einen Engländer, um die Mutter zu lockern.* The workman needed an adjustable wrench to loosen the nut.

englisch This does, of course, mean "English," but in restaurant orders for steak, the word *englisch* is also sometimes used to mean "rare." (The word *blutig* is used for the same thing.)

enorm   **1.** Enormous. *enorme Muskeln* enormous muscles. More common, however, are the following uses: **2.** (adv.) Very/hugely/enormously. *Die Theatertournee war enorm erfolgreich.* The theater tour was hugely successful.   **3.** (adj.) Great, wonderful, fantastic. *Die Art und Weise, wie er die Witze erzählt hat, war enorm.* The way he told the jokes was fantastic.

Enormous (physical) = *riesig;* (infrequently) *enorm* He is enormous. *Er ist riesig; Er ist enorm groß.*

Enormous(ly) (fig.) = *enorm* enormously popular *enorm beliebt*

entern   Not a general word for "to enter," but "to board" (a boat), usually for a hostile purpose. *Die Piraten enterten das Schiff und raubten die Passagiere aus.* The pirates boarded the ship and robbed the passengers.

To enter (rooms, buildings) = (trans.) *betreten*; (intrans.) *hineingehen, eintreten, hereinkommen*

To enter s.o./oneself for a test = *jdn./sich für ein Examen anmelden*

To enter s.t. in a book = *etwas in ein Buch eintragen*

To enter into negotiations = *Verhandlungen aufnehmen*

To enter into a contract = *einen Vertrag schließen/eingehen*

Entree, das   Can be used for the appetizer (BrE starter) in a restaurant, though the usual word for this is *die Vorspeise*. In Swiss German it is a common word (and in Germany and Austria a slightly old-fashioned word) for "entrance."

Entrée: In the English-speaking world, "entrée" means different things to different people. Many hotels and restaurants retain the original French meaning, i.e., a course eaten between the fish course and the main course (from Fr. *entre* = between). The German word for this is *das Zwischengericht*. In some countries, it tends to refer to the main course; here the translation is *das Hauptgericht*. Finally, some English speakers use the word as the Germans do to mean "appetizer." The most frequent German expression for this is *die Vorspeise*.

Epik, die   In German this word has far more restricted use than its English counterpart; it means "epic poetry" only.

An epic film/performance = *ein monumentaler Film/eine monumentale Leistung*

An epic match = *ein gewaltiges Spiel*

Epic poem = *das Epos*

Epitaph, das   Tends to mean the gravestone itself rather than the words of dedication written on it.

Epitaph = *die Grabinschrift*

Esel, der   **1.** Donkey.   **2.** (coll.) A derogatory term meaning "idiot." Easel = *die Staffelei*

Etat, der   Budget, both at the domestic and governmental levels. *Im Bundestag findet morgen die Debatte zum Etat für das nächste Jahr statt.* The debate on next year's budget is taking place in the German parliament tomorrow.

Estate (property and land in the country) = *das (Land)gut*

(jur., after death) = *die Erbmasse, der Nachlaß*

BrE Housing estate = *die Siedlung*

BrE Industrial estate = *das Industriegelände*

Real estate agent (BrE estate agent) = *der Immobilienmakler*

Ethos, das   In isolation, this is not a false cognate for English "ethos"; but it is in the compound *das Berufsethos,* where it means "professional ethics."

Etikett, das   Label, on clothes, wine bottles, etc. Refers to both makers' labels and price labels. *Das Etikett auf der Weinflasche gibt genaue Angaben über die Herkunft des Weines.* The label on the wine bottle gives detailed information about the origin of the wine.

Etiquette = *die Etikette*

evangelisch (rel.)   This is the usual word for "Protestant," though the word *protestantisch* also exists. It also has the more general meaning of "evangelical."

eventuell   This is usually translated by "possible," "possibly," "maybe," "perhaps," or a sentence with "may" or "might." It never means "eventually." *Ich komme eventuell morgen.* I might come tomorrow/Maybe I'll come tomorrow. *Wir sollten eventuelle Schwierigkeiten jetzt schon besprechen.* We should discuss any possible difficulties now. *Wir kaufen eventuell eine Ferienwohnung in Hawaii.* Maybe we'll buy/We may buy a vacation apartment in Hawaii.

Eventually = *schließlich, endlich, letzten Endes*

ex/Ex, der/die   1. (adv.) A word often used when drinking, meaning "Drink up!" "Down the hatch!" etc. The main idea is to drink something down in one draught. *Komm! Wir trinken ex!* Come on! Let's drink up!   **2.** (adj.) Finished, over (usually of relationships). *Meine Freundschaft mit Rodney ist jetzt ex.* My friendship with Rodney is all over now.   **3.** (noun) *der/die Ex.* This is used, as in English, to talk about an old flame. *Ich habe gestern meinen Ex zufällig in der Stadt getroffen.* I happened to bump into my ex-boyfriend/ex-husband downtown yesterday.

exaltiert   A fairly negative word meaning "effusive" or "exaggerated"; its use is generally confined to people's behavior. *Sein Benehmen bei der Gartenparty war so exaltiert, daß niemand mit ihm reden wollte.* His behavior at the garden party was so exaggerated that no one wanted to talk to him.

Exalted (rank, position) = *hoch, hochgestellt*

(idea, ideal, ambition, opinion) = *hochfliegend, hochtrabend, übertrieben*

Exemplar, das When talking of books, magazines, newspapers, etc., this means a copy. *Weißt du was? Ich habe das allerletzte Exemplar von Moby Dick gekriegt!* Do you know what? I got the very last copy of *Moby Dick!* When talking of other things, the word is usually not translated at all, since the translation of another key noun makes the meaning clear. *Vom Sony Trinitron Farbfernseher sind bereits über 25 Millionen Exemplare verkauft worden.* More than 25 million Sony Trinitron color televisions have been sold.

Example = *das Beispiel*

Exemplary = *beispielhaft, beispielgebend, vorbildlich*

exemplarisch As an example. *Der Lehrer hat den Schüler exemplarisch gestraft.* The teacher punished the pupil as an example to the others.

Exemplary = *beispielhaft, beispielgebend, vorbildlich*

exerzieren (esp. mil.) To practice or drill. *Der Feldwebel verbrachte drei Stunden damit, seine Soldaten im Lager zu exerzieren.* The sergeant spent three hours drilling his soldiers in the camp.

To exercise (intrans.) = *sich bewegen*

(a muscle) = *trainieren*

(a dog) = *ausführen*

(horses) = *bewegen*

(control, authority, rights, privilege, influence) = *ausüben*

(mil.) = *exerzieren*

Exhibitionist, der Great care is needed here. This single German word refers both to (a) a person who simply wants to attract attention to himself in some perfectly innocent way, i.e., a "show-off"; and (b) a person who exposes himself sexually in public, i.e., a "flasher." *Auf dem Heimweg durch den Central Park ist mir ein Exhibitionist begegnet, der nur einen Regenmantel anhatte.* On my way home through Central Park I met a flasher wearing only a raincoat.

existentiell Of vital significance, existential, pertaining to one's livelihood. *Das Problem des Treibhauseffekts ist existentiell.* The problem of the greenhouse effect is of vital significance.

Existenz, die **1.** Means either "existence" or "livelihood." *Um eine sichere Existenz zu haben, muß der Fischer täglich mindestens 20 Kilo Fische fangen.* To guarantee a safe livelihood, the fisherman has to catch 20 kilos of fish a day. *das Existenzminimum* Subsistence level. *die Existenzgrundlage* The basis of one's livelihood. **2.** It can also be used pejoratively of people: *eine verkrachte Existenz* a failure, a deadbeat.

Existence = *das Dasein, das Bestehen, die Existenz*

Exkursion, die This has a somewhat more serious ring to it than the English "excursion." It usually refers to a field trip, e.g., an outing arranged by the geology department of a university. It is rarely just a leisure outing.
Excursion (leisure) = *der Ausflug*

Expedient, der (comm.) Dispatch clerk.
Expedient = *das Hilfsmittel, der Notbehelf*

expedieren To dispatch, send off. *Wir müssen drei Traktoren nach Polen expedieren.* We have to dispatch three tractors to Poland.
To expedite = *beschleunigen, vorantreiben*

Expedition, die Can mean "expedition," just as in English, e.g., into the African jungle; but also means "dispatch," "sending off," "dispatch office." *Die 50 Computer für die Versicherungsfirma sind zur Expedition verpackt worden.* The 50 computers for the insurance company have been packed up and are ready for dispatch.

Expertise, die Expert's appraisal/report. *Die Antiquitäten sind mit einer Expertise geliefert worden.* The antiques were delivered with an expert's appraisal.
Expertise (expert knowledge) = *die Sachkenntnis*
　　　　　　(manual skill) = *das Geschick*

Exposé, das The plan or outline of a book or film while it is at the planning stage. *Der Redakteur hat kürzlich ein Exposé für Davids neuesten Roman gelesen.* The editor recently read the outline of David's latest novel. Can also mean "written memorandum/report."
Exposé (of scandal, etc.) = *die Enthüllung, die Aufdeckung*

extra **1.** Specially; deliberately. *Ich habe für deinen Geburstag extra eine Sahnetorte gebacken.* I've baked a cream cake specially for your birthday. *Du hast extra die Hose angezogen, die ich nicht ausstehen kann—nur um mich zu ärgern!* You've deliberately put those pants on that I can't stand— just to annoy me! **2.** Extra. *extra stark* extra strong.
Extra (additional) = *zusätzlich*

Extrakt, der **1.** Synopsis or survey of a book, play, film, etc. *In der Zeitschrift wurde ein Extrakt ihres neuesten Theaterstückes veröffentlicht.* A synopsis of her latest play appeared in the magazine. **2.** In medicine, pharmacy, cooking, etc., it can mean "extract."
Extract (book, film, etc.) = *der Auszug*
　　　　　(med., cul., chem., etc.) = *der Extrakt*

extravagant Not only "extravagant," but also "flamboyant," especially with regard to clothes. *Die Schauspielerin hat bei der Filmpremiere durch ihre extravagante Kleidung viel Aufsehen erregt.* The actress attracted a lot of attention at the film premiere with her flamboyant clothes.

She's extravagant = *Sie gibt das Geld mit vollen Händen aus*
Golden teacups?! That's extravagant! = *Goldene Teetassen?! Das ist wirklich übertrieben!*

Extravaganz, die Flamboyance or extravagance. SEE **EXTRAVAGANT**.
Extravagance = *die Verschwendungssucht, der Luxus*
(claims, demands, etc.) = *die Übertriebenheit*
(ideas, theories) = *die Ausgefallenheit*

F

Fabrik, die Factory. *die Papierfabrik* paper mill.
Fabric (material) = *der Stoff*
The fabric of society = *das Gesellschaftsgefüge, die Gesellschaftsstruktur*

Fabrikation, die Production, manufacture. *Bei der Fabrikation der Motoren haben wir unerwartete Probleme.* We're having unexpected problems with the manufacture of the engines.
Fabrication (lies, stories, etc.) = *die Lügengeschichte, das Lügenmärchen*
(manufacture) = *die Herstellung, die Fabrikation*

fabrizieren **1.** (coll., pej., or hum.) To produce, make in an amateurish way. *Mein Gott! Was hast du da wieder für ein Essen fabriziert?! Das ist ja ungenießbar!* My God! What sort of meal have you produced this time?! It's uneatable! **2.** (inf.) To get up to (s.th. mischievous). *Kaum läßt man die Kinder unbeaufsichtigt spielen, fabrizieren sie etwas!* Leave the children playing alone for more than a moment, and they get up to something! **3.** To concoct, fabricate, cook up (lies, stories, excuses, etc.). *Mein Bruder fabriziert immer die unglaublichsten Geschichten, um vom Sportunterricht freigestellt zu werden.* My brother fabricates the most unbelievable stories just to get out of doing sport. **4.** (old) To manufacture, produce, make (on a production line). *Die Firma Drusig fabriziert Gummienten.* The Drusig firm produces rubber ducks.
To fabricate (lies, excuses, etc.) = *erfinden, ersinnen, zusammenbasteln, fabrizieren*

fad(e) Insipid, tasteless, dull, bland, uninteresting. Is usually used to describe character or food. *Diese Tomatensuppe schmeckt unheimlich fad.* This tomato soup tastes really bland. *Mikes neue Freundin wirkt etwas fad.* Mike's new girlfriend seems somewhat dull.

Fad = *der Fimmel, der Tick, die Masche*
To fade = *verbleichen, verblassen*
(flowers) = *verblühen*

Fagott, das (mus.)   Bassoon.
BrE faggot (meatball) = *die Frikadelle*
Faggot (sl., homosexual) = *der Schwule*
Fagot (BrE faggot, sticks) = *das Reisigbündel*

Fahrt, die   Journey, trip.
Fart = *der Furz*

fakultativ   Optional. *Dieser Kurs ist fakultativ.* This course is optional.
Facultative (univ.) = *von der Fakultät*

Fall, der   (Down)fall or drop, but frequently also "case," "instance." Less often it is used to describe the hang or drape of curtains, dresses, etc. *"Tja," sagte Sherlock Holmes, "das ist wirklich ein sehr interessanter Fall."* "Well," said Sherlock Holmes, "this really is a very interesting case." *auf jeden Fall* In any case, at any rate. *für den Fall, daß er kommt, . . .* In case he comes, . . . *in dem Fall* In that case. *im Falle eines Falles* If it comes to it.
Fall (BrE autumn) = *der Herbst*
　　(defeat of town, castle, etc.) = *die Eroberung, die Einnahme*
　　(administration, government; people or animals falling from heights) = *der Sturz*
　　(temperature) = *der Abfall, der Sturz*
Rainfall = *der Regenfall*

Falle, die   Trap, both physical (as in "animal trap") and nonphysical, e.g., "verbal trap," "trick," "catch." *Der Fuchs ist in die Falle geraten.* The fox got caught in the trap. *Der Einbrecher ging der Polizei in die Falle.* The burglar walked into the trap laid by the police.
Fall (BrE autumn) = *der Herbst*
　　(defeat of town, castle, etc.) = *die Eroberung, die Einnahme*
　　(administration, government; people or animals falling from heights) = *der Sturz*
　　(temperature) = *der Abfall, der Sturz*
Rainfall = *der Regenfall*

fallen   Usually means "to fall," "to drop," or "to go down"; but in war contexts usually means "to die," "to be killed." *Sein Großvater ist im Zweiten Weltkrieg gefallen.* His grandfather was killed in the Second World War.
To fall = *stürzen, hinfallen*
(temperature, prices) = *sinken*
(night) = *hereinbrechen*

familiär Not "familiar," but "family" (adj.). When describing atmosphere, it can also mean "cozy," "intimate." *Aus familiären Gründen, kann ich leider nicht zu deinem Geburstag kommen.* Unfortunately, for family reasons, I can't come to your birthday. *Das neue Weinlokal hat eine sehr familiäre Atmosphäre.* The new wine bar has a very cozy atmosphere.
Familiar = *vertraut, bekannt*

famos A dated word meaning "great" or "super." Corresponds roughly to the old words "spiffy," "champion," or "capital."
Famous = *berühmt*

Fang, der **1.** Catch, whether of fish, criminals, or a football. **2.** Fang.
Fang (snakes) = *der Giftzahn*
(dogs, wolves, game animals) = *der Reißzahn, das Maul, der Fang*
(vampires) = *der Vampirzahn*

Fantasie, die (mus.) Fantasia. *Kennst du die Tallisfantasie von Vaughan Williams?* Do you know Vaughan Williams' Tallis Fantasia? SEE **PHANTASIE.**
Fantasy (erotic, etc.) = *der Tagtraum*

Fassade, die **1.** This is used to refer to the front of almost any building, not just the front of grander buildings, as tends to be the case in English. **2.** It can be used, just as in English, to talk about false appearances and pretense. **3.** The important false cognate is its informal use, meaning "face." *Hast du den neuen Freund von meiner Schwester gesehen? Er hat vielleicht eine komische Fassade!* Have you seen my sister's new boyfriend? He really does have a funny face!
der Fassadenkletterer Cat burglar.

fast Nearly, almost. *fast nie* almost never/hardly ever.
Fast (adj.) = *schnell*
(of films to light) = *empfindlich*
(adv., quickly) = *schnell*
(adv., completely) = *fest, tief*
This window is stuck fast = *Dieses Fenster steckt fest*
To be fast asleep = *fest/tief schlafen*
Fast (noun denoting abstinence from food) = *das Fasten*

fatal The main point is that *fatal* is used to mean "death-bringing" far less frequently than the English "fatal." *Fatal,* like "fatal," is, however, used as a synonym for a wide variety of adjectives, e.g., "awkward," "embarrassing," "annoying," "unpleasant," "dire," "fateful." *Bei seiner Buchhaltung machte Fritz einen fatalen Fehler.* Fritz made a serious mistake with the bookkeeping. *Bei der Bergwanderung machte der Leiter einen fatalen Irrtum; als Ergebnis mußten alle eine Nacht im Freien bei einer Temperatur von zwei Grad verbringen.* The leader of the hiking party made an embarrassing/a serious mistake; as a result, the party had to spend a night in the open, with the temperature down to 36 degrees Fahrenheit.

Fatal (death-bringing) = *tödlich*. a fatal accident *ein tödliches Unglück* (fig.) = *verhängnisvoll, verheerend, fatal*

Fatalität, die (Rare)   Great misfortune; embarrassing situation.

Fatality (case of death) = *der Todesfall, das Todesopfer*

(BrE inevitability) = *die Unabwendbarkeit*

faul   **1.** (of people) Lazy. *Annas Sohn ist sehr faul: er bleibt bis mittags im Bett.* Anna's son is very lazy: he stays in bed till lunchtime.   **2.** (of food, wood, eggs, etc.) Rotten. *Igitt! Diese Eier sind faul!* Ugh! These eggs are rotten!   **3.** (of situations, circumstances) Fishy, funny, suspicious, dubious. *Da ist etwas faul an seiner ungewohnten Höflichkeit.* There's something fishy about his unaccustomed politeness. *eine faule Ausrede* A feeble/poor excuse. *ein fauler Kompromiß* An uneasy compromise. *ein fauler Witz* A stupid/rotten joke.

Foul (adj.) = *sehr schlecht*

(for crimes) = *abscheulich*

You're in a foul mood today = *Du bist aber heute schlecht gelaunt!*

Fazit, das   Used at the end of reports, surveys, summaries, etc., to mean "overall," "all in all," "on balance," etc., or a rewrite with "take stock of." It is important to realize that, although *Fazit* (without an article) often starts a sentence, it nearly always comes after some (often lengthy) detailed discussion of a conference, course, book, etc. *. . . waren ebenfalls gut. Fazit: der Kurs war das Geld wert. . . .* were good as well. On balance the course was worth the money. *Lassen Sie uns aus den letzten 20 Jahren das Fazit ziehen.* Let us take stock of the last 20 years.

Facet = *die Facette, die Seite, der Aspekt*

Feder, die   This not only means "feather," but also "spring" (e.g., in a mattress). The meaning "feather" is quite rare in compound nouns: *der Federantrieb* clockwork; *der Federball* (the game) badminton; *der Federball* (ball) shuttlecock; *der Federkrieg* war of words; *die Federung* (on car) suspension; *das Federbett* duvet, quilt

Fee, die   Fairy. *die gute Fee* the good fairy; *die böse Fee* the bad fairy.

Fee (entrance, registration, etc.) = *die Gebühr*

(doctor's, lawyer's, painter's, etc.) = *das Honorar*

(actor's, singer's) = *die Gage*

School fees = *das Schulgeld*

Membership fee = *der Mitgliedsbeitrag*

fehlen   To be missing, to be lacking, to be away/absent; other meanings according to context. *Ohne Tom hat die Atmosphäre gefehlt.* Without Tom, the atmosphere was missing/there was no atmosphere. *Professor Col-*

lins fehlt heute. Professor Collins is away today. *Mir fehlen 50 Pfennig am Fahrgeld.* I'm 50 pfennigs short for my fare. *Großmutter fehlt uns allen sehr.* We all miss grandmother very much. *Was fehlt dir denn?* What's the matter with you, then?

To fail (general) = *keinen Erfolg haben*
    (tests) = *durchfallen, nicht bestehen*
    (attempts, ambitions, marriages, plans) = *scheitern, fehl-schlagen, mißlingen*

Feier, die   Celebration, ceremony. *die Hochzeitsfeier* Wedding reception. *zur Feier des Tages* In honor of the occasion.

Fire = *das Feuer, der Brand*

feiern   To celebrate; to hold, have. *Gestern abend haben wir meinen Geburtstag gefeiert.* Yesterday evening we celebrated my birthday. *Wir feiern eine Party am Wochenende.* We're having a party over the weekend.

To fire (employee) = *feuern, entlassen*
    (a shot) = *einen Schuß abfeuern*
    (a pot in a kiln) = *einen Topf brennen*

fein   (material, hair, nailfile, guy, etc.) fine; (humor, irony) delicate; (used in praise or approval) good/well, beautiful(ly). *Du hast dich heute aber fein gemacht.* You've really dressed up today. *Das hast du wirklich fein gemacht.* You really did that well/beautifully. *Sie ist ihren Schwiegereltern nicht fein genug.* She's not good enough in the eyes of her in-laws.

That's fine = *Gut/In Ordnung*
Fine weather = *schönes Wetter*
A fine mess! = *eine schöne Sauerei!*
Monday is fine with me = *Montag paßt mir gut*

Feld, das   Means "field" or "open country," but in graphs, sketches, plans, illustrations, board games, etc., it means "area" or "square." *Die braunen Felder auf meiner Landkarte stellen Sumpfgebiete dar.* The brown areas on my map indicate bogs. *Ein Schachbrett hat 64 Felder.* A chessboard has 64 squares. *Er ist im Feld gefallen.* He died on the battlefield.

Field (cultivated) = *der Acker, das Feld*
    (grass or meadow) = *die Wiese*
    (for grazing) = *die Weide*
    (football, other sports) = *der (Fußball)platz*
    (area of study) = *das Gebiet, das Feld*
Oilfield = *das Ölfeld*
Battlefield = *das (Schlacht)feld*

Fell, das   The fur, skin, coat, or fleece of an animal. *Dieses Rentier hat ein wunderschönes Fell.* This reindeer has a wonderful coat. Occasionally it is also used informally to describe insensitive people, in the expression *dickes Fell*. *Er hat ein dickes Fell*. He's thick-skinned.

BrE Fell (mountain) = *der Berg*

(hill) = *der Hügel*

(moor) = *das Moorland*

Fest, das Celebration(s), party, festival. *Im August feiern wir das Fest des fünfzigjährigen Bestehens des Sportvereins*. In August we're holding the fiftieth anniversary celebration of the Sports Club. *das Hochzeitsfest* Wedding reception. *das Weinfest* Wine festival. *das Sportfest* Sports day.

Feast = *das Gelage, das Festessen*

Fete, die A colloquial word for "party." *Die Studenten organisieren eine Fete für Samstag*. The students are organizing a party for Saturday.

BrE *Fête:* No exact equivalent in German: church or garden fêtes to raise money for charity are rare in German-speaking countries. In the following phrases, *der Basar* (also spelt *der Bazar*) comes near, but the word does not include games, coconut shies, tug-of-war, etc.

Church fête = *der Kirchenbasar*

Charity fête = *der Wohltätigkeitsbasar*

Garden fête = *das Gartenfest*

Village fête = *das Dorffest*

Fett, das Usually does mean "fat," e.g., the fat on a piece of beef or bacon. In cooking, however, it is often used inexactly to denote anything you might choose to cook with: margarine, dripping, oil, butter, or lard. *das Schmierfett* Grease. *die Fettcreme* Skin cream. *der Fettbauch* Beer belly, paunch. *der Fettdruck* Bold type. *ins Fettnäpfchen treten* To put one's foot in one's mouth (BrE to put one's foot in it).

fett 1. (of food) Greasy, rich, fatty. *Gestern wurde uns ein sehr fettes Essen aufgetischt*. We were served up a very greasy/fatty meal yesterday. 2. (of people) Fat—to a distinctly unhealthy extent. (SEE **DICK,** which means "fat" in a less unhealthy sense.) *Er ist ganz schön fett*. He's really fat. *ein fettarmer Käse* A low-fat cheese.

feudal Feudal, but also (coll.) "fancy," "posh." *ein feudales Restaurant* a fancy restaurant

Fieber, das The English word "fever" is usually used for more dramatic medical conditions than the German word *Fieber*, which in everyday conversation simply refers to a high temperature. *Ich fühle mich sehr unwohl; ich glaube, ich habe Fieber*. I don't feel at all well; I think I have a temperature. *jdm. das Fieber messen* To take s.o.'s temperature.

Fever = *das Fieber*

Hay fever = *der Heuschnupfen*

Scarlet fever = *der Scharlach*

Yellow fever = *das Gelbfieber*

(fig.) = *die Aufregung, die Erregung, das Fieber*

Election fever = *das Wahlfieber, der Wahlrausch*

Figur, die 1. (human) Figure, physique, build. 2. (geom.) Shape. 3. (novel, film, play) Character. *eine gute Figur abgeben* To cut a fine figure. *auf seine Figur achten* To watch one's figure.

Figure (number) = *die Zahl, die Ziffer*

(price, sum of money) = *die Summe*

(physique) = *die Figur, die Gestalt*

Public figure = *die Persönlichkeit*

Figure of speech = *die Redewendung, die Redensart*

Filiale, die Branch of a company. *Er ist in unsere Nürnberger Filiale versetzt worden.* He has been transferred to our branch in Nuremberg.

Filial (adj.) = *Kindes-/eines Kindes, Sohnes-/eines Sohnes, Tochter-/ einer Tochter/töchterlich*

With filial affection = *mit der Liebe eines Sohnes/einer Tochter*

Finale, das Not only "finale" (in music, circus, or a variety show) but also "final" or "finals," mainly in sporting events. *das Halbfinale der Basketballmeisterschaft* the semifinal of the basketball championships

Finesse, die Skill, refinement, trick; (pl.) finer points. The point here is that, though often similar in meaning to its English counterpart, the German *Finesse* is frequently used in contexts where it would be impossible to use "finesse" in English. *Er beherrscht alle Finessen der Fahrtechnik.* He knows all the finer points about driving. *mit allen Finessen* With all the latest gadgets, with all the trimmings.

Finesse (diplomacy) = *die Gewandtheit, das Geschick*

(BrE slyness) = *die Schlauheit, die Finesse*

fingieren The basic idea is of pretence and deception: to feign, fake; to think up, fabricate, invent. *Er hatte den Unfall fingiert, um die Versicherungsgesellschaft zu betrügen.* He had faked the accident to defraud the insurance company.

To finger (touch) = *anfassen*

(play with) = *(herum)fingern an*

Fink, der Finch (bird).

Fink (despicable person) = *der Saftsack*

(strikebreaker) = *der Streikbrecher*

(police informer) = *der Spitzel*

Firma, die 1. Company, firm. 2. The official name of a company, as registered in the *Handelsregister* (official register of companies). *Die Gesellschaft wurde unter der Firma Lenz eingetragen.* The company was registered under the name of Lenz.

firmieren To trade under a particular name. SEE **FIRMA**. *Seit 1989 firmiert die Gesellschaft als Lenz & Söhne.* Since 1989 the firm has been trading under the name of Lenz & Sons.
To firm (up) = *festmachen*

First, der Ridge (of roof).
(The) first = *der (die, das) Erste*

fix Usually colloquial, denoting speed or quick intelligence. *In der Cafeteria geht es ganz fix, aber hier muß man immer eine Ewigkeit warten.* It's really quick in the cafeteria, but you always have to wait for ages here. *Der neue Abteilungsleiter soll ein ganz fixer Junge sein.* The new department manager is supposed to be a really sharp guy.

fix und fertig **1.** Totally exhausted. *Nach drei Stunden Einkaufen mit zwei Kindern war sie fix und fertig.* She was completely worn out after three hours shopping with two children. **2.** Finished (with a job, etc.). *In zwei Stunden dürften wir mit dem Tapezieren fix und fertig sein.* We should be completely finished with the wallpapering in two hours' time. **3.** (with *machen*) To give s.o. a hiding/thrashing. *Wenn ich den Typ finde, der meine Antenne abgebrochen hat, mach' ich ihn fix und fertig.* If I find the guy who snapped off my antenna (BrE aerial) I'll break his neck.

eine fixe Idee An obsession, a "thing" (about s.t.): an *idée fixe*. *Daß man mit dreißig Kinder haben muß, war bei ihr eine fixe Idee.* It was an obsession of hers that one had to have children by the age of thirty.

To fix (make firm) = *festmachen, befestigen*
(time, price, etc.) = *festlegen*
(settle, sort out) = *in Ordnung bringen*
(intend) = *vorhaben*
(repair) = *reparieren*

fixieren Occasionally corresponds to "fix." *einen Termin fixieren* to fix a time/date. But also: **1.** To stare at. *Man konnte nicht lügen, wenn er einen so fixierte.* It was impossible to lie when he stared at one in this way. **2.** To set down, record (esp. in writing). *Alle Einzelheiten der Baubeschreibung müssen schriftlich fixiert sein.* All the specifications of the building must be set down in writing. **3.** (in participle form) To have an obsession of some kind. *Es ist nicht normal, daß ein Mann in seinem Alter auf Schulmädchen fixiert ist.* It is not normal for a man of his age to have a fixation about schoolgirls.

To fix (make firm) = *festmachen, befestigen*
(time, price, etc.) = *festlegen*
(settle, sort out) = *in Ordnung bringen*
(intend) = *vorhaben*
(repair) = *reparieren*

Flair, das Particular quality or atmosphere that is felt to be positive and even captivating. *Das besondere Flair von Hamburg hat natürlich viel mit*

dem Hafengebiet zu tun. The special atmosphere of Hamburg has of course a great deal to do with the dockside area. *Sie hatte ein Flair von Eleganz und Kultiviertheit.* She had an aura of elegance and refinement.
Flair (talent) = *das Talent, die Begabung*
(style) = *der Stil, das Format*

Flanke, die **1.** Flank. Also used to denote the side of a vehicle. *Er war einem Bus voll in die Flanke gefahren.* He had driven smack into the side of a bus. **2.** Used in various sports, esp. soccer, to refer to a type of pass (the cross or center-pass) or a section of the field (the wing). *Die scharfen Flanken der Stuttgarter machten der Braunschweiger Abwehr schwer zu schaffen.* The crisp crosses of the Stuttgart players gave the Braunschweig defense a lot of trouble. *Auf der rechten Flanke war wieder kein Kölner da.* Once again there was no one from the Cologne side on the right wing.

flanken To cross, center (a ball, in soccer, etc.: SEE **FLANKE**).
To flank = *flankieren*

flankieren To flank. Also used metaphorically, esp. in the phrase *flankierende Maßnahmen* = accompanying measures.

flattern **1.** To flutter, flap. *Die Fahne flatterte im Wind.* The flag was fluttering in the wind. *Die Taube flatterte mit den Flügeln und ließ sich dann nieder.* The pigeon flapped its wings and then settled down. **2.** Also used idiomatically to denote the arrival of a communication. *Dieser anonyme Brief ist mir heute ins Haus geflattert.* This anonymous letter turned up in my mailbox today.
To flatter = *schmeicheln*

Fleck, der **1.** Most commonly denotes a stain or (unwanted) spot; also a splotch, blob, patch (of color, etc.): it thus does not normally indicate something as small as a fleck. *Wo kommen diese ganzen Flecken her?* Where do all these stains come from? *An einem Bein hatte diese sonst schwarze Katze einen weißen Fleck.* This otherwise black cat had a white patch on one leg. **2.** Also "place," "spot" (esp. in certain fixed expressions). *Rühr' dich nicht vom Fleck!* Don't move [i.e., from that spot]!
Fleck = *der Tupfen, der Spritzer*

Fleisch, das Flesh (in relation to human beings, esp. in such fixed expressions as *Fleisch und Blut* = flesh and blood). But also the normal word for "meat." *Ich esse fast kein Fleisch mehr.* I hardly eat meat any more. *Zahnfleisch* Gum(s) (of teeth).

flicken To mend, repair, specifically by applying a patch. *Ich brauchte nur zehn Minuten, um den Reifen zu flicken.* It only took me ten minutes to repair the puncture. Colloquially, it may refer to other forms of repairing.
To flick (s.t. away with finger) = *(weg)schnippen*

Fliege, die 1. Fly (insect). 2. Bow tie. *Ich habe keine Ahnung, wie man eine Fliege bindet.* I've no idea how to put on a bow tie.

Flinte, die Shotgun. *In einer halben Stunde hatte er mit seiner Flinte zehn Wachteln erlegt.* Within half an hour he had shot ten quails with his shotgun. *die Flinte ins Korn werfen* To throw in the towel/sponge.

Flint = *der Feuerstein*

Flipper, der A pinball machine. *Wenn er jeden Nachmittag nur am Flipper steht, statt zu lernen, wird er die Prüfung bestimmt nicht bestehen.* If he spends every afternoon on the pinball machine instead of studying, he certainly won't pass the exam.

Flipper (zool.) = *die Flosse*

flippern To play pinball. SEE **FLIPPER**. *Wir haben den ganzen Abend geflippert.* We played pinball all evening.

Flirt, der Flirtation.

She's a flirt = *Sie flirtet gern*

Flocke, die Flake (of snow, cereal, etc.) *Der Schnee fiel in großen Flocken.* The snow was falling in large flakes.

Flock (sheep) = *die Herde*

(birds) = *der Schwarm, die Schar*

floppen To do the Fosbury flop (athletics, high jump).

To flop (fail) = *durchfallen*

Floß, das Raft. *Er wollte mit diesem Floß den Atlantik überqueren.* He wanted to cross the Atlantic on this raft.

Floss (dental) = *die Zahnseide*

Flosse, die Fin (of fish); flipper (of dolphin, diver, etc.). Also slang for "hand": mitt, paw.

Floss (dental) = *die Zahnseide*

Fluidum, das Aura, atmosphere emanating from s.o. or s.t. *Ich habe technisch bessere Tenöre gehört, aber dieser hat ein gewisses Fluidum, das den Zuhörer bannt.* I've heard tenors who are technically better, but this one has a certain mysterious quality that captivates the listener.

Fluid = *die Flüssigkeit*

Flur, der 1. Hall (of apartment or house). *Als die Kinder den Flur betraten, schleuderten sie einfach ihre Gummistiefel von sich.* When the children came into the hall, they just kicked off their galoshes/gumboots. 2. Landing (on upper floor of house). *Sehr peinlich—ich kam splitternackt aus dem Badezimmer und stieß auf dem Flur auf Tante Erna.* Very embarrassing—I walked out of the bathroom stark naked and bumped into Aunt Erna on the landing. 3. Corridor (in large public building). *Frau Schmidt? Ich habe sie vor fünf Minuten auf dem Flur im Gespräch mit Herrn Meyer gesehen.* Frau Schmidt? I saw her in the corridor five minutes ago, talking to Herr Meyer.

Floor (in room) = *der Fußboden*

(stor(e)y) = *der Stock, das Stockwerk, das Geschoß*

Flur, die **1.** A literary or poetical word for "field," "meadow." **2.** "Parcel," "plot" of (agricultural) land.

Floor (in room) = *der Fußboden*

(stor(e)y) = *der Stock, das Stockwerk, das Geschoß*

flüstern To whisper. *Das ist nicht schön, wie die beiden ständig miteinander flüstern.* It's not nice the way those two keep whispering to each other. Note also the following colloquial phrases. *Dem werde ich was flüstern!* I'll give him a piece of my mind/tell him a thing or two! *Das kann ich dir flüstern!* You'd better believe it!/I can tell you! *Den würde ich nie im Leben heiraten—das kann ich dir flüstern!* I would never marry him—you'd better believe it!

To fluster = *nervös machen, aus der Fassung bringen*

Flut, die **1.** Flood (in the metaphorical sense). *Es gab eine Flut von solchen Artikeln.* There was a flood of articles of this sort. **2.** High tide. *Um 8.07 Uhr ist Flut.* High tide is at 8:07 A.M.

Flood (literal) = *die Überschwemmung*

Föhre, die Scotch pine (tree).

Fir (tree) = *die Tanne*

Folklore, die May denote "folklore" in the sense of the stock of stories, songs, dances, and so on handed down from generation to generation. But more often used to refer specifically to folk songs (and dances) as entertainment. *Wir bieten Ihnen heute abend eine bunte Sendung mit Folklore aus aller Welt.* Tonight we bring you a colorful program with folksong and dance from all over the world. *Die Platte finden Sie unter internationaler "Folklore."* You'll find the record in the international folk(song) section.

Fond, der **1.** Back, rear (of car). *Es gibt keinen Aschenbecher im Fond.* There's no ashtray in the back. **2.** Background (of picture, pattern, etc.). **3.** Juices from roast meat (e.g., as used for making gravy).

Fund = *der Fonds*

foppen To pull s.o.'s leg, tease. The word is a little dated or literary in flavor. *Sie wollten dich wahrscheinlich nur foppen.* They probably just wanted to pull your leg.

Fop (noun) = *der Geck*

forcieren To speed up (a process in order to achieve an aim). *Die Bauarbeiten wurden unter dem neuen Architekten stark forciert.* The building work was speeded up dramatically under the new architect. *das Tempo forcieren* To force the pace.

To force = *zwingen*

Form, die Form, shape. *Der Anzug hat seine Form verloren.* The suit has lost its shape. Also specifically a "mold" of some sort. *Das weiß-glühende Metall wird dann in geeignete Formen gegossen.* The white-hot metal is then poured into suitable molds. *Dann tat sie den ganzen Teig in eine ovale (Back)form.* She then put all the mixture into an oval baking tin. Form (official) = *das Formular, der Vordruck*

Format, das **1.** Format. **2.** The quality that makes a person stand out above the rest: stature, class. *Inzwischen ist er ein Schachspieler von internationalem Format.* He is now a chess player of international stature. *Trotz dieser Fehler wird er als Politiker von Format in die Geschichte eingehen.* Despite these mistakes he will go down in history as a politician of stature. *Du kannst sagen, was du willst—die Frau hat Format.* You can say what you like—the woman has class.

formen To form, shape; also "to mold." SEE **FORM.**

förmlich Formal. But also a strengthening adverb, meaning "really," "properly." *Er hat mich förmlich beschwindelt.* He really swindled me.

Formular, das (Official) form, blank. *Auf jedem Formular finde ich eine Frage, die ich nicht beantworten kann.* On every form I find a question I can't answer.

Formula (math., chem.) = *die Formel*
(recipe, for success, etc.) = *das Rezept*

formulieren To formulate, but often "put" will provide a more natural translation. *Was er sagte, war richtig, aber er hat es ziemlich taktlos formuliert.* What he said was right, but he put it rather tactlessly.

Fotograf, der Photographer. *Dieser Fotograf hat sich auf Tieraufnahmen spezialisiert.* This photographer has specialized in animal pictures.

Photograph = *das Foto, die Fotografie, die Aufnahme*

Fotografie, die Photography, but also "photograph" (though the shorter form *das Foto* is now more commonly used). *Als der Detektiv ihm die Fotografie zeigte, wurde er blaß.* When the detective showed him the photograph, he went pale.

Fox, der A short form for *Foxtrott* (or, very occasionally, *Foxterrier*). Fox = *der Fuchs*

Fraktion, die **1.** A collective term for the representatives of a political party within a parliamentary assembly: parliamentary party. *Die Fraktion der SPD tritt morgen zusammen, um über diesen Vorschlag zu diskutieren.* The parliamentary party of the SPD is meeting tomorrow to discuss this proposal. **2.** A group within a group: faction. *Es hat sich bereits unter den Bauern eine Fraktion gebildet, die weit drastischere Maßnahmen befürwortet.* A faction has already formed among the farmers that advocates much more drastic measures.

Fraction (math.) = *der Bruch, die Bruchzahl*
(small part) = *der Bruchteil*

Fraktur, die Fracture (med.). Also, in printing, the typeface known as "Gothic" (or "black letter"), formerly much used for German texts but now rarely encountered.

Fracture (med., usual term) = *der Bruch*

frankieren To pay for the carriage of a letter, parcel, etc., either by putting a stamp on it or, as many firms do, "franking" it with a postage meter (a special machine). *Wenn er mir schon solche Briefe schicken muß, könnte er sie wenigstens frankieren.* If he really has to send me letters like this, he could at least put a stamp on them.

To frank (cancel postage stamp with postmark) = *abstempeln*

frei Corresponds to "free" in most contexts. Particular uses where "free" is not a satisfactory translation include: **1.** Vacant, unoccupied. *Es sind noch einige Plätze frei in der hinteren Reihe.* There are still some vacant seats in the back row. *In fast jedem Fenster hing ein Schild mit "Zimmer frei."* A sign saying "Vacancies" hung in practically every window. **2.** Not for working (of a day, etc.). *Ja, morgen ist frei—es ist Himmelfahrt.* Yes, tomorrow's a holiday—it's Ascension Day. **3.** Clear (of traffic, etc.). *Ist die Straße frei auf deiner Seite?* Is the road clear on your side? *freier Journalist* Freelance journalist; *die freie Wirtschaft* Industry, private enterprise; *frei ab 12 Jahren* Authorized for showing to those aged 12 and over (film censorship); *freie Fahrt geben (für etwas)* To give the go-ahead/all-clear (for s.t.); *einen Vortrag frei halten* To deliver a lecture without notes. SEE **FREIMACHEN, FREISCHWIMMEN.** Free (i.e., without cost, charge): *frei* may have this meaning (as in *Eintritt frei* = Admission free), but the more usual word is *kostenlos*.

Freier, der A dated word for a "suitor." But nowadays a colloquial term for a prostitute's customer, client, "john." *Wie die meisten Prostituierten empfindet sie nur Verachtung für ihre Freier.* Like most prostitutes she feels only contempt for her clients.

A free man (or, historically, "freeman") = *der Freie* (as a nominalized adjective, declined accordingly)

BrE Freeman (of a city) = *der Ehrenbürger*

freilich **1.** But, though, however, admittedly. *Die Festung wurde zurückerobert, freilich mit starken Verlusten.* The fort was recaptured, though with heavy losses. **2.** Also, esp. in South Germany, a strong affirmative adverb. *"Wird er die Prüfung bestehen?"—"(Ja) freilich!"* "Will he pass the test?"—"Yes, of course."

Freely (generously) = *großzügig*

(without restriction) = *frei, ungehindert*

freimachen Not "to make free," but: **1.** To put a stamp on a letter. *Einen Brief ins Ausland müssen Sie natürlich freimachen.* Of course you have to put a stamp on a letter you're sending abroad. **2.** To take time off work. *Morgen ist Feiertag und übermorgen mache ich frei.* Tomorrow's a public holiday and I'll take the day after tomorrow off.   **3.** (reflexive) To remove clothing (as far as the waist). *"Machen Sie sich bitte frei,"* sagte die etwas *streng wirkende Ärztin.* "Strip to the waist, please," said the rather forbidding (woman) doctor.

To make free (liberate) = *befreien*

freischwimmen   Not "to swim freely" or "to swim free of s.t." Instead this is used as a reflexive verb to indicate that one has passed the (fifteen-minute) swimming test that proves one can swim unaided. There is no obvious succinct translation for this. The term is occasionally used metaphorically, however, to indicate that s.o. can work independently, etc., and can stand on his or her own two feet. *Ich kann nicht immer da sein—du mußt dich auch mal freischwimmen.* I can't always be here—you've got to learn to stand on your own two feet.

frequentieren   A formal word, which can mean "to frequent" (i.e., visit repeatedly). But it is most commonly used today in the past participle to indicate how often a road or place is used. *Dieser Teil der Autobahn ist besonders stark frequentiert.* There is especially heavy traffic on this part of the highway.

Frequenz, die   Frequency (tech., e.g., of radio waves). Generally, it denotes the number of people using a road or place; it is rather formal in tone. SEE **FREQUENTIEREN.** *Wegen der starken Frequenz an dieser Kreuzung soll eine Ampel aufgestellt werden.* Because of the heavy traffic at this junction traffic lights are to be installed. *Ich weiß nicht, ob sich das Land Schulklassen mit diesen niedrigen Frequenzen leisten kann.* I don't know if the state can afford these classes with a low pupil–teacher ratio.

Frequency (how often s.t. happens) = *die Häufigkeit*

Freund(in), der (die)   Friend, but also, in the appropriate context, "boyfriend" or "girlfriend." *Mein Freund möchte, daß wir bald heiraten.* My boyfriend wants us to get married soon.

It should also be remembered that *Freund(in)*, even in its nonromantic sense, will normally indicate a close friendship. Many less intimate relationships, where English still uses "friend," would be denoted by *Bekannte(r)* in German, rather than *Freund.*

frivol   Normally means "indecent," "dirty," "risqué." *Ich meine, du solltest nicht dauernd diese frivolen Witze vor den Kindern erzählen.* I don't think you ought to keep telling these smutty jokes in front of the children.

Frivolous (careless) = *leichtsinnig, leichtfertig*

(silly) = *albern*

Frivolität.   SEE **FRIVOL.** *Ich finde, solche Frivolitäten sind hier fehl am Platz.* I think such risqué comments are out of place here.

Frivolity (carelessness) = *der Leichtsinn, die Leichtsinnigkeit*

(silliness) = *die Albernheit*

Frontal- "Frontal" in some compounds. *Frontalangriff* frontal attack. But note: *Frontalunterricht* Teacher-centered teaching, BrE "chalk and talk"; *Frontalzusammenstoß* Head-on collision.

Fuge, die 1. (mus.) Fugue. 2. A joint or gap (e.g., between bricks, tiles). *Die Fugen zwischen den Fliesen sind viel zu weit.* The gaps between the tiles are much too wide.

füllen 1. To fill. *Er füllte den Kessel mit Wasser.* He filled the kettle with water. 2. To pour or to put (of the substance that goes into a container). *Er füllte das Wasser in den Kessel.* He poured the water into the kettle. 3. (cul.) To stuff. *gefüllte Weinblätter* stuffed vine leaves.

Füller, der Fountain pen. *Kannst du mir deinen Füller leihen?* Can you lend me your fountain pen?

Filler (for cracks) = *der Spachtel, die Spachtelmasse*

fummeln To fumble. Also, by extension, "to grope," in the sexual sense. *Hinter ihm fummelten zwei Teenager, was ihn vom Film irgendwie ablenkte.* Behind him two teenagers were groping (one another), which somehow distracted him from the film.

Fund, der Find, discovery. *Die Archäologen machten einen erstaunlichen Fund.* The archaeologists made an amazing discovery.

Fund (fin.) = *der Fonds*

fundieren To back up, substantiate. Esp. common in the past participle. *Dies ist natürlich nur eine Vermutung, die erst mit Beweisen zu fundieren ist.* Of course this is only a supposition that still has to be substantiated. *Er ist sicher ein geistreicher Biograph, aber es fehlt ihm leider an fundiertem Wissen.* He is certainly a witty biographer, but unfortunately he is lacking in sound knowledge. *fundierte Kritik* Sound/well-founded criticism; criticism that is backed up with facts.

To found (establish) = *gründen*

Funk, der Radio (as a communications system and medium). *Er appellierte per Funk an die Bevölkerung.* He appealed to the population by radio. The word is a little dated in this general sense and tends now to be applied more usually to private communications. *CB-Funk* CB radio.

To be in a funk = *Bammel haben, Schiß haben, Muffe haben*

Funktionär, der Functionary, though the German word does not always carry the slightly pejorative association of the English. It is, for example, the normal word to denote a labor union (BrE trade union) official (*Gewerkschaftsfunktionär*).

funktionieren To function. But "work" is often the better translation when the word carries its normal meaning of "functioning properly." *Wenn du den Stecker nicht einsteckst, wird der Mixer natürlich nicht funktionieren.* If you don't put the plug in, of course the mixer won't work.

To function as (i.e., act in a particular capacity) = *fungieren als*

Fusion, die Fusion, in various technical contexts (e.g., nuclear physics). But in business contexts a "merger," "amalgamation." *Die Fusion dieser beiden Unternehmen ergäbe, wie einige befürchten, ein Kartell.* The merger of these two companies would lead, some people fear, to a cartel. Fusion (coalescence) = *die Verschmelzung*

fusionieren To merge. SEE **FUSION.** *Die beiden Unternehmen werden in den nächsten Tagen fusionieren.* The two companies will merge in the next few days.

To fuse (atoms, metals) = *verschmelzen*

G

Gabel, die Fork (for eating, gardening). Also the "cradle" on which a telephone handset is placed when the telephone is not being used. Gable = *der Giebel*

Gaffer, der S.o. who stares in a stupid or insensitive manner: a gawper, gaper. *Bei jedem Verkehrsunfall gibt es solche Gaffer.* You get these sorts of gapers whenever there's a road accident. Gaffer (old man) = *der Alte*

Gag, der 1. Does not usually signify a "gag" in the sense of a joke delivered by a stand-up comedian. It normally denotes s.t. amusing based on a technical device or special effect. *Das wäre ein toller Gag, in diesem Tigerfell auf die Party zu gehen!* That would be a great stunt to go to the party in this tiger skin! *Gestern hat ein Mann in der Fußgängerzone in einer Wanne voll Bier gebadet—es war natürlich ein Werbegag.* Yesterday a man took a bath in a tub full of beer in the pedestrian zone—of course it was a publicity stunt. *Die meisten von Steven Spielbergs Filmen enthalten phantasievolle Gags.* Most of Steven Spielberg's films contain imaginative special effects. 2. It may also denote special devices without any humorous connotation. *Diese elektronische Schreibmaschine hat wirklich all die neuesten Gags.* This electronic typewriter really has all the latest gadgets.

Gag (joke) = *der Witz*
(over mouth) = *der Knebel*

Gage, die Fee, esp. as paid to an actor, musician, etc. *Die Gage, die solch ein weltberühmter Solist verlangen würde, könnten wir nie bezahlen.* We could never pay the fee such a world-famous soloist would demand. Gauge (measuring instrument) = *das Meßgerät*
(of railroad track) = *die Spur(weite)*

galant   Gallant, either in the sense of "chivalrous" or "attentive to women" or in an amatory context, but not in the sense of "brave." *ein galantes Abenteuer* An affair of the heart. An essentially dated or ironical expression.

Gallant (brave) = *tapfer*

Galerie, die   **1.** Corresponds to "gallery" in most cases. In the context of painting, however, *Galerie* may denote not only a (public) art gallery (*Gemäldegalerie*) but also an artshop that sells and exhibits paintings.   **2.** Less usually, it may denote a (shopping) arcade with an upper floor.

Gang, der   The noun from *gehen*, with a correspondingly large number of uses.   **1.** A walk, or way of walking. *Er hatte den Gang eines Matrosen.* He had a sailor's walk.   **2.** A corridor, passage. *Frau Horn wartet draußen im Gang.* Frau Horn is waiting outside in the corridor.   **3.** Course (of a meal; of an event). *Schon nach dem zweiten Gang war ich satt.* I was already full after the second course. *Wir lassen die Dinge ihren Gang gehen.* We'll let things take their course.   **4.** Gear (of car, etc.). *Ich kann den dritten Gang nie finden.* I can never find third gear.

Gang (criminal) = *die Gang*
　　(of laborers) = *der Trupp, die Kolonne*

garni.   See **Hotel garni.**

Gast, der   Guest, but with a wider range of applications than the English word. It is, for example, the normal word to refer to a customer in a restaurant, bar, pub, etc.

Gasthaus, das   An inn, i.e., a pub/restaurant that often offers accommodations as well. Its connotations vary from person to person—it is felt by some to have a South German flavor. *Wir haben ein wunderschönes Gasthaus im Dorf gefunden.* We found a wonderful inn in the village.

Guest house = *die Pension*

Gastronomie, die   May denote gastronomy, i.e., haute cuisine, cordon bleu cooking. But also indicates the catering trade generally. *Ich glaube, die Gastronomie wäre gerade der richtige Berufszweig für Sie.* I think that catering would be just the right career for you.

Gaul, der   A pejorative term for a horse: nag, hack.

Gaul (country) = *Gallien*
　　(inhabitant) = *der (die) Gallier(in)*

Gaze, die   Gauze.

Gaze = *der (starre) Blick*

Geist, der   May mean "ghost." *der Heilige Geist* the Holy Ghost. But this is a subordinate meaning compared with its main senses of "mind," "intellect," "spirit."

Ghost (also) = *das Gespenst*

geistlich Spiritual, religious; also "clerical," "ecclesiastical" (as seen in the nominalized form *der Geistliche* = clergyman). *Die geistliche Musik Bachs interessiert mich besonders.* I'm especially interested in Bach's sacred music.

Ghostly = *gespenstisch, geisterhaft*

Generaldirektor, der "Chairman" or "president" of a large company.

genial Denotes the presence of genius: "brilliant" is normally a suitable translation. *Es war eine geniale Idee, die beiden Länder gegeneinander auszuspielen.* It was a brilliant idea to play off the two countries against each other. *Ein genialer Mensch bestimmt, aber ohne jede Wärme.* A brilliant man certainly, but totally lacking in warmth.

Genial = *freundlich*

Genialität, die Brilliance, genius. SEE GENIAL.

Geniality = *die Freundlichkeit*

Genie, das Genius (quality or person). *Ein solches Werk zeugt von echtem Genie.* Such a work demonstrates true genius. *Er hält sich für ein Genie.* He thinks he's a genius.

Genie = *der dienstbare Geist*

(in a bottle) = *der Flaschengeist*

Genus, das Gender (grammatical). *Es gibt bestimmte Substantive im Französischen, deren Genus ich mir einfach nicht merken kann.* There are certain nouns in French whose gender I simply can't remember.

Genus (biol.) = *die Gattung*

Germane(-nin), der (die) Refers to a member of the tribes originally inhabiting parts of Northern and Central Europe: "Teuton."

German = *der (die) Deutsche*

gewinnen 1. To win. 2. To extract, to obtain (with reference to natural resources and also their processing). *Aus diesem Erz wird Eisen gewonnen.* Iron is extracted from this ore. *Unser Mehl wird nur aus organischem Weizen gewonnen.* Our flour is produced only from organic wheat.

Gift, das Poison, venom. *Blausäure ist ein besonders schnell wirkendes Gift.* Prussic acid is a particularly quick-acting poison.

Gift (present) = *das Geschenk*

(talent) = *das Talent, die Begabung*

Glanz, der This noun expresses the concept of shining, and the context will determine which of the many English synonyms will be used in each case: shine, gleam, glitter, sparkle, sheen, etc. *Er war stolz auf den Glanz des nagelneuen Lacks.* He was proud of the gleam of the brand-new paintwork.

Glance = *der (flüchtige) Blick*

glänzen To shine, gleam, glitter, etc. SEE **GLANZ**. *durch Abwesenheit glänzen* To be conspicuous by one's absence.

To glance = *blicken*

To glance at s.t. = *einen kurzen Blick auf etwas werfen*

Glas, das **1.** Glass; jar. *Geben Sie mir bitte ein Glas Himbeermarmelade.* Could I have a jar of raspberry jam, please? **2.** Lens of a pair of spectacles. *Die Brille fiel auf den steinernen Boden und dabei zerbrach eines der Gläser.* The glasses fell onto the stone floor and as a result one of the lenses broke.

(Pair of) glasses (spectacles) = *die Brille*

Glashaus, das Does not indicate a glass-producing factory, but a greenhouse, hothouse (BrE also: glasshouse), though the words *Treibhaus* and *Gewächshaus* are more commonly used in this sense, and *Glashaus* is perhaps most familiar in the proverb *Wer (selbst) im Glashaus sitzt, soll nicht mit Steinen werfen* People who live in glass houses shouldn't throw stones.

Glasshouse (factory) = *die Glashütte*

       (BrE slang = military prison) = *der Bau, der Bunker*

Glosse, die Gloss, in the sense of a note on a word or passage in a text or manuscript (as in English). Also a concise commentary in one of the media on some current topic, usually polemical in nature; or a mocking comment generally. *In einer bissigen Glosse nimmt der Journalist die Scheinamateure aufs Korn.* In a vitriolic commentary the journalist lashes out at shamateurs. *Er muß unbedingt zu jeder Diskussion seine Glossen machen.* He simply has to make his snide comments on every discussion.

Gloss (of paint, etc.) = *der Glanz*

       (superficial outward appearance) = *der Schein*

glossieren To gloss (a text). Also: to write a (polemical) commentary on s.t.; to snipe at, to sneer at. SEE **GLOSSE**. *Eine Demokratie braucht freche Journalisten, die das Tun der Politiker glossieren.* A democracy needs impudent journalists to comment on the conduct of politicians.

To gloss over (conceal) = *vertuschen*

       (play down) = *beschönigen*

Glut, die Heat, glow; (fig.) ardor. *Nur die Glut seiner Zigarette verriet seine Anwesenheit.* Only the glow of his cigarette betrayed his presence.

Glut (abundance of fruit) = *die Schwemme*

       (excess supply) = *das Überangebot*

Gobelin, der Tapestry, tapestry fabric. The word is more familiar and general in German than the rather technical "Gobelin" in English, with its definite reference to the Gobelin works in Paris.

Goblin = *der Kobold*

goldig Not "golden," but "sweet," "cute" (of children, etc.) *Sie haben drei ganz goldige Töchterchen.* They've got three really sweet daughters.

Golden = *golden, aus Gold*

Golf, der   Gulf, bay. *der Golf von Mexiko* the Gulf of Mexico; *der Golf von Biskaya* the Bay of Biscay.

Golf = *das Golf*

Gondel, die   1. Gondola (Venetian; also of balloon or airship).   2. Car on a cable railway or ski lift. *Bei dieser Seilbahn kann jede Gondel höchstens 12 Personen befördern.* On this cable railway each car can carry a maximum of 12 persons.

Grad, der   Degree (temperature; academic; also = "extent"). *Ich gehe nie schwimmen, wenn das Wasser weniger als 20 Grad hat.* I never go swimming if the water is less than 20 degrees. *Welchen akademischen Grad hat er erworben?* What degree did he obtain? *Bis zu einem gewissen Grad haben Sie recht.* You're right to a certain extent.

Grade (class, level) = *die Stufe, die Klasse*

(mark in test, etc.) = *die Note, die Zensur*

Grafik, die.   SEE **GRAPHIK.**

grafisch.   SEE **GRAPHISCH.**

grandios   This is normally used positively, whereas English "grandiose" usually has a pejorative flavor (trying too hard to impress: too grand). Thus translations such as "magnificent" or "grand" are more suitable. *Zu seinem Geburtstag gab es einen grandiosen Kuchen.* There was a magnificent cake for his birthday. *Die neunte ist bestimmt die grandioseste von Beethovens Symphonien.* The ninth is certainly the grandest of Beethoven's symphonies.

Grandiose (scheme) = *größenwahnsinnig, hochtrabend*

(architecture) = *bombastisch*

Graphik, die   Graphics, graphic arts; also specifically a "print," "woodcut," or "engraving" (though there are other terms for these). But also a "diagram," which in some cases may take the form of a graph. *Anhand dieser Graphik kann man die Entwicklung der Verkaufszahlen verfolgen.* One can follow the development of the sales figures with the aid of this diagram.

Graph (math.) also = *der Graph, das Schaubild*

graphisch   Graphic (art, etc.). But also "diagrammatic." SEE **GRAPHIK.**

Graphic (vivid) = *plastisch, lebendig, anschaulich*

grassieren   To be rampant, rife (of diseases, etc.). *In den Großstädten grassiert die Drogensucht.* Drug addiction is rampant in the big cities.

To plant grass (on a piece of ground) = *mit Gras bepflanzen*

Gratifikation, die   Financial bonus given (to employees) on special occasions, esp. at Christmas. *Die Weihnachtsgratifikation ist dieses Jahr etwas dürftig ausgefallen.* The Christmas bonus is a bit thin this year.

Gratification (feeling of satisfaction) = *die Genugtuung*

(of desires, etc.) = *die Befriedigung*

graue Star, der.   SEE **STAR.**

graziös   Graceful. *Diese Inderinnen tanzen außerordentlich graziös.* These Indian women dance extraordinarily gracefully.

Gracious = *gütig, gnädig*

Grieß, der   Semolina, cream of wheat.

Grease = *das Fett*

Grill, der   **1.** Grill (in indoor cooking); barbecue. *Er tat mehr Holzkohle auf den Grill und ging ins Haus, um die Bratwürste zu holen.* He put some more charcoal on the barbecue and went into the house to fetch the sausages.   **2.** Grille of a car radiator (i.e., *Kühlergrill*).

grillen   To broil, grill (food). Also "to (have a) barbecue." *Das Wetter ist so schön, daß wir heute abend wieder grillen wollen.* The weather's so nice that we want to have another barbecue this evening.

To grill (interrogate) = *in die Zange nehmen; vernehmen, verhören*

grinsen   "Grin" may often be a suitable translation, but there is a slight difference between the two words in that *grinsen* usually has a negative connotation, denoting the sort of smile associated, for example, with malice: a smirk.

To grin (smile broadly in a friendly way) = *strahlen, lächeln*

Grippe, die   Influenza, flu. Many Germans claiming to have the *Grippe* look remarkably fit and well, and "cold" might sometimes be a more precise diagnosis. *Ich hatte in diesem Winter keine Grippe.* I didn't have the flu this winter.

Grip (hold) = *der Griff*

(traveling bag) = *die Reisetasche*

(film, photo) = *der Handgriff*

Grips, der   (coll.) Common sense. *Für diesen Job hat er nicht den nötigen Grips.* He doesn't have the necessary (common) sense for this job.

Grip (hold) = *der Griff*

(traveling bag) = *die Reisetasche*

(film, photo) = *der Handgriff*

groß   **1.** Big, large. *ein großes Haus* a big house.   **2.** Great. *eine große Leistung* a great achievement.   **3.** Tall. *ein großes Mädchen, bestimmt 1,80* a tall girl, all of 5 feet 11.

Gross (not net) = *brutto, Brutto-*

(coarse) = *grob*

(error) = *kraß*

Grund, der   This has a large number of uses, but it is not the normal term for "ground" in the sense of "soil," "land." Note, however, *Grund und Boden* land (in the context of real estate).   **1.** It may refer to the bottom or bed of a sea, lake, etc., and, less usually, to the bottom of a glass or other vessel. *Vor dieser Küste liegen viele Wracks auf dem (Meeres)grund.* Off this coast there are many wrecks on the seabed.   **2.**

Background (paintings, designs, etc.). *Der Grund ist zu dunkel, als daß man das Muster richtig erkennen könnte.* The background is too dark for one to be able to see the pattern properly. **3.** The most common meaning is "reason" (for an action, etc.). *Der Minister ist aus zwei ganz verschiedenen Gründen zurückgetreten.* The Minister has resigned for two quite different reasons.

Ground (soil) = *der Boden*

Grounds (premises) = *das Gelände*

> (including gardens, etc.) = *die Anlagen* (pl.)

gründen **1.** To found, establish. *Die Firma wurde 1888 gegründet.* The firm was established in 1888. **2.** To base (s.t. on s.t.): the reflexive use is especially common. *Seine ganze Theorie gründet sich auf diese Annahme.* His whole theory is based on this assumption.

To ground (ship) = *auflaufen lassen*

> (plane, for mechanical reason) = *aus dem Verkehr ziehen*
> (pilot) = *sperren*

To be grounded (of plane because of weather, etc.) = *nicht starten können*

grundieren To (apply) undercoat (to). *Wenn du diese Flächen nicht richtig grundierst, blättert die ganze Farbe früher oder später ab.* If you don't put a proper undercoat on these surfaces, all the paint will flake off sooner or later.

To ground (ship) = *auflaufen lassen*

> (plane, for mechanical reason) = *aus dem Verkehr ziehen*
> (pilot) = *sperren*

To be grounded (of plane because of weather, etc.) = *nicht starten können*

Grundierung, die (Application of) undercoat. SEE **GRUNDIEREN.**

Grounding (basic knowledge) = *das Grundwissen, die Grundlagen* (pl.)

> (of plane) = *das Startverbot*
> (of pilot) = *das Sperren*

Gründung, die **1.** Establishment, foundation. *Die Gründung des Vereins erfolgte kurz nach dem Krieg.* The association was founded shortly after the war. **2.** (tech.) The laying of foundations in building. *Die Gründung wird teuer sein, weil das Grundwasser sehr hoch liegt.* Laying the foundations will be expensive because the water table is so high.

Grounding (basic knowledge) = *das Grundwissen, die Grundlagen* (pl.)

> (of plane) = *das Startverbot*
> (of pilot) = *das Sperren*

grüne Star, der. SEE **STAR.**

Gully, der A drain (most commonly in the gutter of a road). *Dummerweise waren meine Autoschlüssel in einen Gully gefallen.* Unfortunately my car keys had fallen into a drain.

Gully = *die Schlucht*

gültig Not "guilty," but "valid." *Tut mir leid, aber dieser Fahrschein ist nicht mehr gültig.* I'm sorry, but this ticket is no longer valid.

Guilty = *schuldig*

Gummi, der or **das** In its primary meaning this denotes the material "rubber": in this meaning it is usually neuter.

Certain abbreviated and colloquial uses have established themselves, with varying gender usage: **1.** (masc.) Eraser, BrE rubber (i.e., *Radiergummi*). *Kann ich schnell deinen Gummi haben?* Can I borrow your eraser for a moment? **2.** (neut.) Rubber band (i.e., *Gummiband*). *Das Gummi ist zu klein für diese Rolle.* The rubber band's too small for this roll. **3.** (masc.) Rubber, in the sense of "condom." *"Die meisten Freier wollen keinen Gummi benutzen,"* sagte die Prostituierte. "Most clients don't want to use a condom," said the prostitute. **4.** (usually neut.) Gum arabic (i.e., *Gummiarabikum*). **5.** (usually neut.) Gum resin (i.e., *Gummiharz*).

BrE Gum (for sticking things) = *der Klebstoff*

(chewing gum) = *der, das Kaugummi*

(of teeth) = *das Zahnfleisch*

Gurgel, die Throat; gullet. *Der Schäferhund sprang ihm an die Gurgel.* The German shepherd (BrE Alsatian) leapt at his throat.

Gurgle (of water, etc.) = *das Gluckern*

(of baby) = *das Glucksen*

gurgeln This may mean "to gurgle," with reference to the sound made by water, etc. But more commonly it means "to gargle." *Wenn du gurgelst, hört man das durchs ganze Haus!* You can hear it all over the house when you gargle!

To gurgle (water, etc.) = *gluckern*

(baby, etc.) = *glucksen*

Gusto, der Taste, appetite (for s.t.). Most common in *nach eigenem Gusto* Just as one likes. *Als verantwortungsbewußter Arbeitgeber darf man die Leute nicht nach eigenem Gusto einstellen und entlassen.* As a responsible employer one cannot hire and fire people just as one likes.

With gusto = *mit Schwung*

Gut, das 1. Good (econ., most often used in the plural). *Diese Güter werden zum größten Teil importiert.* These goods are imported for the most part. **2.** Also "good" in a moral sense, esp. in fixed expressions like *Gut und Böse* (good and evil); otherwise the nominalized adjective *das Gute* is more usual. **3.** (country) Estate. *Er hatte ein großes Gut in*

Ostpreußen. He had a large estate in East Prussia. **4.** Property, esp. in fixed expressions. *fremdes Gut* other people's property.

Gut (intestine) = *der Darm*

Guts (i.e., courage) = *der Mumm* (coll.), *der Mut*

gutsituiert. SEE SITUIERT.

Gymnasium, das The highest level (in academic terms) of secondary school in the German tripartite system (i.e., "above" the *Realschule* and *Hauptschule*). It corresponds, in effect, to the high school in the U.S.A., though the German school is selective and the American is not. In Britain it would correspond to the grammar school (of which there are now few). It is often better in translation to retain the German word. *Wenn er auf dem Gymnasium war, wird er Latein gemacht haben, oder?* If he went to high school/BrE grammar school/the 'Gymnasium' he'll have done Latin, won't he?

Gymnasium = *die Turnhalle*

H

Habitus, der A formal word, denoting, according to the context, a person's manner, appearance, or disposition. *Seinem Habitus nach war er Vertreter oder so etwas.* To judge by his appearance/manner he was a sales rep or something like that.

Habit (custom) = *die Gewohnheit*

(bad: also) = *die Angewohnheit*

hacken This may mean "to hack," but has a much wider range of uses than the English word. **1.** To chop (wood, etc.). *Wenn du heute abend ein Feuer willst, mußt du jetzt Holz hacken.* If you want a fire this evening, you'll have to chop some wood now. **2.** To grind, mince, chop (meat, onions, etc.). *Dieses Rindfleisch ist sehr zäh—ich glaube, es würde gehackt am besten schmecken.* This beef is very tough—I think it would taste best ground (BrE minced). *das Hack, das Hackfleisch* Ground meat; BrE mince, minced meat. **3.** To cut oneself (accidentally). *Bei dieser Arbeit hackte er sich ins linke Bein.* In doing this he cut his left leg. **4.** To hoe (gardening). *Ich muß nur noch dieses Blumenbeet hacken.* I just have to hoe this flowerbed.

May also mean "to peck" (of birds), though *picken* is the more normal term. Note, however, *die Hackordnung* Pecking order.

Hafen, der   Haven (in its figurative sense). But also the normal word for "harbor," "port." *Als Hafen ist Liverpool nicht so wichtig wie vor 50 Jahren.* As a port Liverpool is not as important as it was 50 years ago.

halb (sechs)   German measures the time to go *before* the next hour. *Es ist halb sechs.* It's half past five.

halbwegs   No longer used to mean "halfway." Instead the meaning is "reasonably," "moderately." *Ein halbwegs intelligenter Mensch hätte das gleich erkannt.* A reasonably intelligent person would have realized that right away.

Halfway: no single translation, but the following list contains some of the more common equivalents. The precise context will determine the appropriate selection: *auf halbem Weg, zur Hälfte, auf halber Höhe, halb (hinauf, hinunter).*

Halle, die   Denotes a very large and usually high-ceilinged room used for various purposes. There is no single English translation, and in certain contexts "hall" may be suitable. *Die Fabrik bestand aus drei riesigen Hallen.* The factory consisted of three enormous (work)shops. *Wenn du Tennis in der Halle spielen willst, brauchst du andere Schuhe.* If you want to play indoor tennis you'll need different shoes. *Nichts ist so ungemütlich wie eine Bahnhofshalle.* Nothing is as cheerless as a station concourse. *In der Halle des Hotels saß ein älterer Herr.* An elderly gentleman was sitting in the hotel lobby.

Ausstellungshalle Exhibition building/hall; *Schwimmhalle* Swimming pools/baths; *Flugzeughalle* Aircraft hangar.

Hall (for receptions, dancing, etc.) = *der Saal*

    (in house, apartment) = *der Flur*

    (BrE: for students, AmE dormitory) = *das Studenten(wohn)heim*

hallo!   This and "hello" or BrE "hallo" are equivalent in most cases. Peculiar to German is the use to attract s.o.'s attention, sometimes in a less than friendly manner. *Hallo, Sie haben ihre Autoschlüssel vergessen!* Hey, you've forgotten your car keys. *Hallo, Sie da! Was machen Sie?* Hey, you there! What are you doing?

halt   A particle commonly used in South Germany, Austria, and Switzerland: it should not be confused with the exclamation *halt!* (meaning "halt!"). As with so many German particles, it is difficult to give clear translation equivalents: it tends to indicate resigned acceptance of the situation by the speaker. *Mehr als zwei Prozent werden wir halt in diesem Jahr nicht kriegen.* (Oh well,) we won't get more than two percent this year.

Halt, der   **1.** Halt or stop in a journey.   **2.** Hold or support (physical or psychological). *Ich suchte vergeblich nach einem festen Halt, als der Busfahrer anfing, mit 60 in die Kurven zu gehen.* I looked in vain for something firm to hold onto when the bus driver began taking the curves at

60. *Diese jungen Leute brauchen einen moralischen Halt im Leben.* These young people need a firm moral support/base in life.

BrE Halt (small railroad station) = *der Haltepunkt*

To come to a halt = *zum Stillstand kommen*

halten   To stop, halt. But this is a key verb in German with a very wide range of meanings, the most important being "to hold," "to regard/ consider," "to think (s.t. of s.t./s.o.)," "to keep" (also of food, etc.).

Halter, der   1. Owner (of a vehicle: *Fahrzeughalter;* of an animal: *Tierhalter*). *Auch wenn Sie selbst nicht am Steuer waren, haften Sie als Halter des Fahrzeugs.* Even if you weren't at the wheel yourself you are liable as the owner of the vehicle.   2. Holder (for an object). *Wir brauchen einen neuen Halter für die Küchenrolle.* We need a new holder for the kitchen towels.

Halter (for horse) = *das Halfter*

(noose) = *die Schlinge*

(type of blouse) = *das (rückenfreie) Top (mit Nackenträger)*

Hamburger, der   Now a normal term in German for the mainstay of the fast-food industry. But it can of course also denote an inhabitant of Hamburg. *Die Hamburger essen besonders gern Fischgerichte.* The inhabitants of Hamburg are particularly keen on fish dishes.

Hammer, der   1. Hammer.   2. (coll.) A bad mistake, howler. *Seine Übersetzungen wimmeln immer von solchen Hämmern.* His translations are always full of such howlers.   3. According to context, something marvelous or outrageous. *das ist ein Hammer! Du hast den Job gekriegt? Das ist ja ein Hammer!* You got the job? That's great/fantastic! *Das ist ein Hammer! Tante Marianne hat ihr ganzes Geld ihrer Katze vermacht.* I've never heard anything like it! Aunt Marianne has left all her money to her cat.

Hamster-   Although *der Hamster* does mean "hamster," compounds with *Hamster-* usually have nothing to do with hamsters and instead refer to the hoarding of food and panic buying. *Zu Krisenzeiten sind Hamsterkäufe an der Tagesordnung.* Panic buying is quite normal in times of crisis. SEE **HAMSTERN.**

hamstern   Denotes various phenomena associated with a shortage (present or impending) of goods, esp. food.   1. To engage in panic buying; to hoard (food). *Es gibt immer Leute, die schon bei der geringsten Kriegsgefahr anfangen zu hamstern.* There are always people who start hoarding food when there is the slightest danger of war.   2. To barter (illegally) goods in exchange for food, esp. in the context of the postwar food shortage in Germany after 1945.

Handapparat, der   Handset (of telephone). But also a set of reference books on a particular subject, normally one made available on open shelf for consultation rather than borrowing: it is a term associated with seminar work at German universities and there is no ready English translation. *Der Handapparat für mein Schiller-Seminar besteht aus 30 Büchern.* I've assembled 30 books for students to consult who are taking my Schiller seminar.

Handel, der 1. Trade, commerce; (drugs, etc.) traffic(king). *Der Handel zwischen den beiden Ländern ist rapide gewachsen.* Trade has increased rapidly between the two countries. *Drogenhandel* drug trafficking. **2.** An individual deal or transaction. *Dieser Handel war für uns nicht sehr vorteilhaft.* That was not a very profitable deal for us.

There is also a homonym, formal in style and normally used in the plural, *Händel,* meaning "argument," "dispute," "quarrel."

Handle (suitcase, etc.) = *der Griff*
  (door) = *die Klinke*
  (cup, etc.) = *der Henkel*

handeln A wide variety of uses. **1.** To trade, deal. *Meine Eltern handelten mit gebrauchten Möbeln.* My parents dealt in secondhand furniture. **2.** To haggle, bargain. *In diesem Land ist es selbstverständlich, daß man handelt, bevor man kauft.* In this country it's the usual thing to haggle before you buy. **3.** To act, take action. *Wir haben lange genug geredet—jetzt müssen wir handeln!* We've talked long enough—now we must act! **4.** To act, behave. *Ich finde, er hat in der ganzen Sache sehr egoistisch gehandelt.* I think he has behaved very selfishly in the whole business. **5.** (with *von*) To deal with, be about. *Das Buch handelt von seinen Erlebnissen im Krieg.* The book is about his experiences in the war. *es handelt sich um* In some contexts, this may mean "It's a question of . . . ," "It's about . . . ," but often it means no more than simply "It is . . ." *Sie wollen also zu Herrn Zahn? Worum handelt es sich?* So you want to see Mr. Zahn? What's it about? *Er nahm eine Flasche in die Hand und sagte, "Es handelt sich hier um den feinsten Wein der Gegend."* He picked up a bottle and said, "This is the finest wine in the area."

To handle (tackle: a matter, etc.) = *behandeln*
  (know how to use s.t.) = *mit etwas umgehen können*
  (pick up) = *anfassen, in die Hand nehmen*
  (cope with) = *fertig werden mit*

Händler, der Trader, dealer. SEE **HANDEL, HANDELN.** Often forms compounds. *Gebrauchtwagenhändler* secondhand car dealer.

Handler (i.e., dog-handler) = *der Hundeführer*

Hang, der 1. Slope. *Es wird nicht leicht sein, an einem solchen Hang ein Haus zu bauen.* It won't be easy to build a house on a slope like this. **2.** Tendency, inclination. *Sie hat einen ausgeprägten Hang zur Melancholie.* She has a distinct tendency toward melancholy.

hantieren 1. To be busy. *Wie immer hantierte sein Vater in seiner kleinen Werkstatt.* As always, his father was busy in his little workshop. **2.** To (know how to) handle s.t. *Man muß es bewundern, wie er mit diesem* *komplizierten Gerät hantiert.* One has to admire the way he handles this complicated piece of equipment. **3.** (esp. in the compound *herumhantieren*) To tinker with s.t. (often without success). *Helmut hantiert schon seit zwei Stunden an diesem Vergaser herum.* Helmut's been tinkering with that carburetor for two hours now.

To haunt (ghost) = *spuken (in)*
(torment, of nightmares, etc.) = *quälen, heimsuchen*

happig (coll.) Expensive, steep. *Diese Anwaltsgebühren sind ganz schön happig.* These legal fees are pretty steep.

Happy = *glücklich*

Happy-End, das Pseudo-anglicism for "happy ending."

harken To rake (lawn, flowerbed, etc.).

To hark, hearken = *lauschen, horchen*

harmlos Harmless, but the German word is used in a wider range of contexts than the English, and other translations may be preferable. *Warum hat er sich so aufgeregt? Es war doch eine ganz harmlose Frage.* Why did he get so worked up? It was a perfectly innocent question. *Ein harmloser Typ wie Hartmut wird nicht hinter dieser Intrige stecken.* An innocuous guy like Hartmut won't be behind this conspiracy.

harsch May mean "harsh," but its commonest use is to refer to snow that is frozen over with a layer of ice. *harscher Schnee* frozen snow.

Harsh = *rauh, hart*

Harsch, der Frozen snow. SEE **HARSCH**.

Haus, das House. But whereas the English word normally denotes a private dwelling, *Haus* is also used to indicate office blocks, conference centers, etc. *"Ich möchte Herrn Jahn sprechen." "Tut mir leid, er ist nicht im Haus."* "I'd like to speak to Mr. Jahn." "I'm sorry, he's not in the building." *Wenn Sie aus dem Haus kommen, müssen Sie nach links gehen.* When you leave the building, you have to turn left.

Hausarbeit, die Housework (washing, cleaning, etc.). But also a lengthy paper or essay prepared by a college student: term paper. *Letztes Jahr habe ich eine Hausarbeit über Schillers Balladen geschrieben.* Last year I wrote a term paper about Schiller's ballads.

Hausarrest, der House arrest (for political opponents, etc.). But also used informally to refer to grounding children or young people as a punishment. *Nein, Peter kann nicht spielen—er hat zwei Tage Hausarrest.* No, Peter can't play—he's being grounded for two days. SEE **ARREST.**

hausen **1.** To live, dwell (but with the connotation of poor living conditions). *Tausende hausen in solchen Slums.* Thousands live in slums of this sort. **2.** To wreak havoc, cause destruction (of storms, people, etc.). *Söldner hatten im Dorf schrecklich gehaust.* Mercenaries had wrought terrible havoc in the village.

To house (provide accommodation for) = *unterbringen*

Haushalt, der   **1.** Household.   **2.** Budget. *Unser Haushalt für das kommende Jahr sieht keine Investitionen auf diesem Gebiet vor.* Our budget for the coming year does not allow for any investment in this field.   **3.** (biol.) A (chemical) balance. *Dieses Medikament bringt den Hormonhaushalt leicht durcheinander.* This drug can easily upset the hormone balance.

Haushälter(in) der (die)   Housekeeper. *Zwanzig Jahre später heiratete dieser Junggeselle seine Haushälterin.* Twenty years later this bachelor married his housekeeper.

Householder (occupant) = *der (Haus)bewohner*
(owner of house) = *der Hauseigentümer*
(owner of apartment) = *der Wohnungseigentümer*

hausieren   To peddle, hawk (also figuratively). *Hausieren verboten* No hawkers. *Mit diesen naiven revolutionären Ideen hausiert er schon seit Jahren.* He's been peddling those naive revolutionary ideas for years.

To house (provide accommodation for) = *unterbringen*

Hausmann, der   This is now used to denote a man who runs the household, looks after the children, etc. (while his wife goes out to work). *Die wenigsten Männer sind bereit, ihre Karriere dadurch zu gefährden, daß sie für ein paar Jahre Hausmann werden.* Only very few men are prepared to jeopardize their careers by staying at home and running the household for a few years.

Houseman (general worker in hotel, etc.) = *das Faktotum, das Mädchen für alles*
(BrE = AmE "intern") = *der Medizinalassistent*

Hausmeister, der   Caretaker, janitor. *Er hatte diesen mißtrauischen Blick, den so viele Hausmeister haben.* He had that suspicious look that so many caretakers have.

BrE Housemaster: there is no real German equivalent for the concept expressed by this term for a boarding school teacher who is responsible for the pupils in his "house."

heftig   **1.** Strong, violent, severe, intense: the context will determine the choice of adjective. *Sie wurde von heftigen Kopfschmerzen geplagt.* She was tormented by severe headaches. *Wir können heute mit heftigen Regenschauern rechnen.* We can expect heavy showers today.   **2.** (of persons) quick-tempered, having a violent temper. *Er kann sehr leicht heftig werden.* It takes very little to make him lose his temper.

Hefty (strong: of person) = *kräftig*
(restaurant bill, etc.) = *saftig*
(fat: of person) = *dick*
(heavy: of object) = *schwer*

heilen   **1.** (wound, etc.) To heal.   **2.** To cure. *Diese Krebsart läßt sich relativ leicht heilen.* This type of cancer can be cured relatively easily. *Kein*

Arzt kann dich vom Alkoholismus heilen. No doctor can cure you of alcoholism.

Heilige, der (die) This could conceivably mean a "holy man" or "holy woman." But it is the normal word for "saint," and this will be the usual translation. *Bilder von verschiedenen Heiligen standen auf dem Kaminsims.* Pictures of various saints stood on the mantelpiece.

Heim, das 1. This may refer to a private home, but it then has a strong emotional connotation as the seat of domestic happiness and security. *Ich habe lieber ein eigenes Heim als teure Autos und solche Sachen.* I prefer to have my own home rather than expensive cars and that sort of thing. **2.** More commonly, it has an institutional sense: a "hostel" (e.g., for the homeless), a "home" (e.g., for orphans), a student "dormitory" (BrE hall of residence), etc. In this sense it forms a large number of compounds, e.g., *Schullandheim* (a sort of country retreat where school classes can be taught for a few days away from home). Home (as larger area, country, etc.) = *die Heimat*

heimlich Secret, clandestine. *Sie trafen sich heimlich in einem kleinen Café.* They met secretly in a little café.

Homely (home-loving) = *häuslich*
(BrE, of atmosphere) = *gemütlich*
(of person) = *wenig attraktiv*

Hektik, die This noun denotes the same concept as that denoted by the English adjective "hectic," but a variety of translations may be needed. *Sie konnte die Hektik dieser Schlußverkäufe nicht ausstehen.* She could not stand the hectic rush of these sales. *Sie erklärt immer mit einer solchen Hektik, daß keiner sie versteht.* She always explains things at such a frantic pace that no one understands her. *Ach diese deutsche Hektik!* Ah, the way these Germans are always rushing about! *Nur keine Hektik!* Take it easy!

Hectic (adj.) = *hektisch*

hell 1. Light, bright (of colors, light, etc.). *Ein helles Blau wäre für dieses Zimmer gerade richtig.* A light blue would be just right for this room. **2.** High-pitched (of sound). **3.** Intelligent, bright. *Anna ist ein helles Kind.* Anna's a bright child. **4.** (coll.) Used as an intensifying adverb: "utterly," etc. *Alle waren von meinem Vorschlag hell begeistert.* Everybody was extremely enthusiastic about my suggestion.

Hell (noun) = *die Hölle*

Helm, der Helmet. Often short for *Sturzhelm* = crash helmet. *Es ist leichtsinnig, ohne (Sturz)helm Motorrad zu fahren.* It's foolish to ride a motorcycle without a (crash) helmet.

Helm (of ship) = *das Steuer, das Ruder*

hemmen To hinder, obstruct, inhibit. *Dieser Protektionismus hemmt den Handel zwischen den beiden Ländern.* This protectionism inhibits trade between the two countries.

To hem (dress, etc.) = *säumen*

herb **1.** Bitter, tart (taste), sharp (smell); dry (wine). *Ich mag diesen etwas herben Geschmack.* I like this rather tart taste. **2.** It is also used metaphorically to mean "bitter," "harsh," "austere," etc. *Seine Untreue war eine besonders herbe Enttäuschung für sie.* His unfaithfulness was a particularly bitter disappointment for her.

Herb = *das Kraut*

Herd, der **1.** Range, cooking stove, BrE cooker. *Ich kann mit einem elektrischen Herd nicht umgehen.* I don't know how to use an electric range. **2.** Also the center of some trouble or disturbance, and, specifically, the focus of an infection (*Krankheitsherd*).

Herd = *die Herde*

Hering, der **1.** Herring. **2.** Tent peg. *Du hast die Heringe nicht richtig in den Boden geschlagen.* You haven't driven the tent pegs into the ground properly.

herzig Cute, sweet, delightful (e.g., of child); a dated expression that can sound rather ridiculous today. *Friederike hat zwei ganz herzige Töchterchen.* Friederike has two really cute little daughters.

Hearty (welcome) = *herzlich*

(meal) = *kräftig, herzhaft*

Highlife, das High life. But the word is used in expressions where other translations are needed. *Bei uns ist Highlife heute abend: wir feiern Stephans Verlobung.* We'll really be living it up tonight: we're celebrating Stephan's engagement. *Wir können bei unserem Verdienst nicht jedes Wochenende Highlife machen.* We can't paint the town red every weekend on what we earn.

hindern To hinder, impede. But it may also have the stronger meaning of "to prevent" (s.o. from doing s.t.). *Dieser Schnee wird uns (daran) hindern, heute weiterzufahren.* This snow will prevent us driving any farther today.

Hippe, die Two homonyms coincide in this word. Together they present a variety of meanings, though few native speakers seem to be familiar with all of them. **1.** Pruning knife. **2.** The "scythe" carried by Death in allegorical pictures. **3.** Goat. **4.** (pej., of woman) Cow, bitch.

Hip (anat.) = *die Hüfte*

Rosehip (fruit) = *die Hagebutte*

hissen To raise, hoist (flag, etc.). *Die amerikanische Flagge wurde gehißt.* The American flag was hoisted.

To hiss = *zischen*

Hitliste, die Denotes a "hit list" in the sense of a "hit parade" of popularity (for records, but also other things, and persons). *Ich weiß nicht, was zur Zeit ganz oben auf der Hitliste steht.* I don't know what's at the top of the charts at the moment.

Hit list (for assassins, etc.) = *die Abschußliste*

hitzefrei Not "free of heat" or "heatproof." Instead it denotes the German practice of sending pupils home from school early if the weather is unusually hot. (There are exact regulations based on temperature readings!) *Mann, ist das warm! Heute kriegen wir bestimmt hitzefrei.* Hey, it's hot! They're bound to send us home today.

Heatproof = *hitzebeständig*

Hochschule, die University, college: the German term refers to higher/tertiary education generally, and there is no exact English equivalent. *In den sechziger Jahren wurden mehrere neue Hochschulen gegründet.* Several new colleges were founded in the sixties.

There are various compounds for which only approximate English equivalents can be given. There is also a tendency for terminology to change regularly in all countries, and the translations given here are only indicative in nature. *Fachhochschule* Polytechnic; *Kunsthochschule* College of art/art college; *Musikhochschule* College of music; *Technische Hochschule* College of (advanced) technology; *Pädagogische Hochschule* College of education, teacher training college.

High school = *die Oberschule*

Hochzeit, die 1. When pronounced with a short *o:* wedding. *Wieviele Gäste waren auf der Hochzeit?* How many guests were there at the wedding? 2. When pronounced with a long *o:* a golden age. *die Hochzeit des amerikanischen Journalismus* the golden age of American journalism. In this latter sense *die Blütezeit* is more usual.

It's high time that he retired = *Es ist höchste Zeit, daß er in Rente geht.*

hocken 1. To squat, crouch. *Ein sehr schmutziges Kind hockte in der Ecke und aß ein Stück verschimmeltes Brot.* A very dirty child crouched in the corner, eating a piece of moldy bread. 2. (coll.) To sit. *Warum hockst du vor dem Fernseher? Komm' doch mit in die Kneipe!* Why are you sitting in front of the TV? Come to the pub with us!

To hock (pawn) = *versetzen, verpfänden*

hohl Hollow. *Diese Wand ist hohl—vielleicht ist der Schatz dahinter verborgen.* This wall is hollow—perhaps the treasure is hidden behind it.

Hole (noun) = *das Loch*

Höhle, die Cave; (if inhabited by animal) den, etc. *Die Kinder sollten nicht in diesen Höhlen spielen—sie könnten sich leicht verlaufen.* The children shouldn't play in these caves—they could easily get lost.

Hole = *das Loch*

Hölle, die   Hell. *Glaubst du, daß es eine Hölle gibt?* Do you believe there's a hell?

Hole = *das Loch*

Honorar, das   Honorarium; fee (for professional services). *Das Honorar, das dieser Architekt verlangen würde, könntest du gar nicht bezahlen.* You simply couldn't afford the fee this architect would charge.

Honor = *die Ehre*

honorieren   **1.** To honor, in the sense of giving recognition for achievements, etc. *Wir wollen mit diesem Denkmal seine Arbeit für unser Volk honorieren.* With this monument we wish to honor his work for our people.   **2.** To pay a fee for. SEE **HONORAR.** *Seine Leistungen als Hauptanwalt in der Sache wurden mit 50.000 Mark honoriert.* He received a fee of 50,000 marks for his work as the main attorney in the case.

To honor (person, etc.) = *ehren*

(a check) = *annehmen*

(credit card) = *anerkennen*

hoppla!   Not associated with the patter of acrobats and jugglers. Instead, it is more common as an interjection made when minor mishaps (e.g., tripping up) occur: whoops, oops. *Hoppla! Da wäre ich fast ausgerutscht.* Whoops! I nearly slipped. *Hoppla, jetzt komm' ich!* Look out, here I come! (This is a phrase often associated with arrogant people who have an exaggerated sense of their own importance and who expect to attract everyone's attention.)

hören   **1.** To hear. But also "to hear with attention," i.e., "listen." *So, ich habe genug gearbeitet—jetzt werde ich ein bißchen Musik hören.* Right, I've done enough work—I'm going to listen to a bit of music now. Also used with reference to attending university lectures. *Ich habe letztes Semester eine Vorlesung bei Staiger gehört.* I went to a series of lectures by Staiger last term.   **2.** (with *auf*) To answer to (of animal). *Die Katze hört auf den Namen Quasimodo.* The cat answers to the name of Quasimodo.

Hörer, der   **1.** Hearer, but more commonly "listener." *Die meisten Hörer haben nach fünf Minuten ausgeschaltet.* Most listeners turned it off after five minutes.   **2.** Student (attending a lecture). *Professor Nissop hat nie mehr als zwei Hörer.* Professor Nissop never has more than two students at his lectures.   **3.** Receiver of a telephone. *Ich traute mich nicht, den Hörer abzunehmen.* I didn't dare to pick up the receiver.

Horn, das   **1.** Horn (animal, musical).   **2.** (coll.) Bump, lump (e.g., after an insect bite). *Er hatte ein ganz schönes Horn, wo die Wespe ihn gestochen hatte.* He had a huge bump where the wasp had stung him.

hornig   Horny, but only literally, not in the sexual sense.

Horny (sexually excited) = *geil, scharf*

Hose, die (A pair of) pants, trousers. *Wann kaufst du dir endlich eine neue Hose?* When on earth are you going to buy a new pair of pants?

Hose (for watering) = *der (Garten)schlauch*

hospitieren Nothing to do with hospitals or hospitalization. The word is applied to trainees sitting in on classes in order to learn from the example of an experienced teacher. *Die ersten drei Wochen haben wir nur hospitiert—selbst unterrichtet haben wir überhaupt nicht.* For the first three weeks we only sat in on other people's classes—we didn't do any teaching ourselves.

To hospitalize = *ins Krankenhaus einweisen*

Hosteß or **Hostess, die** Hostess with reference to airline, trade fair, tour operator staff, etc., and also to the "hostesses" who work in night clubs. But it is not the term used for the hostess of a private party, e.g., dinner party: the appropriate word here is *die Gastgeberin.*

Hotel garni, das Nothing to do with garnishing. It denotes a hotel that serves breakfast, but no other meals.

human **1.** Human*e*, civilized. *Der Strafvollzug in diesem Land ist alles andere als human.* The penal system in this country is anything but humane. Also "not ruthless": "considerate," "decent." *Der Oberst hat seine Macken, aber im großen und ganzen ist er human.* The colonel has his funny ways, but on the whole he's a considerate sort. **2.** May mean "human" in medical contexts, e.g., *Humanmedizin.*

Human = *menschlich*

humanistisch Humanist(ic). But also "classical," referring to Greek and Latin language and literature and the education based thereon. *Er meint, mit einer humanistischen Bildung sei man für jeden Beruf bestens ausgerüstet.* He thinks that a classical education equips one for all careers. *humanistisches Gymnasium* a **GYMNASIUM** (Q.V.) that puts the emphasis on Greek and Latin.

Hummer, der Nothing to do with low-pitched sounds or BrE bad smells: it denotes a lobster. *Ich bin nicht ganz sicher, wie man überhaupt einen Hummer ißt.* I'm not quite sure how one actually eats a lobster.

Humor, der Humor. But also "sense of humor." *Du darfst sie nicht auf den Arm nehmen—sie hat keinen Humor.* You mustn't pull her leg—she has no sense of humor.

Humpen, der Mug, tankard (for beer, etc.).

Hump (hill) = *der Hügel*

    (camel) = *der Höcker*

    (deformity on back) = *der Buckel*

Hund, der Dog (the normal word).

Hound (for hunting) = *der Jagdhund*

husch! **1.** This interjection does not call for quiet, but speed. *So Kinder, husch, ins Bett!* So, kids, off you go to bed, on the double. **2.** Shoo.

Husch, ihr dummen Gänse! Shoo, you stupid geese! **3.** Sometimes used as an adverb, normally in the doublet form *husch husch*. *Wenn du alles so husch husch reparierst, hält das nicht lange.* If you do all your repairs as quickly as that they won't last very long.

Hush! = *sch!, pst!*

huschen To move quickly, lightly and silently: to flit, dart, scurry; flash (of light, etc.). *Eine Spitzmaus huschte über den Weg.* A shrew darted across the path. *Ein Sonnenstrahl huschte über den See.* A ray of sunshine flashed across the lake.

To hush (make s.o. be quiet) = *zum Schweigen bringen*

Hut, der Hat.

Hut = *die Hütte*

Hut, die Guard. Most commonly used in the fixed expression *auf der Hut sein* = to be on one's guard.

Hut = *die Hütte*

Hütte, die Hut, shack; kennel (for dog). But also an industrial "plant," "works" for producing metal from ore or bricks, glass, etc. In this meaning appropriate compounds are formed: *Eisenhütte, Glashütte,* etc. *Die letzte Eisenhütte wurde 1964 stillgelegt.* The last iron works was closed in 1964.

Hymne, die Hymn. But also a shorter form of *Nationalhymne* = national anthem. *Nach der Siegerehrung wird die jeweilige (National)hymne gespielt.* After the presentation ceremony the appropriate national anthem is played.

I

Idee, die Idea. But note its use to mean "a little," "a bit." *Eigentlich müßte das Fenster eine Idee breiter sein.* The window really ought to be a shade wider.

Igel, der Hedgehog.

Eagle = *der Adler*

Ignorant, der Ignoramus. *Der Mann ist doch ein Ignorant—wir können ihm unmöglich die Stelle geben.* The man's an ignoramus—we can't possibly give him the job.

Ignorant (adj.) = *ignorant, unwissend*
　　　　　(uneducated) = *ungebildet*

immanent The word is used more frequently than English "immanent," which is largely restricted to philosophical contexts. As such, *imma-*

nent corresponds more to "intrinsic," "inherent." *Diese Schwäche ist, wie er meint, dem kapitalistischen System immanent.* This weakness is, in his view, inherent in the capitalist system.

immateriell   Not existing physically, but in the mind or as an emotion: intangible, spiritual. *Der Mensch hat natürlich auch immaterielle Bedürfnisse.* Naturally man has spiritual needs too. *Schmerzensgeld wird für einen erlittenen immateriellen Schaden bezahlt.* Compensation for personal suffering is paid for damage of an intangible nature.

Immaterial (irrelevant) = *nebensächlich, nicht relevant*

Immaturen-   Most commonly found in the compound *Immaturenprüfung*. This is not concerned with maturity in the general English sense. Instead, it denotes a test administered to those without the formal qualification usually necessary for university entry (the *Abitur*). It establishes whether they should be admitted to higher education despite their lack of formal qualifications.

Immature = *unreif*

Immobilie, die   A piece of "immovable property": most commonly found in the plural, it corresponds to "real estate," "property" (and is, unlike "immovable property," an everyday expression). *Immobilien sind zur Zeit eine gute Investition.* Real estate is a good investment at present.

Immobile (adj.) = *unbeweglich*

imposant   Imposing, but, unlike the English word, which tends to be used of things that are impressive by virtue of their size, *imposant* also means impressive in other contexts too. *Eine höchst imposante Leistung, das muß ich schon sagen.* A very impressive performance, I must say.

Impressum, das   The "imprint" in a book, newspaper, or journal that gives details of the publisher and also of the editorial team, etc. *Das Impressum finden Sie auf Seite 16.* You'll find the publisher's details on page 16.

Impress (noun) = *der Abdruck*

Impression (effect produced on mind, feeling, etc.) = *der Eindruck*
           (of foot, fingerprint, etc.) = *der Abdruck*
           (imitation) = *die Imitation, die Nachahmung*

inadäquat   Inappropriate, unsuitable. SEE ADÄQUAT.

Inadequate (not enough) = *nicht ausreichend*
           (not good enough) = *unzulänglich*

indezent   Indiscreet, insensitive. SEE DEZENT.

Indecent = *unanständig, obszön*

Indikation, die   Indication (medical). The word has become popularized as a result of the discussion of abortion legislation, and other English expressions are more appropriate in such contexts. *Für strenggläubige Katholiken wird die soziale Indikation für einen Schwangerschaftsabbruch* *nie akzeptabel sein.* For strict Catholics abortion on social grounds will never be acceptable.

Indication = *das Zeichen*

Initiative, die   Initiative. But also (often in the compound form *Bürger-initiative*) a pressure group formed by citizens, generally in response to a particular situation or problem. *Jedesmal, wenn eine neue Autobahn gebaut werden soll, bildet sich über Nacht eine (Bürger)initiative dagegen.* Every time a new highway is to be built a (citizens'/civic) pressure group forms overnight to oppose it.

inkonsequent   Inconsistent, illogical. SEE **KONSEQUENT.**

Inconsequential (unimportant) = *unbedeutend, unwichtig*

Inland, das   **1.** This may mean "inland" as opposed to "by the sea." *Im Inland ist Regen fast unbekannt.* Rain is almost unknown inland.   **2.** But more often it signifies "not foreign": home, domestic (i.e., not *Ausland*). *Diese Güter werden zum größten Teil im Inland verkauft.* These goods are sold mainly on the domestic market.

Inland (waterway, etc.) = *Binnen-* (as in *Binnenwasserstraße*)

To travel inland = *landeinwärts fahren*

To live inland = *im Landesinneren wohnen*

inserieren   To advertise (in a newspaper in the form of a small advertisement). *Ich habe unsere Garnitur letzte Woche inseriert, aber bis jetzt hat keiner angerufen.* I advertised our suite (in the paper) last week, but so far no one's called.

To insert = *hineinstecken, einführen*

Inspektion, die   May mean "inspection" in a general sense. But most commonly it denotes (regular) service for a vehicle. *Morgen muß ich mein Auto zur Inspektion bringen.* I've got to take my car in for a service tomorrow.

Inspection = *die Prüfung, die Kontrolle*

Installateur, der   Not s.o. engaged in installing things generally, but more particularly a plumber, an electrical fitter, or a gas fitter, the last two often being denoted by the compounds *Elektroinstallateur* or *Gasinstallateur. Unser Installateur wird sich das Abflußrohr ansehen.* Our plumber will take a look at the waste pipe.

Instanz, die   **1.** Instance, in the judicial sense of one of the various stages through which a court case can go. But whereas the English word is a technical term, *Instanz* is freely used by the layman too. *Er gewann den Prozeß in der zweiten Instanz.* He won the case at the second hearing/after an appeal.   **2.** Also used to denote an official authority responsible for a particular matter. *Ich weiß gar nicht, an welche Instanz ich mich wenden soll.* I've no idea what department I'm supposed to apply to.

Instance (example) = *das Beispiel*

integer   Having integrity: honest, incorruptible. *Ich gebe zu, daß es sich bei ihm um einen integeren Politiker handelt, aber er ist trotzdem nicht sehr beliebt.* I admit that he is a politician of integrity, but he is still not very popular.
Integer (noun) = *die ganze Zahl*

Intelligenz, die   Intelligence. But also used as a collective term for intellectuals: intelligentsia. *Unter der Naziherrschaft wurde die polnische Intelligenz weitgehend vernichtet.* The Polish intelligentsia was largely annihilated under the Nazi rule.

Intendant, der   Not s.o. with any particular intentions, or an "intendant" in the historical or specialist senses of the word. Instead, the (artistic and commercial) manager or director of a theater; also the head of a (public) broadcasting corporation. *Wie heißt der neue ZDF-Intendant?* What's the name of the new head of the ZDF (Channel 2)?

intensiv   Intensive. Also "intense" in the sense of "strong," "powerful" with reference to sensory perceptions, etc. *Die sehr intensiven Farben der Tapete machten mich unruhig.* The very intense colors of the wallpaper made me restless.

Interpret(in), der (die)   Interpreter, but in relation to music, etc., not the oral translation of languages. *Brendel ist ein bekannter Interpret der Klaviersonaten Schuberts.* Brendel is a well-known interpreter of Schubert's piano sonatas. It often simply means "singer." *Er hat viele Platten von Mireille Mathieu, der berühmten französischen Interpretin.* He has many records by Mireille Mathieu, the famous French singer.
Interpreter (linguistic) = *der Dolmetscher*

Invalidität, die   This corresponds to the English word "invalidity" only as it is used in certain fixed expressions, such as BrE "invalidity pension." Otherwise the usual translation is "disability." *Die Versicherung zahlt Ihnen DM 800 pro Monat bei 60% Invalidität.* The insurance pays you 800 marks a month in the event of 60% disability.
Invalidity (of ticket, etc.) = *die Ungültigkeit*

Inventar, das   Inventory (list). SEE **INVENTUR.** *Wieso fehlen diese Güter im Inventar?* Why aren't these goods on the inventory? Also all the things in a household (fittings, etc.) that could be listed. *Nachdem die alte Frau gestorben war, machte man eine Liste des Inventars.* After the old woman died, a list was made of all the furniture and fittings.
Inventor = *der (die) Erfinder(in)*

Inventur, die   The process of drawing up an inventory; BrE stocktaking. SEE **INVENTAR.** *Morgen machen wir Inventur, und der Laden ist zu.* We're taking inventory tomorrow and the shop'll be shut.
Inventor = *der (die) Erfinder(in)*

irritieren   To put off, distract. *Pfeifen Sie gefälligst nicht, wenn ich beim Zeichnen bin: es irritiert unheimlich.* Kindly refrain from whistling when

I'm drawing: it's terribly distracting. *Das Kichern der Mädchen irritierte ihn: gefiel er ihnen, oder fanden sie ihn nur dumm?* The giggling of the girls confused him: did they like him or did they just think he was stupid? It would appear that *irritieren* is occasionally used in the English sense of "to annoy"—which would make most uses of it at least potentially ambiguous. But there is disagreement among native speakers on this point.

To irritate (annoy) s.o. = *jdn. ärgern, jdm. auf die Nerven gehen*

(eyes, skin, etc.) = *reizen*

Island (das)   Iceland (the country).

Island = *die Insel*

Isolation, die; Isolierung, die   **1.** Isolation.   **2.** Insulation. *Eine bessere Isolierung des Daches würde ihre Heizkosten bestimmt senken.* Better insulation of the roof would certainly reduce your heating costs. The form *Isolation* is the less frequent of the two in this technical sense, though it is found, esp. in electrical contexts.

isolieren   **1.** To isolate.   **2.** To insulate. SEE **ISOLATION.** *Das Gerät ist schlecht isoliert: du bekommst vielleicht einen Schlag, wenn du es anfaßt.* The appliance is badly insulated: you may get a shock if you touch it.

Isolated (of village, etc.) = *abgelegen*

J

Jacke, die   Jacket. But today it more often means "cardigan" (i.e., *Strickjacke*). *Diese Jacke hat ein sehr schönes Muster—schade, daß die Knöpfe so häßlich sind.* This cardigan has a very nice pattern—it's a pity the buttons are so ugly.

Jacket (of suit) = *das Jackett*

Sports jacket = *der* or *das Sakko*

Jalousie, die   Venetian blind. *Bei einem solchen Klima braucht man unbedingt Jalousien.* You've really got to have venetian blinds in a climate like this.

Jealousy = *die Eifersucht*

Job, der   There is an increasing tendency for this word to be used in the same general way as English "job," but it still denotes primarily a temporary post, e.g., of the sort students take on during vacations.

jobben   To work, in a job of a temporary nature. SEE **JOB.** *Ich habe eine Zeitlang als Sekretärin in Boston gejobbt.* I worked as a temp in Boston for a time.

Jubiläum, das Most commonly denotes an anniversary of some sort, often connected with work. *Morgen feiert Herr Daniel sein 25jähriges Jubiläum bei uns.* Tomorrow Herr Daniel will be celebrating 25 years of work with our firm.

jüngst- **1.** Youngest. *mein jüngster Sohn* my youngest son. **2.** Latest, most recent. *Die jüngsten Nachrichten sind besonders besorgniserregend.* The latest news is especially disturbing.

Junior, der **1.** Junior (a man's son). The German word is often used in humorous contexts. **2.** Junior (sport). **3.** Junior partner. **4.** The son of the head of a firm (often in the form *Juniorchef*). **5.** In relation to fashion and so on, it indicates the teenage/adolescent group. *Wir präsentieren unsere neueste Kollektion für Junioren.* We are presenting our new collection for young people.

Junior (student in next-to-last year): No real German equivalent, as the German system is more open-ended from the point of view of study time.

BrE Juniors (primary schoolchildren) = *die Grundschüler* (pl.)

Juror, der Rather than having a legal sense, this normally refers to a person whose task it is (as a member of a panel or committee) to judge the entries in a competition, e.g., a quiz, beauty competition, film festival: judge. *Der italienische Juror hat immer gegen die anderen gestimmt.* The Italian member of the panel consistently voted against the others.

Juror (at trial, referring to American and British systems) = *der (die) Geschworene.* The German system has "lay judges" who are similar in some respects to jurors: these are known as *der (die) Schöffe(-in).*

Jury, die This may mean "jury" in the legal sense, when referring to the American or British systems. But it normally denotes (a panel of) judges with reference to a competition of some sort (an occasional meaning of English "jury"). SEE **JUROR.** *Für Teilnehmer aus dem eigenen Land darf die jeweilige Jury nicht stimmen.* Judges are not allowed to vote for participants from their own country.

Jury (American or British trial) = *die Geschworenen* (pl.)

Justiz, die May occasionally mean "justice," as an abstract ideal. More commonly it denotes a country's legal machinery: the courts. *Bis jetzt wußte die Justiz nicht so recht, wie sie solche Fälle behandeln soll.* Up to now the courts have not really known how to deal with such cases.

Justice (abstract ideal) = *die Gerechtigkeit*

K

Kabel, das   Refers not only to thicker, heavy-duty cable, but also to thinner insulated wires used for conducting electricity to household appliances, telephones, etc., where English normally does not use "cable." *Er stolperte über das Fernsehkabel.* He tripped over the TV cord (BrE: flex/lead).

Kabine, die   Cabin (on board ship, aircraft, etc.). But also a small room or cubicle for changing clothes, or a booth for listening to s.t. in privacy. *Probier's doch an! Die Umkleidekabinen sind da drüben.* Try it on! The changing rooms are over there. *Sie können sich die Platte in Kabine 3 anhören.* You can listen to the record in booth 3. *Dieses Sprachlabor hat 24 Kabinen.* This language lab has 24 booths.
Log cabin = *die Blockhütte*

Kabinett, der or **das**   When used as a neuter noun, this corresponds to English "cabinet" in various senses, notably the political one. As a masculine noun, it is short for *Kabinettwein* and indicates one of the official quality designations for German wine. SEE **PRÄDIKAT.**

Kadaver, der   Carcass (dead body of animal, or pejoratively with reference to the human body). *Der Kadaver wurde zuerst von einem Tierarzt untersucht, weil Verdacht auf Maul-und Klauenseuche bestand.* The carcass was inspected by a vet first since there was a suspicion of foot-and-mouth disease.
Cadaver (human dead body) = *die Leiche*

Kalender, der   Calendar (Gregorian, etc.; as hung up on wall). But also an appointment book (BrE diary). *Ich glaube, ich habe am Freitag keine Sitzung—ich sehe in meinem Kalender nach.* I don't think I have a meeting on Friday—I'll just check my appointment book. *Mein Terminkalender ist immer voll—ich habe keine Zeit für die Familie.* My appointment book is always full—I have no time for my family.

Kaltblut, das   Carthorse.
Cold-blooded animal = *der Kaltblüter*

Kamera, die   Camera, but it should be noted that there is a tendency for this word to denote a film camera or video camera rather than one that takes still pictures, though the latter use is by no means uncommon.

Kamerad(in), der (die)   **1.** (mil.) Comrade.   **2.** A companion, in the sense of a close lifetime partner. This use is rather dated, however, and is now essentially restricted to the language of obituaries (the normal term is *der (die) Lebensgefährte(-tin)*. *Die zehn Jahre jüngere Maria*

Heinold war bis zu seinem Tod seine treue Kameradin. Maria Heinold, ten years his junior, was his faithful companion till his death.

Comrade (left-wing ideology) = *der Genosse, die Genossin*

Kameraderie, die   A normally pejorative term denoting an insincere, exaggerated display of "comradely" feeling and chumminess. *Laß dich von seiner Kameraderie nicht irreführen—er denkt nur an sich selbst.* Don't let yourself be misled by his hail-fellow-well-met manner—he only thinks of himself.

Camaraderie = *die Kameradschaft*

Kampagne, die   1. (mil., advertising, etc.) Campaign.   **2.** The busiest time in a business characterized by seasonal work. *Jetzt während der Kampagne findest du in der Zuckerfabrik bestimmt einen Job.* It's the busy time of the year now and you're bound to find a job in the sugar factory.

Kanal, der   1. Canal.   **2.** Channel, in most senses (including radio and TV). *Ein ganzes Netz von Kanälen sorgt für die Bewässerung.* Irrigation is provided by a whole network of channels. *Die Nachricht gelangte über offiziöse Kanäle an die Öffentlichkeit.* The news reached the public through semiofficial channels. *Er schaltete alle Kanäle nacheinander ein, aber er fand keine einzige interessante Sendung.* He tuned into all the channels one after another, but he didn't find a single interesting program. *Die Überfahrt über den Ärmelkanal ist nicht immer ein guter Auftakt zum Englandbesuch.* The trip across the English Channel is not always a good start to a visit to England. *Abwasserkanal* Sewer.

Kanalisation, die   This rarely means "canalization" (i.e., the making of canals), and normally denotes a sewerage system, or the installation of such a system. *Riesenbeträge werden für die Sanierung der Kanalisation unserer Großstädte benötigt.* Enormous sums are required for the renovation of the sewerage systems of our big cities.

Kandis, der   Longer form: *Kandiszucker.* This is the type of sugar, resembling large crystals, that is used in particular by the inhabitants of East Frisia (*Ostfriesland*) to sweeten the tea they drink in such large quantities.

Candy (general = BrE sweets) = *Süßigkeiten* (pl.)

Kanne, die   Usage varies, as with most container words, but *Kanne* never means "can" in the sense of an airtight container for storing food or drink. It often indicates a "pot" or "pitcher" (BrE: jug), though in this sense it is often used in the diminutive form *das Kännchen. Er trinkt jeden Morgen eine ganze Kanne Tee zum Frühstück.* He drinks a whole pot of tea for breakfast every morning. *Gieß bitte die Milch von der Flasche in das Kännchen.* Pour the milk out of the bottle into the pitcher, please. The nondiminutive form may denote larger containers. *Die Milch stand* *in riesigen Kannen zum Abholen bereit.* The milk was stored in huge churns, ready to be collected.

Can (of beer, peas, etc.) = *die Dose, die Büchse*

Kanone, die **1.** May denote a cannon (i.e., the artillery of previous centuries), but the German word is more general and can also denote a piece of modern artillery: gun. *Die Armee verfügt nur über Kanonen aus dem Zweiten Weltkrieg.* The army only has guns dating from the Second World War. There are various colloquial uses: **2.** Revolver. *Schmeißt die Kanonen weg! Das Haus ist umstellt!* Throw down your guns! The house is surrounded! **3.** Expert (esp. sporting). *Helmut ist eine echte Sport(s)-kanone!* Helmut's a real sporting ace! **4.** *unter aller Kanone* Denotes quality so low that it defies description. *Der Service in diesem Hotel ist unter aller Kanone.* The service in this hotel is the pits. **5.** *Gulaschkanone* (mil. sl.) Field kitchen.

Kapazität, die **1.** Capacity. **2.** Recognized expert in a particular field. *Herr Braun ist im Bereich der Halbleitertechnik eine anerkannte Kapazität.* Herr Braun is a recognized expert in the field of semiconductor technology.

Kapelle, die **1.** Chapel (small church or section of church). **2.** (rather dated) A band of musicians (playing dance music). *Zu dieser Zeit konnte jeder, der über einen Keller und eine Kapelle verfügte, einen Nachtklub aufmachen.* At that time anyone with a cellar and a band could open a nightclub.

kapern **1.** To capture and seize a ship (in historical contexts). *Mit nur zwölf Mann hatte er das französische Kriegsschiff gekapert.* He had captured the French man-of-war with only twelve men. **2.** (coll.) To get hold of (s.t. or s.o.), to win (s.o.) over (to one's side).

To caper = *herumtollen*

kapital **1.** (hunting) A particularly magnificent specimen of an animal, esp. in the phrase *ein kapitaler Hirsch* = a magnificent/prize stag. **2.** In other contexts it also indicates s.t. out of the ordinary, in which case it may correspond to the rather dated English "capital," though not when applied to negative things like mistakes. *Damit hat er einen kapitalen Fehler gemacht.* He made a real blunder when he did that.

Capital (excellent) = *ausgezeichnet*

kappen First and foremost a nautical term, meaning "to cut" (ropes, etc.); occasionally used in other contexts too. *Die Matrosen kappten schnell die Leinen.* The sailors quickly cut the lines. *Diese langen Äste müßten eigentlich gekappt werden.* These long branches really ought to be cut.

To cap (bottle) = *verschließen*

Karaffe, die   Carafe (for serving wine); decanter.

Karikatur, die   Caricature. Also the normal term for a (single) "cartoon" (in a newspaper, etc.). *Diese berühmte Karikatur zeigt Hitler und Stalin, wie sie sich nach der Unterzeichnung des Nichtangriffspakts höflich voreinander verneigen.* This famous cartoon shows Hitler and Stalin politely bowing to each other after the signing of the nonaggression pact.

Karriere, die   Not quite the same as English "career," in that *Karriere* always denotes a successful career, usually involving rapid promotion: unlike the English word, it is not used merely to denote a job one chooses on a lifetime or at least long-term basis. *Sie verließ die Schule mit sechzehn Jahren und machte schnell Karriere.* She left school at sixteen and rapidly made a successful career for herself.
Career (job) = *der Beruf*
Career guidance = *die Berufsberatung*

Karte, die   **1.** Card.   **2.** Map (*Landkarte*). *Warum sollte ich eine Karte von Chile haben?* Why should I have a map of Chile?   **3.** Menu (*Speisekarte*). *Herr Ober, kann ich noch einmal die Karte haben?* Waiter, can I have the menu again?   **4.** Ticket (*Fahrkarte, Eintrittskarte*). *Eine Karte nach Ulm kostet über 200 Mark.* A ticket to Ulm costs over 200 marks.

Karton, der   **1.** A (large) carton, cardboard box. *In jedem Karton waren 12 Dutzend Dosen Erbsen.* In each carton/box there were 12 dozen cans of peas.   **2.** Also the material: cardboard. *Du darfst dich nicht auf die Kiste setzen—die ist ja nur aus Karton.* You mustn't sit on that box—it's only made of cardboard.
Carton (small container for milk, juice, etc.) = *die Tüte, die Packung*. (There is considerable variation in individual usage, and some native speakers use *Karton* in this sense too.)

kartonieren   To bind (a book) in boards. *Das Buch gibt es nur in der kartonierten Ausgabe.* The book is only available in a hardback edition.
To carton (i.e., pack in cartons) = *in Kartons verpacken*

kaschieren   **1.** To conceal. *Warum versuchst du, deine Glatze mit diesem absurden Toupet zu kaschieren?* Why are you trying to hide the fact you're bald with that ridiculous toupee?   **2.** (tech.) To laminate.
To cash (check) = *einlösen*

Kasino, das   **1.** Casino (for gambling).   **2.** A room where meals are taken, either in military contexts or (less commonly) with reference to (large) firms. *Im Offizierskasino herrschte eine ungewöhnliche Ruhe.* It was unusually quiet in the officers' mess. *In der obersten Etage befindet sich das Kasino für die ganz hohen Tiere.* The cafeteria for the real big shots is on the top floor.

Kasse, die   The place where money is paid, in a supermarket, bank, etc.: the translation varies according to the context. *Bei Realkauf gibt es fast 20 Kassen.* There are almost 20 checkouts at Realkauf. *Ich packe Ihnen das*

ein, während Sie an der Kasse da drüben bezahlen. I'll wrap it up for you while you pay at the cashier over there. *Wir mußten uns zwei Stunden an der Kasse anstellen, um Karten für das Konzert zu bekommen.* We had to stand in line (BrE queue up) at the box office for two hours to get tickets for the concert. *Ich löse meine Reiseschecks ein, sobald eine Kasse frei wird.* I'll cash my traveler's checks as soon as there's a cashier free.
Cash = *das Bargeld*

Kassette, die   1. Cassette (audio, video).   **2.** Small box for safeguarding money, valuables, etc. *Das Geld war zwar in der Kassette, aber sie war nicht verschlossen.* Although the money was in the (cash) box, it wasn't locked.   **3.** Boxed set, of books or records. *Beethovens Symphonien gibt es auf sieben Platten in Kassette.* Beethoven's symphonies are available in a boxed set of seven records.

kassieren   1. To receive payment, take money (of a shop assistant, etc.). *Darf ich jetzt kassieren? Wir schließen in zehn Minuten.* Would you mind paying now? We're closing in ten minutes' time. *Unsere Vertreter dürfen die Prämien nicht kassieren.* Our agents are not allowed to receive payment for premiums.   **2.** (coll.) To receive money (for oneself, as profit, etc.). *Jedesmal wenn er eine solche Wohnung vermittelt, kassiert der Makler 2000 Mark.* Every time he finds a tenant for a flat like this the realtor (BrE estate agent) makes 2000 marks. *Ich habe keine Erben—wenn ich sterbe, kassiert nur der Staat.* I have no heirs—when I die, the state will be the only one to collect.   **3.** (coll.) To confiscate. *1,2 Promille—da hat die Polizei natürlich seinen Führerschein kassiert.* He had a blood alcohol level of 120 mg—as you can imagine, the police confiscated his driver's license.   **4.** (coll.) To catch (fugitive, etc.). *Den letzten entflohenen Häftling hat die Polizei gestern kassiert.* The police picked up the last escaped prisoner yesterday.   **5.** (jur.) To quash (a verdict).
To cash (check) = *einlösen*

Kassierer, der   Cashier; also a "teller" or "clerk" at a bank. The term can also denote the "treasurer" of a club or society.

Katalysator, der   Catalyst—chemical or figurative. In recent years the word has become an everyday one in its new meaning of "catalytic converter," to reduce pollution from car exhausts: it is often abbreviated to *Kat. Wenn dein Auto einen Kat(alysator) hat, darfst du kein verbleites Benzin tanken.* If your car has a catalytic converter, you mustn't fill up with leaded gas.

Katarrh, der   Catarrh, in the strict medical sense. Unlike English "catarrh," it is not used popularly to denote the profuse nasal mucus produced during a bad cold. The German word is also used to denote a bad cold and/or cough.
Catarrh (nasal mucus) = *der (Nasen)schleim*

Kater, der　**1.** A tomcat.　**2.** (coll.) A hangover. A very common expression. *Wenn du einen Kater hast, mußt du ein kräftiges Frühstück essen, auch wenn du keinen Appetit hast.* If you have a hangover you must eat a hearty breakfast, even if you don't have an appetite.

kauen　To chew. *Seitdem ich diese Füllung verloren habe, tut es richtig weh, wenn ich kaue.* Ever since that filling came out, chewing has been really painful. *der* (also *das*) *Kaugummi* Chewing gum.

　To cow (intimidate) = *einschüchtern*

kauern　To cower, if the idea of fear is present. But it may also mean simply "to crouch," "to squat." *Wir kauerten (uns) in der Ecke des Wintergartens, in die die Sonne noch schien.* We crouched in the corner of the conservatory into which the sun was still shining.

　To cower (if squatting) = *kauern*
　　　　　(cringe) = *sich ducken*

Kaution, die　The basic idea is that of a financial surety, specifically:　**1.** Bail. *Der Angeklagte wurde gegen eine Kaution von 20.000 Mark freigelassen.* The accused was released on bail of 20,000 marks.　**2.** Deposit (esp. for rented accommodation). *Die Miete für die Wohnung beträgt 800 Mark im Monat, und Sie müssen eine Kaution von 1.000 Mark hinterlegen.* The rent for the apartment is 800 marks a month and you must pay a deposit of 1,000 marks.

　Caution (prudence) = *die Vorsicht*

Kavalier, der　Cavalier (hist.). Also a "gentleman," who is "chivalrous" in his conduct toward women (or, as he would call them, ladies): the term is often tinged with irony. *Er weiß, wie ein Mann sich in der Gesellschaft einer Dame zu verhalten hat—er ist ein echter Kavalier der alten Schule.* He knows how a man should behave in the company of a lady— he's a real gentleman of the old school. The word has formed some interesting compounds: *das Kavaliersdelikt* A trivial offense, one most people would not regard as worth prosecuting; *der Kavalier(s)start* A racing start, e.g., by a driver at traffic lights.

Keeper, der　Keeper, goalkeeper (in soccer). But also used occasionally as an abbreviation of **BARKEEPER** (Q.V.).

Keks, der　Cookie, BrE biscuit. *Iß nicht so viele Kekse, sonst wirst du dick!* Don't eat so many cookies or you'll get fat!

　Cake = *der Kuchen, die Torte*

Kerbe, die　Notch, nick (in wood, etc.). *Für jeden Feind, den er tötete, schnitt er eine kleine Kerbe in seinen Bogen.* He carved a small notch in his bow for every enemy he killed.

　Curb (of sidewalk; BrE kerb, of pavement) = *der Bordstein, die Bordsteinkante*

kerben　To (cut a) notch (in). SEE **KERBE.**

　To curb (restrain) = *zügeln*

Kessel, der   **1.** Kettle.   **2.** Boiler (e.g., of central heating system). *Mit diesem alten Kessel verbrauchen Sie viel zu viel Gas.* You're using much too much gas with this old boiler.   **3.** A large pot, cauldron, vat. *In diesen Riesenkesseln wird das Bier gebraut.* The beer is brewed in these enormous vats.   **4.** A valley surrounded by hills or mountains: basin. *Stuttgart liegt in einem Kessel.* Stuttgart is situated in a basin.   **5.** (mil.) An encircled area. *Wir müssen uns ergeben—aus diesem Kessel kommen wir nie raus.* We must surrender—we're completely surrounded and we'll never break out. *das Kesseltreiben*   **1.** A hunt using a circle of beaters.   **2.** (by extension) A witchhunt conducted against a person or persons.

kicken   **1.** To kick (a ball).   **2.** To play (soccer). *Seit Oktober kickt er für Werder Bremen.* He's been playing for Werder Bremen since October.
To kick (general) = *treten*

Kicker, der   **1.** Soccer player. *Die Südamerikaner haben die besten Kicker der Welt.* The South Americans have the best soccer players in the world. Also the often frantically exciting replica of soccer played in pubs or amusement arcades by two or four participants on a sort of large table: (BrE) "table football," "bar football." *Wenn er in die Kneipe geht, spielt er stundenlang Kicker.* When he goes to the pub, he plays bar football for hours.

kielholen   To keelhaul (a sailor). But also "to career" (of a ship).

killen   To kill, but the German word is informal and denotes cold-blooded murder in particular (e.g., as committed by gangsters). *Er ist völlig gefühlskalt—er killt jeden, wenn er damit Geld verdienen kann.* He's completely without feeling—he'll murder anyone if he can earn money by doing so.
To kill = *töten*

Kind, das   Child.
Kind (noun: type) = *die Art, die Sorte*

kindlich   Childlike. *Er hat die kindliche Gewohnheit, immer Fragen zu stellen.* He has the childlike habit of constantly asking questions.
Kindly (adj.) = *freundlich, gütig*

kippen   To tip, tilt. *Die Asche wird dann auf diese Halde gekippt.* The ashes are then tipped onto this heap. *Diese alten Fenster kann man nicht kippen.* You can't tilt these old windows.
BrE To kip (sl., = sleep) = *pennen*

Kipper, der   Dump truck, BrE tipper. *Mit einem Kipper schaffen wir diese Erde schnell weg.* We'll soon clear away this earth with a dump truck.
Kipper (smoked herring) = *der geräucherte Hering, der Räucherhering*

Kissen, das   Cushion, pillow. *Wir brauchen nicht so viele Kissen auf dem Sofa.* We don't need so many cushions on the sofa.
Kiss = *der Kuß*
Kissing = *das Küssen*

Kitt, der   Putty (for windows). Also used metaphorically to denote a bond of some sort. *Dieser Staatsbesuch wird als Kitt zwischen den beiden bis vor kurzem verfeindeten Ländern dienen.* This state visit will serve to cement relations between the two countries, which were enemies until recently.
Kit (equipment, etc.) = *die Ausrüstung*
    (set of tools) = *das Werkzeug*
    (for model-making, etc.) = *der Bastelsatz, der Bausatz*

Kittchen, das   Not a kitchen, but a slang word for "jail": jug, clink, hoosegow. *Dieser Junge landet irgendwann mal im Kittchen.* That boy'll end up in the clink one day.
Kitchen = *die Küche*

kitten   To stick together (with cement, glue, etc.). Often used metaphorically of relationships, etc., in the sense of "to mend," "to patch up." *Das ist eine Ehe, die sich nicht mehr kitten läßt.* It's a marriage that can no longer be held together.
BrE To kit (s.o. out with s.t.) = *(jdn. mit etwas) ausrüsten*

Klamm, die   An uncommon word for "gorge." *Wir haben in einer Klamm neben einem Bach gezeltet.* We camped in a gorge, next to a stream.
Clam = *die Venusmuschel*

klamm   **1.** Damp and cold. *Das ist doch nicht gesund, in einem klammen Bett zu schlafen.* It's not healthy to sleep in a cold, damp bed.   **2.** Numb. *Meine Finger waren klamm und ich konnte den Deckel nicht aufmachen.* My fingers were numb and I couldn't open the lid.   **3.** (coll.) Short of money, hard up, in the (now rather dated) expression *klamm sein*.
Clammy (humid, BrE close) = *schwül*
    (moist, of handshake) = *feucht*

Klang, der   Sound (esp. with reference to tonal quality). *Diese Gitarre hat meines Erachtens einen zu metallischen Klang.* In my opinion this guitar has too metallic a sound.
Clang (metallic, high-pitched) = *das Klirren*
    (low-pitched) = *das Dröhnen*

Klapp-   Compounds with *Klapp-* denote s.t. that folds (for storage, etc.), e.g., *Klappstuhl* = folding chair. SEE **KLAPPEN**.

Klappe, die   This has many different meanings (but not "clap"!). The most important include   **1.** Flap (i.e., s.t. that moves or folds). *Die Katze kann durch diese Klappe rein- und rausgehen, wie sie will.* The cat can use this flap to come in and go out as she likes.   **2.** Valve (heart,

trumpet, etc.). **3.** (coll.) Mouth, trap. *Halt' die Klappe!* Shut your trap!
Clap(ping) (applause) = *das (Beifall)klatschen*

klappen **1.** To fold (up, together, away, etc.). *Dieses Bett läßt sich ganz einfach zusammenklappen.* This bed can be folded up very easily. **2.** To lift up, raise (a flap, etc.). *Der Deckel wird dann mit der rechten Hand nach oben geklappt.* The lid is then lifted up with the right hand. **3.** (coll.) Come out smoothly, meet with success (often impersonal). *Mit deiner Fahrprüfung klappt es bestimmt.* I'm sure your driving test will go all right. *Mit der Schlichtung hat es leider nicht geklappt.* Unfortunately the arbitration didn't work out. **4.** To bang (door, etc.). *Das macht mich verrückt, wie diese Tür klappt!* That door banging is driving me mad!
To clap (applaud) = *(Beifall) klatschen*

klasse/Klasse, die (coll.) Excellent, great, fantastic. *"Ich habe bestanden!"—"Das ist ja Klasse!"* "I've passed!" "That's fantastic!" *Er hat eine klasse Frau geheiratet.* He married a fantastic woman.

Klassenarbeit, die Not classwork in general (as opposed to homework), but a written test administered in class under supervision (and counting toward assessment). *Wie war die Klassenarbeit in Mathe?* How was the math test?
Classwork = *das Anfertigen von (schriftlicher) Arbeit in der Klasse*

Klassik, die Classicism; classical period. *Er interessiert sich nur für die Klassik und hat für die Romantik nichts übrig.* He is only interested in classicism and has no time for romanticism.
Classic (noun) = *der Klassiker*

Klause, die **1.** Cell (of monk). **2.** Hermitage (i.e., hermit's dwelling). **3.** By extension, also a small dwelling place offering peace and quiet and privacy: a retreat, den. **4.** In North Germany it also denotes a small bar or pub, nearly always in compounds giving the name of the establishment, e.g., *"Waldklause," "Harzklause."*
Clause (of contract) = *die Klausel*
Main clause (grammar) = *der Hauptsatz*
Subordinate clause = *der Nebensatz*

Klinge, die Blade (of sword, etc.). *die Rasierklinge* Razor blade.
Cling (sound) = *das Klingeln*

klingen May occasionally denote a specifically high-pitched tone, but the general "to sound" is more usually the English equivalent. *Ihre Stimme klingt sehr ruhig.* Her voice sounds very restful. *Ja, das klingt gut.* Yes, that sounds fine.
To cling to s.t. or s.o. (hold on) = *sich an etwas/jdn. klammern*

Klinke, die **1.** (Door) handle. *Entsetzt sah sie, wie sich die Klinke langsam nach unten bewegte.* Horrified, she saw the door handle slowly move downward. **2.** There are various specialist technical uses, e.g., a "jack" in telecommunications connections.

Clink (sound) = *das Klirren*

    (sl., = prison) = *der Knast*

Klippe, die (Large) rock (rising out of the sea). *Wir fuhren mit dem Boot zwischen die Klippe und den Strand.* We sailed the boat between the rock and the beach. Metaphorically also a difficulty, a "reef" one has to circumnavigate.

Clip (for attaching things, etc.) = *die Klammer*

Klischee, das Cliché. But also, in printing contexts, a "plate" or "block."

Klosett, das Lavatory, toilet. It is hardly the normal term nowadays (though the shorter form *das Klo* is extremely common in colloquial speech) and is often used with humorous intent. *Seit er diese Muscheln gegessen hat, muß er ständig aufs Klosett.* Ever since he ate those mussels, he's had to keep going to the toilet (BrE loo).

Closet (BrE, cupboard) = *der Wandschrank*

Kloster, das Monastery, nunnery. *Es lebt sich hier wie in einem Kloster.* It's like living in a monastery here.

Cloister(s) (covered walk of cathedral, etc.) = *der Kreuzgang*

Knabe, der Not a "knave," but a now rather dated or literary word for "boy." *Diese Schule ist für Knaben zwischen 11 und 14.* This school is for boys between 11 and 14.

Knave (villain) = *der Schurke*

    (in cards—BrE) = *der Bube*

Knack, der Short, sharp sound; crack. *Mit einem lauten Knack zerbrach das Brett.* The plank snapped with a loud crack.

Knack (special technique) = *der Kniff, der Trick*

    (special talent) = *das Talent, das Geschick*

Knicker, der Scrooge, skinflint.

BrE (Pair of) knickers (panties) = *der Schlüpfer, das Höschen*

kochen **1.** To cook (i.e., do the cooking, be able to cook). *Kochst du heute abend?* Are you (doing the) cooking tonight? *Warum heiratest du ein Mädchen, das nicht kochen kann?* Why are you marrying a girl who can't cook? **2.** To boil (water, vegetables, or eggs in water). *Das Wasser kocht schon.* The water's already boiling. *gekochte Eier* boiled eggs. **3.** To make (coffee, tea, soup, or other heated liquids). *Kannst du den Tisch decken, während ich den Kaffee koche?* Can you set the table while I make the coffee?

To cook (prepare food by heating it) = *zubereiten.* (But German tends to use the specific word for the method of cooking used, e.g., *braten, grillen.*)

Koffer, der   Suitcase. *Mehr als einen Koffer dürfen Sie nicht mitnehmen.* You are not allowed to take more than one suitcase.

Coffer (chest) = *die Truhe*

(specifically for money and other valuables) = *die Schatulle*

Kognak, der   Brandy. More general than English "cognac," which is normally only applied to French brandy from the Cognac area.

Kohl, der   Cabbage.

Coal = *die Kohle*

Kollege, der   Colleague. *Ich finde den neuen Kollegen nicht sonderlich sympathisch.* I don't think our new colleague is particularly nice. It should be noted that *Kollege* and *Kollegin* are used more widely than English "colleague": German manual workers, for example, use the term freely whereas their American or British counterparts would not normally use "colleague" except perhaps with ironical intent. *"Fragen Sie meinen Kollegen da drüben,"* sagte der Müllmann. "Ask my buddy (BrE mate) over there," said the garbage collector.

College (university) = *die Universität, die Hochschule*

(referring to a part of a university) = *das College*

Kollier, das.   SEE **COLLIER.**

Kollision, die   Collision. Peculiar to German is the application to clashes in appointments or times. *Wenn die Sitzung am Dienstag stattfindet, dann gibt es leider für mich eine Terminkollision.* If the meeting takes place on Tuesday it'll unfortunately conflict with another appointment I have.

Kolonie, die   1. Colony.   **2.** One of the areas set aside to provide small parcels of land rented out for the purpose of cultivation, known in BrE as "allotments" (there is no American equivalent). *Wir haben einen sehr schönen Schrebergarten in der Kolonie "Edelweiß."* We've got a really nice allotment in the "Edelweiss" allotments.

Kolonne, die   1. Column (of figures; troops).   **2.** Convoy (of motor vehicles, etc.). *Wegen dieser verdammten Kolonne kommen wir mit mindestens einer Stunde Verspätung an.* Because of this damned convoy we'll be at least an hour late.   **3.** Line, queue (of slow-moving cars). *In einer Kolonne zu fahren, verlangt großes Konzentrationsvermögen.* It requires great concentration to drive in a line of slow-moving traffic.   **4.** Gang (of workers). *Die Kolonne, die die Straße ausbesserte, bestand zum größten Teil aus Fremdarbeitern.* The gang repairing the road consisted for the most part of foreign workers.

kolossal   May be used to indicate great size, but rather more common as a colloquial epithet to mean "tremendous," "fantastic," etc. *"Das ist ein kolossaler Film,"* sagte sie. "That's a fantastic film," she said.

Colossal = *riesig*

Kombination, die   1. Combination.   **2.** The process of arriving at a conclusion by (logical) reasoning. *Durch geschickte Kombination gelang es* *ihm festzustellen, daß nur der Anwalt die Witwe getötet haben konnte.* With the aid of skillful deduction he succeeded in establishing that only the attorney could have killed the widow.

kombinieren 1. To combine. 2. To reason, to deduce, to conclude. SEE **KOMBINATION.** *Er hat falsch kombiniert, daß ich an dem Verbrechen beteiligt war.* He concluded wrongly that I was involved in the crime.

Komfort, der May be equivalent to "comfort," but the German word has strong technological connotations: it refers not so much to a general abstract concept of physical ease as to those "extras" that can make life less strenuous and more pleasant: modern conveniences, etc. *Gesucht: Komfortwohnung (3 Zi.) in City-Nähe für alleinstehenden Geschäftsmann.* Wanted: 2-bedroom luxury apartment with all mod(ern) con(venience)s near city center for single businessman. *Ein Auto mit allem Komfort zu diesem Preis—wo gibt's das sonst?* A car with all the luxury features at this price—where else will you get that?

Comfort (physical) also = *die Bequemlichkeit*
(consolation) = *der Trost*

komfortabel Comfortable (esp. of accommodations, less commonly of furniture; not applied to persons). It usually means rather more than "comfortable," implying the presence of (all) modern conveniences: "well-appointed," "luxurious." SEE **KOMFORT.** *Ich muß sagen, die Wohnung ist äußerst komfortabel.* I must say the apartment is extremely well-appointed.

Comfortable (furniture) = *bequem*
(pleasant, of life, etc.) = *angenehm.* I don't feel very comfortable about this decision. *Mir ist es nicht ganz wohl bei dieser Entscheidung.*

Komik, die The comic side or element of s.t. *Es war ein tragischer Zwischenfall, der aber leider auch einer gewissen Komik nicht entbehrte.* It was a tragic incident which, however, was unfortunately not devoid of a certain comic element.

Comic (comedian) = *der (die) Komiker(in)*
(magazine) = *der Comic*

komisch Comic(al), funny—but also "funny" in the sense of "strange," "odd." *Er hält seine eigenen Witze für sehr komisch.* He thinks his own jokes are very funny. *Es ist komisch, daß er dir nie gedankt hat.* It's odd that he never thanked you.

Komma, das Comma. But also "(decimal) point." *Zehn Komma acht— das ist ein neuer Rekord!* Ten point eight—that's a new record!
The decimal point is in fact represented by a comma in German texts: thus, what an American would write as 10.8 would appear as 10,8 in a German text.

kommandieren   The basic idea of "command" is always present, but the various special uses should be noted.   **1.** To command, be in command of. *Die Kompanie wurde von einem Sachsen kommandiert.* The company was commanded by a Saxon.   **2.** To give an order. *"Stillgestanden!" kommandierte der Feldwebel.* "Attention!" ordered the sergeant.   **3.** (coll.) To order, boss (people) around, often in the compound form *herumkommandieren. Er kommandiert so gern—ich glaube, er hat Minderwertigkeitskomplexe.* He likes ordering people around so much—I think he suffers from an inferiority complex. *Ich lasse mich nicht länger von ihm herumkommandieren.* I'm not going to let myself be ordered around by him any more. *abkommandieren* To post (s.o. to a different duty, etc.). *Er hatte Angst, an die Ostfront abkommandiert zu werden.* He was afraid of being posted to the Eastern Front. *Nächste Woche werde ich in die Finanzabteilung abkommandiert.* I'm being transferred (BrE seconded) to the finance department next week.

To command (order) also = *befehlen*

To commandeer = *requirieren*

Kommando, das   **1.** A concise military or military-style order. *Barsche Kommandos ertönten in seinen Ohren.* Curt orders rang in his ears.   **2.** The authority to give orders, esp. in the phrase *das Kommando haben. "Wer hat hier das Kommando?" fragte der Oberst.* "Who is in command here?" asked the colonel.   **3.** A military unit constituted to carry out special duties: English "commando" may be used in this sense, though the layperson would probably use other expressions. *Der Auftrag, das Dorf nach Terroristen zu durchsuchen, wurde einem Spezialkommando übertragen.* A special unit/commando was given the task of searching the village for terrorists.

Commando (soldier) = *das Mitglied/der Angehörige eines Kommandotrupps*

Kommentar, der   **1.** Commentary (collection of notes on text, etc.).   **2.** Critical assessment of an event or topic (esp. in the media). *Zu den Ereignissen im Libanon jetzt ein Kommentar von unserem Korrespondenten.* Our correspondent now gives an assessment of the events in Lebanon. *Nur der Kommentar in der* Frankfurter Rundschau *sprach sich für eine solche Reform aus.* Only the editorial in the *Frankfurter Rundschau* came out in favor of such a reform.   **3.** (Unhelpful or malicious) comments, remarks. *Sabine muß zu allem ihren blöden Kommentar geben.* Sabine has to make stupid remarks about everything. *kein Kommentar* No comment.

Commentary (on sporting event) = *die Berichterstattung*

kommentieren   To comment (on); also "to write a commentary on" (a text). *Professor Bleike hat den Text kommentiert.* Professor Bleike wrote the commentary on the text.

Kommissar, der 1. Commissar (political, esp. communist). **2.** A high-ranking police officer: inspector, etc. *Den Mordfall untersucht Kommissar Holland.* Inspector Holland is investigating the murder. **3.** Commissioner (for administering an area, etc.). *Die Verwaltung der besetzten Gebiete wurde einem Kommissar übertragen.* A commissioner was entrusted with the administration of the occupied territories.

Kommission, die Wider in application than English "commission" (in its sense of a group of experts examining some matter), and "committee" is often the more appropriate translation. *Eine kleine Kommission ist gebildet worden, um dieses Problem zu untersuchen.* A small committee has been set up to examine this problem.

Commission (for work to be carried out) = *der Auftrag*

(of officer) = *das Patent*

(on a sale) = *die Provision*

Kommissionär, der (Commission/trading) agent. *Ich kann zu diesem Geschäft nichts sagen—das läuft alles über unseren Kommissionär.* I can't say anything about this transaction—our agent handles all that.

BrE Commissionaire (hotel doorman) = *der Portier*

Kommode, die Commode, bureau, chest of drawers. *Die Strumpfhosen findest du in der Kommode, zweite Schublade von oben.* You'll find the tights in the chest of drawers, second drawer from the top.

Commode (BrE, for invalids) = *der Nachtstuhl*

kommunal Local, municipal. SEE **KOMMUNE**. *Diese Freizeiteinrichtungen werden kommunal verwaltet.* These leisure facilities are administered locally.

Communal (used by various people) = *gemeinsam, Gemeinschafts-*

Kommune, die 1. Commune (group of persons living together, esp. in an "alternative" lifestyle). **2.** The local (i.e., town or village) level of political administration, below the federal (*Bund*) and state (*Land*) level: *Gemeinde* is another term for this. *Das Geld wird an Bund, Länder und Kommunen verteilt.* The money is being distributed at the federal, state, and local level (of administration). *Diese Frage der Zuschüsse für Umweltschutz beschäftigt die Kommunen schon seit einigen Jahren.* Local authorities have been concerned with this question of subsidies for conservation for some years now.

Kompagnon, der Partner, associate (in business).

Companion (travel) = *der (Reise)gefährte*

kompetent Competent, in the sense of "responsible for," "authorized to deal with." Since English "competent" is used so often to mean "capable," other translations of *kompetent* may be clearer. *Keiner scheint zu wissen, wer für solche Angelegenheiten kompetent ist.* No one seems to know who is responsible for/authorized to deal with such matters. *Das Auswärtige Amt ist wohl das kompetente Ministerium.* The Department of

State (BrE Foreign Office) is probably the responsible/relevant ministry.
Competent (capable) = *fähig*

Kompetenz, die   Competence, in the sense of "area of authority, responsibility, jurisdiction." SEE **KOMPETENT**. *Wir würden Ihnen gern helfen, aber das liegt außerhalb unserer Kompetenz.* We would like to help you, but the matter is outside our jurisdiction. *Damit hat das Finanzamt seine Kompetenzen eindeutig überschritten.* By doing this the Internal Revenue (BrE Inland Revenue) has clearly exceeded its authority.
Competence (capability) = *die Fähigkeit*

Komplementär, der   This refers to the partner who bears full liability in the form of company known as a *Kommanditgesellschaft.*
To be complementary (i.e., complement each other) = *sich ergänzen*

komplett   Complete, but this is not always the most appropriate translation, notably in culinary contexts. *ein komplettes Frühstück* a full breakfast.

Kompositum, das   A compound (in word formation). *Warum benutzen Sie immer diese langen Komposita? Sie machen Ihren Stil nicht schöner.* Why do you always use these long compounds? They don't make your style any more attractive.
Composite (noun, botany) = *der Korbblütler*
           (adj.) = *zusammengesetzt*

Kondensmilch, die   Unlike condensed milk, this is not sweetened and corresponds to "evaporated milk."

Kondition, die   **1.** Condition (i.e., restriction, provision).   **2.** Physical fitness, stamina. *Ich muß etwas für meine Kondition tun.* I must do something to keep fit. *Mit seinen 70 Jahren hat er eine erstaunliche Kondition. Eine 20-Kilometer-Wanderung macht ihm nichts aus.* He's still amazingly fit for a 70-year-old. A 20-kilometer walk doesn't bother him at all.
Condition (restriction, provision) also = *die Bedingung*
           (state) = *der Zustand*
           (ailment) = *das Leiden*
Conditions (circumstances) = *die Verhältnisse* (pl.)

konditionell   Referring to physical fitness or stamina. SEE **KONDITION**. *Er hatte es mit einem Gegner zu tun, der ihm konditionell weit überlegen war.* He was facing an opponent who was physically much fitter than he was.
Conditional (grammar) = *konditional, Konditional-*
To be conditional (up)on s.t. = *von etwas abhängen*

Konfektion, die   Ready-to-wear clothing or the production thereof. *Ich merke gar nicht, ob einer Konfektion oder maßgeschneiderte Anzüge trägt.* I don't notice if someone's wearing ready-to-wear (BrE off-the-peg) clothes or custom-made (BrE made-to-measure) suits. *Durch eine rationelle Technik der Konfektion gelang es der Firma, schicke Kleidung zu Tiefstpreisen* *zu vertreiben.* By using an efficient technique of producing ready-to-wear clothing the firm was able to sell stylish clothes at rock-bottom prices.

Confectionery (candy) = *Süßwaren, Süßigkeiten* (pl.)

Konfektionär, der A now rather dated term for a manufacturer of ready-to-wear clothing, or a manager or executive working in this industry. SEE **KONFEKTION.**

Confectioner (seller of candy) = *der Süßwarenverkäufer*

Konferenz, die Conference. But in many contexts (esp. in relation to business and management) the translation "meeting" may be more appropriate. *Auf unserer letzten Konferenz haben wir vereinbart, vorläufig keine Kredite mehr aufzunehmen.* We agreed at our last meeting not to arrange any more loans for the time being.

Conference (convention) also = *die Tagung*

Konfession, die (Religious) denomination, religion. *Für eine solche Bewerbung brauchen Sie Ihre Konfession nicht anzugeben.* For a job application of this sort you don't need to give your religion.

Confession (of crime, etc.) = *das Geständnis*

(religious, of sins) = *die Beichte*

konfessionell Relating to religious denomination. SEE **KONFESSION.** *Bei solchen Streitigkeiten ist das konfessionelle Moment äußerst wichtig.* The religious factor is extremely important in such disputes.

Confessional (noun) = *der Beichtstuhl*

The secrecy of the confessional = *das Beichtgeheimnis*

konform This adjective, normally used in the phrases *konform gehen* and *konform sein,* indicates agreement. *In diesem Punkt gehe ich mit Ihnen konform.* I agree with you on that point.

To conform (in behavior, etc.) = *sich anpassen*

To conform to (correspond to) = *entsprechen*

Kongruenz, die 1. (math., geom.) Congruence. **2.** (gramm.) Agreement, concord. *Hier stimmt die Kongruenz nicht: das Subjekt steht im Singular, aber das Verb hat die Pluralform.* The agreement is wrong here: the subject is in the singular, but the verb has the plural form.

Konjunktiv, der The grammatical term denoting the **sub**junctive (mood). *Man sagt, der Konjunktiv sterbe aus.* People say the subjunctive is dying out.

Konjunktur, die 1. The (state of the) economy: the word may sometimes denote specifically a good economic period (*Hochkonjunktur*). *Bei der jetzigen rückläufigen Konjunktur ist mit großen Investitionen nicht zu rechnen.* In the present declining economic situation large-scale investments cannot be expected. *Die augenblickliche (Hoch)konjunktur wird bestimmt nicht anhalten.* The present boom will certainly not last. **2.** (by extension) Popularity, being in demand, or situation (of a noneconomic kind). *Autos mit Hecktür haben im Augenblick Konjunktur.* Cars with a tailgate are popular at present. *Die gegenwärtige hochschulpolitische Konjunktur würde solchen Reformen entgegenwirken.* The present situation regarding higher education policy would work against such reforms. Conjuncture (of circumstances, etc.) = *das Zusammentreffen*

Konkurrent, der Competitor. *Diesen Beschluß werden höchstens Ihre Konkurrenten begrüßen, denn so werden Sie bankrott.* Your competitors will be the only ones to welcome this decision, because it will make you bankrupt.
Concurrent (adj., = simultaneous) = *gleichzeitig*

Konkurrenz, die Competition. *Die japanische Konkurrenz macht uns besonders zu schaffen—ihre Produkte sind einfach besser.* The Japanese competition worries us especially—their products are simply better.
Concurrence (agreement) = *die Übereinstimmung*

konkurrieren To compete. *Mit solchen alten Produkten können Sie auf dem Weltmarkt nicht konkurrieren.* You cannot compete in the world market with such old products.
To concur (agree) = *übereinstimmen*

Konkurs, der Bankruptcy, or the legal proceedings connected with it. *Die Aufträge gingen der Firma verloren und sie machte Konkurs.* The firm lost the orders and went bankrupt. *Der Konkurs wird nächste Woche eröffnet.* The bankruptcy proceedings open next week.
Concourse (of railroad station) = *die (Bahnhofs)halle*

konsequent Consistent, logical. *In den letzten Jahren war unsere Politik in dieser Beziehung alles andere als konsequent.* In the last few years our policy has been anything but consistent in this respect. *Algebra ist nicht schwierig, wenn man einigermaßen konsequent denken kann.* Algebra isn't difficult if you're reasonably good at thinking logically. *Er hat seine Nachbarn immer ganz konsequent ignoriert.* He has always ignored his neighbors quite consistently.
Consequent = *daraus resultierend*
Consequently = *deswegen, folglich*

Konsequenz, die 1. Consequence (result). 2. Consistency, logic. SEE **KONSEQUENT.** *Unserer Wirtschaftspolitik fehlt es an Konsequenz.* Our economic policy lacks consistency.
Consequence (result) also = *die Folge*
⠀⠀⠀⠀⠀⠀⠀⠀⠀⠀(importance) = *die Bedeutung, die Wichtigkeit*

Konserve, die 1. Food that has been preserved in jars or cans, or the containers themselves. *Seit er nicht mehr bei seinen Eltern wohnt, lebt er von Konserven.* Ever since he stopped living with his parents he's been living off canned food. *Obst aus der Konserve schmeckt nie ganz richtig.* Canned fruit never tastes quite right. 2. By extension, "canned" entertainment: *Musik aus der Konserve* canned music/Muzak.
Preserve (jam) = *die Konfitüre, die Marmelade*

konservieren   To conserve, but often "preserve" is a better translation. *Man kann die meisten Lebensmittel konservieren, ohne Chemikalien zu benutzen.* Most food can be preserved without the use of chemicals. *Er weiß, wie man alte Bilder konserviert.* He knows how to preserve old pictures.
To conserve (energy, etc.) = *sparen, sparsam umgehen mit*

Konsorte, die   Used in the plural as a pejorative noun to denote people who assist in dubious activities: gang, mob, crowd, cronies. *Unser Bürgermeister und seine Konsorten haben diese Demonstration inszeniert.* Our mayor and his cronies have stage-managed this demonstration.
Consort (spouse) = *der (die) Gemahl(in)*

Konstellation, die   Constellation (astron.), but also a combination of circumstances or general situation. *Bei der jetzigen politischen Konstellation ist mit einer klaren Entscheidung nicht zu rechnen.* In the present political situation a clear decision cannot be expected.
Constellation (astron.) also = *das Sternbild*

konstruieren   1. To construct (math., geom.; also theories, sentences, etc.).   2. To design, with reference to technical expertise. *Ein Team von vierzig Mitarbeitern hat unser neues Auto konstruiert.* A team of forty have designed our new car.
To construct (build) = *bauen*

Konstrukteur, der   Designer. SEE **KONSTRUIEREN.**

Konstruktion, die   1. Construction.   2. (Technical) design. SEE **KONSTRUIEREN.**
Construction (building) = *der Bau*

Kontingent, das   1. Contingent (of troops, police, etc.).   2. Quota (of a material, product, etc.). *Wir haben unser Papierkontingent für dieses Jahr bereits ausgeschöpft.* We've already used up our quota of paper for this year.

Kontrolle, die   1. Primarily denotes checking, inspecting, or supervising. *Die Kontrollen an der Grenze sind nicht sehr streng.* The checks at the border are not very strict. *Wir benötigen eine wirksamere Kontrolle dieser sogenannten Selbstverteidigungsgruppen.* We need more effective monitoring of these so-called self-defense groups.   2. Control. *Der Motorradfahrer hatte die Kontrolle über seine Maschine verloren.* The motorcycle rider had lost control of his machine.
Control (power over) = *die Beherrschung*

Kontrolleur, der   Inspector (of tickets, etc.). *Der Kontrolleur erwischte ihn beim Schwarzfahren.* The inspector caught him traveling without a ticket. *Jedes Gerät wird von einem Kontrolleur auf Herz und Niere geprüft.* Every appliance is thoroughly checked by an inspector.
Controller (person in charge) = *der Leiter*
Air-traffic controller = *der Fluglotse*

kontrollieren   1. Occasionally, to control. *Die Politik in diesem Land wird von ein paar sehr reichen Familien kontrolliert.* Politics in this country is controlled by a few very rich families.   **2.** More usually, to check, to inspect, to monitor. SEE **KONTROLLE.** *Die Radioaktivitätswerte werden laufend kontrolliert.* The radioactivity values are constantly monitored. *Unsere Pässe wurden nicht kontrolliert.* Our passports weren't checked. To control = *beherrschen, steuern*

Konvent, der   A somewhat recondite word with a variety of meanings: **1.** A religious community of monks or nuns: convent, monastery.   **2.** Specifically, a meeting of monks or nuns.   **3.** Certain other assemblies, e.g., of student fraternities.   **4.** All those members of a university who have the postdoctoral qualification known as the *Habilitation.* Convent (i.e., convent school) = *die Klosterschule*

Konventionalstrafe, die   Not a conventional or traditional punishment, but a penalty (for breach of contract). *Die Konventionalstrafen sind sehr hoch, wenn man die Lieferzeiten nicht einhält.* The penalties are very severe if one doesn't keep to delivery dates.

Konvikt, das   A rare word, unfamiliar to many native speakers. It denotes a seminary. In Austria it may also denote a (Catholic) boarding school. Convict (prisoner) = *der Sträfling*

konzentriert   Concentrated (chem., etc.). But also used of a person applying his powers of mental concentration, when "concentrated" is not a possible translation. *Wenn Peter etwas konzentrierter arbeiten würde, würde er bestimmt bessere Noten bekommen.* If Peter worked with more concentration he would certainly get better grades. *Ich bin in letzter Zeit so unkonzentriert—ich brauche eine Woche Erholung.* I haven't been able to concentrate lately—I need a week's rest.

Konzept, das   1. Draft, rough version for text, speech, etc. *Ich mache kein Konzept für solche Übersetzungen—ich tippe sie gleich in die Maschine.* I don't do a draft for this sort of translation—I just type it out right away.   **2.** Plan (e.g., for some sort of project or new development). *Es fehlt der Opposition offensichtlich an einem klaren Konzept im Bereich der Energieversorgung.* The Opposition evidently lacks a clear program as regards energy supply. Concept (idea) = *der Begriff, die Vorstellung*

Konzern, der   Unlike English "concern," this does not denote a company or firm, but a group of companies that work together but remain individually independent. *ein multinationaler Konzern* a multinational combine.

Concern (company) = *die Firma, das Unternehmen*
          (worry) = *die Sorge*
          (matter) = *die Angelegenheit*

Konzert, das This can mean both "concert" and "concerto." *Beethovens Viertes Klavierkonzert* Beethoven's Fourth Piano Concerto.

Konzession, die Concession (though the German word is formal and tends to be found most often in the plural). *Konzession* is also the normal term to denote the official permission to carry out a trade for which a license is required, e.g., taxi driving; English "concession" is relatively rare in this sense. *Der Taxifahrer hatte Angst, seine Konzession zu verlieren.* The taxi driver was afraid of losing his license.

Concession = *das Zugeständnis*

Koppel, das (Leather) belt (as part of a military uniform). *Der Leutnant öffnete sein Koppel und warf es in die Ecke.* The lieutenant undid his belt and threw it into the corner.

Couple (pair) = *das Paar*

(married) = *das Ehepaar*

Koppel, die A piece of enclosed pasture land: paddock. *Wir haben die Pferde sicherheitshalber in der Koppel zusammengetrieben.* We've rounded up the horses in the paddock for safety's sake.

Couple (pair) = *das Paar*

(married) = *das Ehepaar*

koppeln **1.** Denotes linking, combining, joining: "to couple" may sometimes provide an adequate translation (esp. in mechanical contexts), but other expressions are often more idiomatic. *Der Speisewagen wird jetzt an den Zug gekoppelt.* The dining car is being coupled to the train now. *Die beiden Stationen sind über Satellit aneinander gekoppelt.* The two stations are linked by satellite. *Soviel ich weiß, sind diese beiden Phänomene nicht gekoppelt.* As far as I know, there is no connection between these two phenomena. *Wir könnten den Messebesuch mit einem Abstecher in die Alpen koppeln.* We could combine the visit to the trade fair with a trip to the Alps. **2.** To hyphenate (words).

Korn, das Used in a variety of ways, few of which correspond to "corn." **1.** Piece, grain, speck (of salt, dust, wheat, etc.). *Ein paar Salzkörner lagen auf dem Boden.* A few grains of salt lay on the floor. *Sie hat einen echten Putzfimmel—da wird jedes Staubkorn gleich entfernt.* She's crazy about keeping the house clean—every speck of dust is removed right away. *das Hagelkorn* hailstone. **2.** Grain (i.e., cereal crop collectively: this may be rye, wheat, or some other crop according to what is normally grown in a particular area). *Wir ernten das Korn noch in dieser Woche.* We'll be harvesting the grain this week. **3.** Grain (in relation to photography, papermaking, etc.). **4.** Front sight (of a gun). *Beim Gewehr war das Korn leicht verbogen und er konnte nicht genau zielen.* The front sight of the rifle was slightly bent and he could not aim accurately.

Corn (BrE maize) = *der Mais*

(on foot) = *das Hühnerauge*

Korn, der   Short form of *der Kornbranntwein:* a sort of clear spirit (schnapps) derived from grain that is not really very well-known in the U.S.A. or Britain.
Corn (BrE maize) = *der Mais*
(on foot) = *das Hühnerauge*

Korporation, die   1. Corporation (public, municipal, etc.).   2. A not very common term for a student society or fraternity.

Korps, das   1. Corps (mil., diplomatic).   2. A student society or fraternity, esp. one with dueling associations. *Politisch standen die meisten Korps immer ziemlich rechts.* Politically, most student dueling fraternities have always been rather right-wing.

Korrektor, der   May denote a "corrector" in the sense of someone assessing test papers, etc. (esp. in the compounds *Erstkorrektor* and *Zweitkorrektor:* first and second marker). But normally this term denotes a "proofreader" in the publishing world. *Solche Fehler hätte unser Korrektor nie durchgelassen.* Our proofreader would never have let through errors of this sort.

Korrespondent(in), der (die)   Correspondent (press, TV, etc.). But in the compound *Fremdsprachenkorrespondent(in)* it denotes a clerk with foreign language skills dealing with correspondence from abroad. The compound *Auslandskorrespondent(in)* is occasionally used in this sense, but it much more usually denotes the "foreign correspondent" of a newspaper, etc.

Kost, die   1. Food, fare (also fig.). *Einfallsreiche vegetarische Kost gibt es in diesem Restaurant auch.* This restaurant also has imaginative vegetarian food. *Man kann nicht immer intellektuelle Romane lesen—man braucht auch mal leichte Kost.* You can't read intellectual novels all the time—you need some lightweight stuff occasionally as well.   2. Board, esp. in the phrase *Kost und Logis* = (free) board and lodging.
Cost = *die Kosten* (pl.)
(price) = *der Preis*

kosten   To cost. *Wieviel kostet dieses Bild?* How much does this picture cost?
But there is also a homonym meaning "to taste," "to sample," "to try" (a slightly more elevated alternative to *probieren*). *Sie können heute abend den neuen Beaujolais kosten.* You can sample the new Beaujolais this evening.

köstlich   Not "costly," but "splendid," "exquisite," "priceless" (in the figurative sense). *Hast du schon diesen köstlichen Burgunder probiert?* Have you tried this exquisite Burgundy yet? *Wir haben uns gestern auf Richards Geburtstagsparty köstlich amüsiert.* We had a tremendous time at Richard's birthday party yesterday.
Costly = *teuer, kostspielig*

Kostüm, das 1. Costume (theater, fancy dress, etc.). 2. A two-piece (skirt and jacket) suit for women. *Für das Vorstellungsgespräch brauche ich ein schickes Kostüm.* I need an elegant suit for the interview.

BrE Bathing/swimming costume = *der Badeanzug*

Kot, der 1. Excrement, faeces. 2. (fig.) Filth.

Cot (collapsible, portable bed) = *das Klappbett*

(BrE, = small bed for child) = *das Kinderbett*

Koteletten, die (pl.) Sideburns, BrE also sideboards. *Er trug lange Koteletten, weil er wie der junge Elvis Presley aussehen wollte.* He wore long sideburns because he wanted to look like the young Elvis Presley.

Cutlet (of meat) = *das Kotelett* (pl.: *Koteletts*)

Krabbe, die There are difficulties here, since native speakers of German do not always agree about the range of meanings borne by *Krabbe.* Some maintain that, strictly speaking, the word does indeed denote certain types of crustacean that in English would be called "crab." But in everyday usage (e.g., with reference to the ubiquitous *Krabbencocktail* in restaurants) it denotes a shrimp or prawn.

Crab = *die Krabbe, der Krebs*

Kraft, die Strength, power, force. *Mit dieser neuen Technologie nutzen wir die Kraft der Sonne.* With this new technology we harness the energy of the sun. *Der Patient hatte keine Kraft mehr.* The patient had no strength left.

Craft (handicraft, artistic) = *das (Kunst)handwerk, das Kunstgewerbe*

(boat) = *das Boot*

(hist., = guild) = *die Zunft*

kräftig 1. Strong, powerful, forceful. SEE **KRAFT**. 2. Big, massive, etc. *In letzter Zeit gibt es kräftige Mieterhöhungen.* There have been big rent increases lately.

Crafty (clever) = *schlau*

kramen 1. To rummage (about). *Er kramte lange in seiner Schublade, bevor er seinen Paß fand.* He rummaged about in his drawer for a long time before he found his passport. 2. To fish out (what one has located by rummaging). *Er kramte den Paß aus der Schublade.* He fished the passport out of the drawer.

To cram (fill) = *vollstopfen*

(learn for test) = *pauken, büffeln, ochsen*

Krampf, der 1. (Muscular) cramp. 2. Also, more serious manifestations: spasm, convulsion, fit. *Solche Krämpfe sind typisch für Epilepsie.* Such convulsions are typical of epilepsy. 3. (coll.) Frantic (and exaggerated) attempts to achieve a result or create an impression. *Was soll der ganze Krampf? Es ist mir egal, ob ich gewinne.* What's the point of all this fuss? I don't care if I win or not.

kraulen   To do the crawl (swimming).

But there is also a homonym meaning "to fondle" (an animal or person), using the tips of one's fingers. *Meine Katze ist im siebten Himmel, wenn ich sie unter dem Kinn kraule.* My cat's in her seventh heaven when I stroke her under the chin.

To crawl (on hands and knees) = *kriechen*
            (baby) = *krabbeln*

Kraut, das   Not surprisingly, this is not used by the Germans as a derogatory term with which to refer to themselves, though they are aware of the expression (the English use was derived from the popular notion that all Germans were addicted to sauerkraut).

The German meanings are exclusively vegetable in nature: **1.** Herb. *Zwei Kräuter, Basilikum und Oregano, dürfen in diesem Rezept nicht fehlen.* Two herbs, basil and oregano, are essential for this recipe.   **2.** Various forms of cabbage, where *Kraut* is used as a short form for compounds, e.g., *Sauerkraut* (sauerkraut, pickled cabbage), *Blaukraut* (South German for *Rotkohl:* red cabbage), *Weißkraut* (white cabbage, esp. as shredded in salads).   **3.** Those stems and leaves of various vegetables that are not used for human consumption: tops, leaves, foliage. *Das Kraut der Rüben wird an die Tiere verfüttert.* The turnip greens are fed to the animals. *wie Kraut und Rüben* In an untidy condition. *In deinem Zimmer liegt alles wie Kraut und Rüben herum.* Everything's always lying all over the place in your room.

Krawatte, die   Necktie, tie. *Ohne Krawatte kommst du in dieses Restaurant gar nicht hinein.* You'll never even get into that restaurant without a necktie.

Cravat (BrE = neckerchief) = *das Halstuch*

Krebs, der   **1.** Denotes various crustaceans: crab, crawfish. SEE **KRABBE**.   **2.** (med.) Cancer. *Beide Eltern sind an Krebs gestorben.* Both parents died of cancer.   **3.** Cancer (the astrological sign).

Kredenz, die   Dresser, buffet, BrE sideboard. The word is now dated, except in Austria.

To attach/give credence to s.t. = *einer Sache Glauben schenken*

Kredit, der   Credit (financial). Unlike English "credit," it may also denote a specific loan. *Um den Sportwagen zu kaufen, hat er einen Kredit in Höhe von DM 10.000 aufgenommen.* He took out a loan of 10,000 marks to buy the sports car.

Credit (credibility) = *die Glaubwürdigkeit*
        (honor) = *die Ehre*
        (for university course) = *der Schein*
        (belief) = *der Glaube* to give a story credit *einer Geschichte Glauben schenken*

Kreuz, das **1.** Cross (shape); crucifix. **2.** (Small of the) back. *Diese Schmerzen im Kreuz machen mich verrückt.* These pains in my back are driving me mad. **3.** Junction, intersection (of highways). *Autobahnkreuz.* **4.** Clubs (suit in cards). *Er hat mit dem Kreuz-König gestochen.* He trumped with the king of clubs.

Cross (hybrid) = *die Kreuzung*

Kreuzung, die **1.** Not a "crossing" (i.e., a crosswalk for pedestrians), but a "junction" or "intersection" of two or more roads. *Sie müssen an der nächsten Kreuzung links abbiegen.* You have to turn left at the next intersection. **2.** A "cross" or "hybrid" between varieties of plant or breeds of animal. *Diese Beere ist eine Kreuzung aus Himbeere und Brombeere.* This berry is a cross between a raspberry and a blackberry.

Crossing (for pedestrians) = *der Fußgängerüberweg*

(by sea) = *die Überfahrt*

(railroad) grade crossing (BrE level crossing) = *der Bahnübergang*

kriechen To crawl, creep; (fig.) to grovel. *Sie sah eine Riesenschlange über den Fußboden kriechen.* She saw a huge snake crawling across the floor.

To creak (door, etc.) = *knarren*

(bed springs, etc.) = *quietschen*

Kriminale(r), der (coll.) *Kriminalbeamter* = a plain-clothes detective.

Criminal (official term) = *der (die) Straftäter(in)*

(general) = *der (die) Kriminelle*

(serious crime) = *der (die) Verbrecher(in)*

Kriminalität, die Not usually "criminality" (as an abstract quality), but "crime" as a collective term. *Die wachsende Kriminalität in den Innenstädten ist besonders besorgniserregend.* The increase in crime in the inner cities is especially disturbing.

Kritik, die Not a critic, but a review (of a book, film, etc.) or a criticism, general or specific. *Die Kritik des neuen Films in der heutigen Zeitung fiel ziemlich positiv aus.* The review of the new film in today's paper was fairly positive. *Er kann keine Kritik ertragen.* He can't stand any criticism.

Critic = *der Kritiker, die Kritikerin*

Krone, die **1.** Crown (also in dentistry), coronet. There are various other technical uses, notably: **2.** Top (of tree). **3.** (bot.) Corolla (*Blumenkrone*). **4.** Krone, krona (unit of currency in Scandinavia); crown (in Czechoslovakia). **5.** (fig.) Height (of emotion, etc.). *Das ist ja die Krone der Arroganz.* That's the height of arrogance. *Das setzt doch allem die Krone auf.* That beats everything. *einen in der Krone haben* To be (slightly) drunk. *Ich glaube, unsere liebe Tante hat einen in der Krone.* I believe our dear aunt is a little tipsy.

kroß   Crisp, crusty (though *knusprig* is the more generally used word). *Das esse ich besonders gern: gebratenen Fisch in ganz krossem Teig.* That's something I particularly like: fried fish in really crisp batter.

Cross (adj.) (angry, annoyed) = *böse*

(transverse) = *Quer-, querstehend, querliegend*

Kruste, die   Crust (of bread, earth's surface, etc.). But also "crackling" (of roast pork), or generally the crisp surface of a roast joint of meat. *Der Schweinebraten hat eine schöne Kruste—aber sie läßt sich nicht so leicht schneiden.* This roast pork has a fine crackling—but it's none too easy to cut.

Küche, die   **1.** Kitchen.   **2.** Cooking, cuisine, food. *Im allgemeinen hat die amerikanische Küche einen guten Ruf.* Generally speaking, American cooking has a good reputation.

Kühler, der   **1.** Cooler, cooling device (in various technical contexts). **2.** Radiator (of a car). *Der Motor läuft heiß, weil der Kühler nicht ganz dicht ist.* The engine's overheating because the radiator isn't quite water-tight.   **3.** An ice bucket (*Sektkühler*) for champagne, etc.

kultiviert   Cultivated, but the German word is used more frequently than the English, and other translations may be preferable. *Ich glaube, ihr Schwiegersohn ist ihr nicht kultiviert genug.* I don't think she finds her son-in-law sufficiently cultured. *Kannst du dich nicht ein bißchen kultivierter benehmen? Schau' mal, wie die alle gucken!* Can't you behave in a more civilized manner? Look at the way they're all staring! *Er liest sehr viel und hat einen sehr kultivierten literarischen Geschmack.* He reads a great deal and has a very sophisticated literary taste. *Endlich ein Restaurant, wo man kultiviert essen kann.* At last a restaurant where you can get a civilized meal.

Kultur-   Culture is a difficult phenomenon to define exactly, but certain German compounds with *Kultur-* are misleading, notably: *Kulturbeutel* Toilet bag, washbag; *Kulturgeographie* Human geography; *Kulturhoheit* Autonomy/independence in educational and cultural matters.

Kultus-   This is used as an official term, particularly in the compounds *Kultusminister* and *Kultusministerium*, to refer to responsibility not only for cultural and artistic matters, but also for education. *Der Kultusminister will mehr junge Lehrer einstellen.* The minister of education wants to appoint more young teachers.

Kupon, der   SEE COUPON.

Kuppe, die   **1.** Tip (of finger).   **2.** Hilltop; hump (e.g., in road).

Cup = *die Tasse*

kuppeln   **1.** This may, like KOPPELN (Q.V.), mean "to couple" in technical contexts.   **2.** To operate the clutch (in a car). *Ich habe sonst nur Automatikwagen gefahren—ich weiß nicht, wie man richtig kuppelt.* I've only driven automatic cars—I don't know how to operate the clutch properly.   **3.** To match-make; to procure (a woman). This usage is rather dated and the compound form *verkuppeln* is more normal.

Kupplung, die   1. (tech.) Coupling.   **2.** Clutch (of a car). SEE **KUPPELN.**

Kur, die   1. A course of treatment (and/or a diet) for a medical condition. *Ich darf nichts Scharfes essen—ich mache eine Kur gegen meine Magengeschwüre.* I mustn't eat anything spicy—I'm taking a course of treatment for my stomach ulcers.   **2.** It also refers in particular to the phenomenon, less familiar in the U.S.A. and Britain, of going away to a health resort (*Kurort*) for a stay of several weeks that combines a supervised course of medical treatment and general rest and recuperation (rather like going to a health farm). Medical insurance schemes often carry all or part of the cost and the *Kur* is big business in Germany. "(Health-) cure" is not an entirely happy translation, but there is no obvious English equivalent. *Ich fahre nächste Woche nach Bad Harzburg zur Kur.* I'm going to Bad Harzburg next week to take a (health)-cure. *Die Versicherung bezahlt meine Kur.* The insurance is paying for my (health)-cure. *der Kurschatten* (hum.) A member of the opposite sex with whom a person develops at least a potentially romantic attachment during a *Kur.*
Cure (medical remedy) = *das Heilmittel*

Kür, die   Free section (e.g., in ice-skating).
Cure (medical remedy) = *das Heilmittel*

küren   To choose, elect (for a position). Elevated style or dated. *Sie wurde zur Weinkönigin gekürt.* She was elected Wine Queen.
To cure (disease, person) = *heilen, kurieren*
            (meat, etc., using salt) = *pökeln*
            (meat, etc., using smoke) = *räuchern*

Kurs, der   1. (navigation; educational) Course.   **2.** Price of a share on the stock market (*Aktienkurs*); exchange rate of currencies (*Wechselkurs*). *Diese Aktien können Sie zur Zeit zu einem sehr günstigen Kurs erwerben.* You can purchase these shares at a very reasonable price at the moment. *Wie steht der Dollarkurs?* What's the exchange rate for the dollar?
Course (of meal) = *der Gang*
         (of events, activity, illness, etc.) = *der Lauf, der Verlauf*

Kursbuch, das   Not a coursebook, but the official railway timetable (in book form). *Wo finde ich im Kursbuch die Strecke Stuttgart–Ulm?* Where do I find the Stuttgart–Ulm route in the timetable?
Coursebook (textbook) = *das Lehrbuch*

kursiv   Italic (script, typeface). *Alle Wörter, die in den Anmerkungen erklärt werden, sind kursiv gedruckt.* All words explained in the notes are printed in italics.

Kurve, die   Curve, but also the normal word for a bend in a road. *Fahr' lieber etwas langsamer—es gibt einige ganz tückische Kurven auf dieser*

Straße. It's better to drive a bit slower—there are some pretty tricky bends in this road. *die Kurve kratzen* To beat it, to make tracks.

kurven **1.** To circle, go round in circles (vehicles, etc.). **2.** (coll.) To drive around, cruise around (aimlessly). *Wir sind 10.000 Kilometer durch ganz Europa gekurvt.* We drove 10,000 kilometers all over Europe. To curve: Many different expressions according to the object being described: *einen Bogen machen* (e.g., of a road passing round s.t.); *sich wenden* (of a road with several bends); *sich schlängeln* (e.g., of a meandering river); *sich wölben* (e.g., of an arch)

Küster, der Sacristan, verger, sexton. *Seitdem wir den neuen Küster haben, ist alles blitzsauber in unserer Kirche.* Ever since we've had our new verger everything's been spick and span in our church.

Coaster (for wineglass, etc.) = *der Untersetzer*
    (BrE: ship) = *das Küstenmotorschiff*
Roller coaster = *die Achterbahn*

Kuvert, das **1.** Place setting at table. **2.** Envelope for a letter—a term still coexisting alongside *(Brief)umschlag. Auf dem Kuvert stand kein Absender:* There was no sender's address on the envelope.

Covert (hiding place; also for game birds, etc.) = *das Versteck*

L

Labor, das Not "labor," but "lab(oratory)." The form is nearly always preferred to the lengthier *Laboratorium. Meine Frau ist im Labor.* My wife's in the lab. *das Sprachlabor* language lab(oratory).

Labor (work) = *die Arbeit*
    (in childbirth) = *die Wehen* (pl.)

laborieren **1.** To labor, in the sense of making long and wearisome efforts, often without success. *Er laboriert schon seit acht Jahren an seiner Doktorarbeit.* He's been laboring away at his doctorate for eight years. **2.** To suffer for a long time from an illness one cannot shake off. *Sie laboriert an dieser Bronchitis seit Monaten—sie braucht dringend eine Luftveränderung.* She's been suffering from that bronchitis for months—she urgently needs a change of air.

To labor (work) = *arbeiten*

Lack, der **1.** Paint(work) (esp. of car). *Der Lack ist stark beschädigt—das kann sehr schnell zu Rost führen.* The paint's damaged—that can lead to rust very quickly. **2.** Varnish, lacquer (for wood, etc.); nail polish (*Nagellack*).

Lack = *der Mangel*

lackieren To paint, varnish, spray (esp. car with paint). SEE **LACK**. *Wenn das Auto neu lackiert ist, wirst du es bestimmt verkaufen können.* Once the car's had a respray you'll certainly be able to sell it.
To lack = *fehlen* (often used impersonally)

Lager, das **1.** Camp, in the literal or metaphorical sense. *Die Gefangenen wurden in ein zentrales Lager gebracht.* The prisoners were taken to a central camp. *Der Politiker wechselte ins konservative Lager über.* The politician went over to the Conservative camp. **2.** Store(room), warehouse. **3.** Stock. *auf Lager haben* to have in stock. **4.** (tech.) Bearing. *das Kugellager* ball bearing.

Lager = *helles Bier, Pils, Lagerbier.* The last expression is not in common use, and these beers are not really the same as American or British lager (nor would many Germans want them to be).

lahm Lame, but also "dull" or "feeble" in the metaphorical sense. *Das ist vielleicht eine lahme Fete!* This is a pretty dreary party.

lamentieren Less serious and dramatic than English "lament" and means "to moan," "to complain." *Marianne lamentiert über jede Kleinigkeit.* Marianne moans about every little thing.
To lament = *(be)klagen, (be)jammern*

Lampe, die **1.** Lamp. **2.** (Street)light: *Diese Kurve ist nachts etwas gefährlich, weil die Lampen so ungünstig stehen.* This bend is rather dangerous at night because the lights are positioned so awkwardly. **3.** (Electric light) bulb, though *die Birne* is the more usual term. **4.** Flashlight (usually in the compound *Taschenlampe*).

lancieren **1.** To launch, in the abstract sense (e.g., a new product). *Das neue Modell wird im Herbst lanciert.* The new model is being launched in the autumn. **2.** To put out (a piece of information). *Die Meldung wurde lanciert, um für Panik zu sorgen.* The announcement was made to create panic. **3.** To maneuver (s.o. into a job or position). *Der Junge ist ein Trottel, aber sein Vater hat ihn in den Vorstand lanciert.* The lad's an idiot, but his father got him on to the board of directors.
To lance (med.) = *aufschneiden, öffnen*

Land, das **1.** Land, country (political, territorial). *Ich möchte in keinem anderen Land wohnen.* I wouldn't like to live in any other country. **2.** Country(side). *Ich möchte nicht auf dem Lande wohnen.* I wouldn't like to live in the country. **3.** State, in certain federal countries. *das Land Niedersachsen* the state of Lower Saxony. (U.S.A. states are referred to as *(Bundes)staaten*.)
Land (real estate) = *Grund und Boden*
(a piece of land) = *das Grundstück*

Landschaft, die Can mean "landscape," but is a more general term: scenery, countryside. *Wir sind hier ziemlich abgeschnitten, aber die Landschaft ist einmalig.* We're a bit cut off here, but the scenery is fantastic.

Landsmann, der   Compatriot, fellow countryman. *Wie viele Emigranten traf er sich ausschließlich mit seinen Landsleuten.* Like many émigrés he only met his fellow countrymen.

Landsman (i.e., landlubber) = *die Landratte*

lapidar   Concise, succinct, terse. *Mit ein paar lapidaren Bemerkungen hat er die zweistündige Rede seines Gegners zunichte gemacht.* He demolished his opponent's two-hour speech with a few succinct remarks.

Lapidary (adj.) = *die (Edel)steinschneidekunst betreffend, in Stein gehauen*

(noun) = *der (Edel)steinschneider*

lasten   **1.** To weigh (heavily): used most normally of abstract burdens. *Die Verantwortung der neuen Stelle lastet auf ihm.* The responsibility of the new post weighs heavily on him.   **2.** (fin.) To encumber s.t., with debts. *Mehrere Hypotheken lasten auf diesem Grundstück.* This piece of real estate is encumbered with several mortgages.

To last (time) = *dauern*

(be durable, of product, etc.) = *halten*

laut   Loud, but also "noisy," of people, rooms, etc. *Es sind eigentlich ganz nette Kinder, aber sehr laut.* They're very nice children really, but very noisy. *Wir wohnen an einer großen Kreuzung im Zentrum und es ist natürlich sehr laut.* We live at a big crossroads in the center, and of course it's very noisy.

There is also a preposition *laut*, meaning "according to," and usually associated with official contexts. *Laut Paragraph 69 haben diese Personen kein Stimmrecht.* According to Section 69 these persons are not entitled to vote.

Loud (person) = *aufdringlich*

(colors) = *grell*

Lebensraum, der   Living space, in a political, territorial context. *Hitlers Ostpolitik zielte darauf hin, Lebensraum für die Deutschen zu schaffen.* Hitler's eastern policy was aimed at creating living space for the Germans. The German word is often retained in translations.

Living room = *das Wohnzimmer*

leeren   **1.** To empty. *Sie leerte das schmutzige Wasser in einen Eimer.* She emptied the dirty water into a bucket. (This usage belongs more to the written language; *gießen* would be the more normal verb in such a sentence as this.)   **2.** To collect (mail from mailboxes). *Wann wird dieser Briefkasten geleert?* When's the next collection from this mailbox? To leer (at): No single verb. Suitable adverbs (*lüstern, boshaft, anzüglich*) must be combined with an appropriate verb (e.g., *(an)blicken* = to look (at), *grinsen* = to grin, smirk).

Legitimation, die Legitimation, but also "authorization" or "justification." *Wenn er keine Legitimation bei sich hat, darf er die Wohnung nicht betreten.* He is not allowed to enter the apartment unless he is carrying some authorization. *Ich kann für seine brutale Vorgehensweise keine Legitimation finden.* I can find no justification for his brutal approach to the matter.

legitimieren To legitimize or make legitimate, but also "to authorize," "to justify," or "to prove one's identity." *Seine Stellung als Minister legitimiert ihn nicht, Gerichtsentscheidungen für ungültig zu erklären.* His position as minister does not authorize him to annul court decisions. *Auch die verzweifelte Lage der Truppen kann solche Ausschreitungen nicht legitimieren.* Even the troops' desperate situation cannot justify such excesses. *Die festgenommenen Ausländer konnten sich alle nicht legitimieren.* None of the foreigners arrested was able to prove his identity.

Leim, der Lime, in *Vogelleim* = birdlime. But normally just "glue." *Ich habe ganz normalen Leim benutzt, um die Bilder auf diese Pappe zu kleben.* I used perfectly ordinary glue to stick the pictures to this cardboard. *jdm. auf den Leim gehen* To be cheated/taken in by s.o.

Lime (mineral) = *der Kalk*
    (fruit) = *die Limone, die Limette*
    (tree) = *die Linde*

leiten **1.** To lead, to manage, to run. *Sein Sohn leitet die Firma schon seit zwei Jahren.* His son has been managing the firm for two years. **2.** Similarly, to chair (a discussion or meeting). **3.** To conduct (heat, electricity, etc.). *Silber leitet sehr gut.* Silver is a good conductor.

To lead (usually) = *führen*

Leiter, der Manager, director, head, etc., rather than "leader." *Herr Steier ist Leiter der Marketingabteilung.* Herr Steier is the head of the marketing division.

Leader = *der Führer*

Leiter, die Ladder. *Kannst du mir deine Leiter leihen?* Can you lend me your ladder?

Leader = *der Führer*

Leitung, die **1.** Management, running, direction, etc. SEE LEITEN, LEITER (DER). **2.** The conducting of an orchestra. *unter der Leitung von Herbert von Karajan* = conducted by Herbert von Karajan. **3.** (tech.) The channel along which something flows: wire, cable (electricity), line (telephone), main, pipe (water, gas). *Jemand könnte über diese Leitung stolpern.* Someone might trip over this wire.

Lektüre, die Can indicate both the act of reading and actual reading material. *Für die Lektüre eines solchen juristischen Textes braucht der Laie sehr viel Zeit.* The layperson needs a great deal of time to read a legal text of this sort. *In seinem Handgepäck war genügend Lektüre für den langen Flug.* There was enough reading material for the long flight in his hand baggage.

Lecture (university) = *die Vorlesung*

(talk) = *der Vortrag*

lernen To learn, but it is also used absolutely, where English would use "to study." *Nein, ich kann heute abend nicht ins Kino—ich muß für den Mathetest lernen.* No, I can't go to the movies tonight—I have to study for the math test. It is also used in the context of vocational training. *Ich habe Klempner gelernt, bin jetzt aber Verkäufer im Heimwerkermarkt.* I trained as a plumber, but I'm a sales assistant at the do-it-yourself center now.

Lexikon, das Unlike English "lexicon," with its tendency to refer to dictionaries of ancient languages, the German word can denote any (large) alphabetically arranged work of reference. *Der Kauf des fünf-zehnbändigen Lexikons kann auch in monatlichen Raten erfolgen.* This fifteen-volume encyclopedia can also be purchased on a monthly install-ment plan. *Mein deutsch—englisches Lexikon ist schon 15 Jahre alt und enthält viele neue Begriffe nicht.* My German—English dictionary is 15 years old and does not contain a lot of new terms.

Libelle, die 1. Dragonfly. 2. (Spirit) level (as used in building, etc.; *die Wasserwaage* is the more usual term). *Kein Wunder, daß alles schief ist, wenn du keine Libelle benutzt hast!* No wonder everything is crooked if you didn't use a (spirit) level!

Libel = *die Verleumdung*

lichten 1. To make less dense, thin out. *Hier müßten die Bäume etwas gelichtet werden.* The trees should be thinned out a little here. *An dieser Stelle lichtete sich der Wald.* The woods became less dense at this point. 2. (elevated style) To make less dark, to lighten. *den Anker lichten* To weigh anchor.

To lighten (a load) = *leichter machen*

To light (illuminate) = *beleuchten*

(cigarette, fire, etc.) = *anzünden*

Lichtung, die Clearing (in a forest, wood, etc.). *Mitten in der Lichtung stand ein Blockhaus.* A log cabin stood in the middle of the clearing.

Lighting = *die Beleuchtung*

lieblich Charming, delightful. Much less general in application than BrE "lovely." Applied to scenery, *lieblich* suggests the gentle in contrast to the forbidding or dramatic. It is also one of the adjectives used to describe wine, when it indicates mild sweetness.

Lovely = *schön, herrlich, wunderschön, reizend*

liften 1. To perform surgical "lifting." *sich das Gesicht liften lassen* to have a facelift. 2. It is occasionally found as a borrowing from the English word in its general sense. *Um solche Blöcke zu liften, braucht man einen Kran.* You need a crane to lift blocks like these.

To lift = *(hoch)heben*

lila Color equivalences between languages are problematical, but *lila* is a dark, not a light, color and corresponds to English "purple" rather than "lilac."

Lilac = *fliederfarben*

Limone, die Not a "lemon," but a "lime."

Lemon = *die Zitrone*

Linie, die Line, in most contexts, but note its use to indicate the number of a particular public transportation service. *Am besten fahren Sie mit der Linie 19.* Your best bet is to take the number 19.

Linien- In connection with transportation services this indicates a regular, scheduled service. Hence *Linienbus, Linienflug(zeug), Linienschiff,* and the general term *Linienverkehr. Bei Linienflügen gibt es normalerweise weniger Verspätungen als bei Charterflügen.* There are normally fewer delays with scheduled flights than with charter flights.

Linse, die Lens (optical), but also "lentil." *In einer solchen Suppe dürfen Linsen nicht fehlen.* A soup like this really needs some lentils in it.

liquid(e) 1. Liquid, in the financial sense, but unlike the English word it is also applied to persons: solvent. *Dem nicht mehr liquiden Geschäftsmann drohte der Konkurs.* The businessman was no longer solvent and faced bankruptcy. 2. It is occasionally used in the physical sense (i.e., neither gas nor solid), but the usual word is *flüssig*.

Liquidation, die Liquidation (of assets, etc.). But the word is also used by some doctors as a heading for the bills they send patients and corresponds to "account." It does not denote any forthcoming drastic treatment.

List, die Cunning; cunning trick, ruse. *Hier wirst du mehr mit List als mit Gewalt erreichen.* You'll achieve more by cunning than by violence in this case. *Auf diese einfache List ist sie hereingefallen.* She fell for this simple ruse.

List = *das Verzeichnis, die Liste*

To have a list (nautical) = *Schlagseite haben*

Literatur, die Literature, but may be used at the end of a scholarly article to head a list of works referred to, where English would use "bibliography."

Lithograph, der Lithographer, not lithograph. SEE **FOTOGRAF**.

Lithograph = *die Lithographie, der Steindruck*

locken To entice, lure, tempt. *Diese Sonderangebote sollen die Verbraucher in die Geschäfte locken.* These special offers are supposed to lure the customers into the shops.

To lock (up) = *abschließen, zuschließen, zusperren*

locker **1.** Loose, not firm. *Der Griff meines Koffers ist locker.* The handle of my suitcase is loose. **2.** Casual, informal. *Bei uns in der Firma geht alles ziemlich locker zu.* In our firm everything's pretty informal.

Locker (noun) (e.g., in changing room) = *der Spind*
(for baggage, etc.) = *das Schließfach*

Lohn, der **1.** Wage(s), pay. *Ihr Lohn wird um 6% erhöht.* Your wages are being increased by 6%. **2.** (fig.) Reward.

Loan (e.g., from bank) = *das Darlehen*

lohnen **1.** To be worthwhile. The verb is normally used reflexively. *Es lohnt sich nicht, in Singapur ein Auto zu mieten.* It's not worth renting a car in Singapore. *Unsere Mühe hat sich gelohnt.* Our efforts were worthwhile. **2.** In the written language, to repay, to reward (s.o. for s.t.). *Er hat uns unsere ganze Hilfe schlecht gelohnt.* He didn't repay us very well for all our help.

To loan (lend) = *leihen*

Lok, die Not "lock," but "locomotive" (short for *Lokomotive*).

Lock (for door, etc.) = *das Schloß*
(on canal, etc.) = *die Schleuse*
(of hair) = *die Locke*

Lokal, das Denotes a fairly wide range of places where one can obtain food and/or drink—a bar, restaurant, pub, etc. *In diesem Lokal gibt es manchmal ganz wunderbare Fischgerichte.* You can sometimes get quite marvelous fish dishes in this restaurant. *Ich kenne ein Lokal, wo es ein tolles Pils gibt.* I know a bar where you can get a great pilsener.

Local (nearby bar, pub one regularly visits) = *das Stammlokal*, (coll.) *die Stammkneipe*

The locals (coll., = local population) = *die Einheimischen*

Looping, der *einen Looping machen* To loop the loop (aircraft). The word is also used with reference to the new generation of roller coasters (BrE big dippers) where riders find themselves performing this alarming maneuver. *Bei der neuen Achterbahn gibt es einen doppelten Looping.* You have to loop the loop twice on this new roller coaster.

losen To draw lots. *Am besten losen wir, wer den Preis gewinnt.* The best thing to do is to draw lots to decide who wins the prize.

To lose = *verlieren*

lösen **1.** To solve (a problem). *Selbst die größten Experten konnten dieses Problem nicht lösen.* Even the greatest experts were unable to solve this problem. **2.** To remove, esp. from a surface. *Zuerst mußt du aber die alte Tapete von der Wand lösen.* First of all you have to remove the old wallpaper. **3.** To make loose, (refl.) become loose. *Eine Schraube hatte sich gelöst.* A screw had come loose. **4.** To buy (a ticket). *Sie müssen den Fahrschein vor Fahrtantritt lösen.* You must buy the ticket before you begin your journey. **5.** To annul, cancel, dissolve. *Dadurch haben Sie den Vertrag praktisch gelöst.* By doing that you have effectively annulled the contract. **6.** To dissolve (solids in liquid). *Salz in Wasser lösen* to dissolve salt in water.

To lose = *verlieren*

Lot, das **1.** Plumb line. *Um eine Mauer ordentlich zu bauen, braucht man unbedingt ein Lot.* A plumb line is essential if you want to build a wall properly. *eine Sache ins Lot bringen* To straighten s.t. out, to put s.t. on an even keel. **2.** (math., geom.) Perpendicular. **3.** Solder (i.e., *Lötmetall*).

A lot of = *viel(e)*

Lot (lottery; auction; destiny) = *das Los*

Lotto, das May denote the game similar to bingo, but for most Germans *Lotto* indicates the great national lottery in which large sums of money can be won. There are various versions, but all are based on selecting numbers from a given set, e.g., "6 from 49," in which the player chooses any six numbers from the numbers 1 to 49 and marks them with a cross. In the weekly draw a random number machine chooses the six numbers that will win the first prize: it is thus purely a game of luck. *Wenn ich eine Million im Lotto gewinnen würde, würde ich mir ein Haus mit Swimmingpool kaufen.* If I won a million in the lottery, I'd buy a house with a swimming pool.

Lump, der A rather dated word for a "rogue," "scoundrel."

Lump = *der Klumpen*

(sugar) = *das Stück*

(in a breast) = *der Knoten*

To have a lump in the throat = *einen Kloß im Hals haben*

lumpen This verb is now really only found in the idiom *sich nicht lumpen lassen* = to be generous, to splash out.

To lump things together (judge in the same way) = *über einen Kamm scheren, in einen Topf werfen*

You'll have to like it or lump it = *Wenn's dir nicht paßt, hast du eben Pech gehabt.*

Lumpen, der Rag. *Wir sammeln alte Lumpen für karitative Zwecke.* We're collecting old rags for charity.

Lump = *der Klumpen*

(sugar) = *das Stück*

(in a breast) = *der Knoten*

To have a lump in the throat = *einen Kloß im Hals haben*

lumpig **1.** Measly, paltry (this is the commonest use). *Solche Arbeit mache ich nicht für lumpige acht Mark die Stunde!* I'm not doing that sort of work for a measly eight marks an hour! **2.** Mean, shabby (action, etc.). **3.** Ragged, tattered.
Lumpy (porridge, etc.) = *klumpig*

Lurch, der Amphibian (zool.).
Lurch (movement) = *der Ruck*
To leave in the lurch = *im Stich lassen*

Lust, die Only rarely indicates strong sexual desire. Instead it normally denotes pleasure in doing something or the inclination to do it. *Diese ganzen Staus haben mir die Lust am Autofahren genommen.* All these traffic jams have taken the pleasure out of driving for me. *Lust haben* To feel like (doing s.t.). *Hast du Lust, heute abend chinesisch zu essen?* Do you feel like having a Chinese meal tonight?
Lust = *die Begierde*

lustig **1.** Funny, amusing. *Diese alten Stummfilme findet er immer noch sehr lustig.* He still finds those old silent films very funny. **2.** Cheerful, merry, jolly. *Das war ein lustiger Abend!* That was a really fun evening!
Lusty (powerful, e.g., of voice) = *kräftig*

Lyrik, die Denotes the whole genre of lyric poetry, "the lyric." *Wie bei so vielen romantischen Dichtern war die Lyrik seine Stärke.* As with so many romantic poets his forte lay in lyric poetry. *Goethes Lyrik* Goethe's lyric poetry.
Lyric (words of pop song) = *der Text*

M

machen This verb performs a vast number of functions in German, for many of which the translation "make" will be unsuitable. These cannot all be listed here, but as a general point it should be noted that *machen* and *tun* are more interchangeable than English "make" and "do." Thus *Was soll ich machen?* and *Was soll ich tun?* both mean "What am I supposed to do?"

Macher, der **1.** A man who gets things done, of the dynamic executive type. *Ich traue ihm nicht—wie so viele Macher handelt er schnell, aber unüberlegt.* I don't trust him—like a lot of dynamic types he acts quickly, but without thinking. It may indicate admiration or scepticism, or both. **2.** (coll., often pej.) A person who actually carries out a plan, scheme, etc. *Die eigentlichen Macher sind nie erfaßt worden.* The people who actually did this were never caught. In compounds *-macher* often corresponds to English "-maker": *Filmemacher* Film maker; *Schuhmacher* Shoemaker.

Maker (manufacturer) = *der Hersteller*
    (creator) = *der Schöpfer*

Magazin, das   **1.** Magazine (publication, radio or TV program; also of a gun).   **2.** Storeroom, stockroom, stack of a library. *Wir haben den Artikel vorrätig, aber er muß erst einmal aus dem Magazin geholt werden.* We have the item in stock, but it has to be fetched from the storeroom first. *Alle Bücher aus dem 16. Jahrhundert werden im Magazin aufbewahrt.* All sixteenth century books are kept in the stack.

Magistrat, der   Apart from historical and dialect uses, this refers to the administrative authority of certain towns and cities. *Alle solche Anträge laufen über den Magistrat.* All such applications are dealt with by the municipal authority.

Magistrate = *der Friedensrichter,* as a term to refer to American or British justices of the peace. There is no close equivalent in the German legal system.

Mähre, die   A pejorative term denoting an old horse that is well past its best: an old nag.

Mare = *die Stute*

Make-up, das   Like the English word, this may be used as a collective term for cosmetic aids, but peculiar to German is the use to denote the specific cosmetic known as "(liquid) foundation."

Make-up (of actor) = *die Maske*
    (person's character) = *die Veranlagung*

managen   **1.** To get s.t. done, but not necessarily in a normal, official, or unexceptionable way. *Ich weiß, es gibt noch das Problem mit der Steuer. Aber keine Angst—das werde ich schon managen.* I know there's still the tax problem. But don't worry—I'll see to that.   **2.** It may also be used in a business context in the sense of "to manage," esp. with reference to professional sports persons or entertainers. *Der angehende Tennis-Star wird von seinem Vater gemanagt.* The aspiring tennis star is being managed by his father.

To manage (succeed) = *gelingen* (impersonal structure, as in *es ist mir gelungen,* etc.), *es schaffen* (coll.)
    (cope financially) = *auskommen*
    (company) = *leiten*

Manchester, der   A type of material: broad-ribbed corduroy, jumbo cord.

Mandat, das   **1.** May have the English meaning of an authorization to act given to a representative body by those who voted for it. *Als unser Abgeordneter haben Sie von Ihren Wählern kein Mandat, für eine solche Gesetzesänderung zu stimmen.* As our representative you have no mandate from your electors to vote for such an amendment. **2.** More commonly, a seat in a parliament or representative assembly. *Nach dem Skandal wurde er gezwungen, sein Mandat niederzulegen.* After the scandal he was forced to give up his seat. *Wie viele Mandate haben die Demokraten im House of Representatives?* How many seats do the Democrats have in the House of Representatives? **3.** The instructions a client gives an attorney to represent him in a legal matter. *Zunächst wollte kein Anwalt das Mandat des Terroristen übernehmen.* At first no attorney wanted to take on the terrorist's case/brief.

Mangel, der **1.** Lack, shortage. *Sein Mangel an Taktgefühl ärgerte mich.* His lack of tact annoyed me. *Der Mangel an möbliertem Wohnraum wird allmählich kritisch.* The shortage of furnished accommodation is beginning to become critical. **2.** Defect, flaw, etc. *Das neue Gerät weist verschiedene Mängel auf.* The new appliance exhibits various defects.

Mangle (laundry) = *die Mangel*

mangeln To mangle (washing, etc.).

But there is also a homonym, the impersonal verb denoting a lack or shortage of s.t. *Es mangelt ihm an den nötigen Qualifikationen.* He lacks the necessary qualifications.

Manifest, das May denote a ship's manifest, but more commonly means "manifest*o*" (political). *Dieses Werk stellt sein politisches Manifest dar.* This work represents his political manifesto.

Manifestation, die (Sw.) Demonstration (political, etc.).

Manifestation = *der Ausdruck, die Erscheinung, das Zeichen*

manifestieren (Sw.) To demonstrate (for political aims, etc.).

Mann, der Man, but in appropriate contexts "husband." *Ihr Mann hat ihr ganzes Geld verspielt.* Her husband gambled away all her money.

Manuskript, das Manuscript, but also full or brief "notes" for a lecture or talk. *Ohne sein Manuskript konnte der Professor seinen Vortrag nicht halten.* The professor was unable to give his talk without his notes.

Mappe, die **1.** A briefcase or bag (for documents, etc.). *Der Griff meiner Mappe hat sich gelockert.* The handle of my briefcase has come loose. *Irgendwo in meiner Mappe habe ich eine Dose Cola.* I have a can of cola somewhere in my bag. **2.** A file, folder. *Den Antrag finden Sie in der blauen Mappe A-F.* You'll find the application in the blue file A-F.

Map = *die (Land)karte*

(of town, city) = *der Stadtplan*

Marine, die Navy. *Er würde seinen Wehrdienst lieber bei der Marine als bei der Bundeswehr ableisten.* He would rather do his military service in the navy than the army. *die Handelsmarine* The merchant marine (BrE merchant navy).

Marine (soldier) = *der Marineinfanterist*

The marines = *die Marineinfanterie*

Mark, die   Mark, as unit of currency (plural [-]: *10 Mark*).

Also (a different word with the plural [-en]) a borderland or border district, "march," mainly in fixed geographical expressions, e.g., *die Mark Brandenburg,* the Mark Brandenburg, the Brandenburg Marches.

BrE Mark (grade, for schoolwork, etc.) = *die Note, die Zensur*

(indication) = *das Zeichen*

(stain) = *der Fleck*

Mark, das   (Bone-)marrow.

Also "purée" (of fruit, etc.). *das Tomatenmark* tomato purée.

Mark (currency) = *die Mark*

BrE Mark (grade, for schoolwork, etc.) = *die Note, die Zensur*

(indication) = *das Zeichen*

(stain) = *der Fleck*

Marke, die   **1.** Mark, in the context of measurements, records, etc. *Die Temperatur hat die 200°-Marke noch nicht erreicht.* The temperature has not yet reached the 200° mark. Other words are needed to translate most other uses.   **2.** Brand, make. *Welche Zigarettenmarke bevorzugst du?* What brand of cigarettes do you prefer?   **3.** Postage stamp (*Briefmarke*). *Zehn Marken zu 80 Pfennig, bitte.* Ten 80-pfennig stamps, please.   **4.** Ticket, voucher (short for *Essenmarke,* etc.). *Jeder Angestellte erhält eine (Essen)marke im Wert von DM 3,00.* Every employee receives a meal voucher worth 3 marks.   **5.** A metal disc, token, badge, etc. (which can be used for a variety of purposes). *Unsere Katze trägt eine Marke mit unserer Adresse.* Our cat wears a tag with our address. *Sie erhalten an der Kasse eine Marke, die Sie dann für die Automaten benutzen können.* You'll get a token at the cashier that you can then use for the vending machines. *Der Polizeibeamte zeigte seine (Dienst)marke.* The policeman showed his badge.

BrE Mark (grade, for schoolwork, etc.) = *die Note, die Zensur*

(indication) = *das Zeichen*

(stain) = *der Fleck*

markieren   **1.** To mark, in sporting contexts (soccer players, etc.), and also in the sense of "to indicate." *Dies markierte einen bedeutenden Wendepunkt in der Geschichte der deutsch-deutschen Beziehungen.* This marked a significant turning point in the history of the relations between East and West Germany.   **2.** To pretend, to put on an act. *Robert markiert gern den starken Mann, aber ich finde ihn im Grunde genommen lächerlich.* Robert likes to play the strong man, but basically I find him ridiculous. *Es ist gar nicht so schlimm—er markiert nur.* It's not so bad—he's just putting it on.

To mark (correct a piece of schoolwork, etc.) = *korrigieren*

(assign a grade to a piece of schoolwork, etc.) = *zensieren, benoten*

Markise, die   Sunblind, awning (e.g., in front of a shop window).
Marquis/marquess = *der Marquis*
Marquise/marchioness = *die Marquise*

Marmelade, die   Refers to all jams, not merely those made from citrus
fruits. *Himbeermarmelade* raspberry jam. *Ich esse nie Marmelade, sie ist
mir zu süß.* I never eat jam—it's too sweet for me.
Marmalade = *Orangenmarmelade, Zitronenmarmelade*, etc.

Marsch, die   "Marsh" is a misleading translation, since the English word
is rarely associated with successful cultivation, whereas *Marsch* indicates very fertile land situated behind dikes (esp. on the North Sea
coast). "Fertile marshland" or "rich fenland" would give a better idea
of what is meant.
Marsh = *der Sumpf*

Maschine, die   **1.** Machine, in its general sense, but the German word has
certain specific uses not translatable by "machine." **2.** Aircraft, airplane (not restricted to earlier models, like English "machine"). *Die
Maschine aus Rom wird mit voraussichtlich 30 Minuten Verspätung ein-
treffen.* The plane from Rome will probably arrive about 30 minutes late.
3. Typewriter (a common abbreviation for *Schreibmaschine*). *Die
ersten zehn Seiten habe ich schon mit der Maschine geschrieben.* I've
already typed the first ten pages.   **4.** Occasionally used as a colloquial
expression for "engine" (of a motor vehicle). *Kein Wunder, daß die
Maschine schon nach 50.000 Kilometern kaputt ist—wie du fährst!* It's no
wonder the engine's already had it after only 50,000 kilometers, the way
you drive!

Maske, die   Mask, but also an actor's make-up. *Ich finde, die Maske des
Don Giovanni wirkt etwas zu unheimlich.* I think there's something too
sinister about the make-up Don Giovanni's wearing.
Mask (as worn by a surgeon) = *der Mundschutz*

Maß, die   A liter (of beer: the typical South German unit of measure-
ment). *Nach vier Maß Bier kannst du doch nicht Auto fahren!* You can't
drive after four liters of beer!
Mass (phys.) = *die Masse*
   (church) = *die Messe*

Maß, das   **1.** Measure(ment). *Ich habe die Maße des Zimmers aufgeschrie-
ben.* I've made a note of the room's measurements/dimensions. Note,
however, that "measure" in the sense of "course of action" = *die
Maßnahme*. *Wir müssen jetzt schon Maßnahmen ergreifen.* We must take
measures now.   **2.** Extent, degree (i.e., *Ausmaß*). *Das haben wir in
hohem Maße deinem Großvater zu verdanken.* We have your grandfather
to thank for that to a large extent.   **3.** Tape measure (short for *Meter-*

maß, Bandmaß). **4.** Moderation, usually in fixed phrases such as *in Maßen* In moderation; *über alle Maßen* Beyond all measure.

Mass (phys.) = *die Masse*

(church) *die Messe*

massiv This does not normally refer to large dimensions. Applied to materials, it denotes something that is solid, i.e., not hollow or not an alloy. *Solche Gipsbüsten sind meistens hohl und selten massiv.* Such plaster busts are usually hollow and are rarely solid. *Alle diese Becher sind massiv Silber.* All these goblets are made of solid silver. Thus the term *Massivbau* used by realtors and builders to describe houses does not denote a huge building, but one built with solid, stable materials, such as brick or concrete (rather than a lighter prefabricated structure). It is also used with abstract nouns to denote severity, e.g., *massive Kritik* Severe criticism; *massive Beleidigung* Gross insult.

Massive = *sehr groß, riesig, wuchtig*

Mast, der Mast, of ship, radio transmitter, etc. Also "pylon" carrying high-voltage cables. *Beim Sturm wurden einige Masten der Hochspannungsleitung stark beschädigt.* The gale severely damaged some of the pylons carrying the high-voltage cable.

Mast, die **1.** Fattening of animals for slaughter. *Zur Mast verwenden wir nur Weizen.* We only use wheat for fattening purposes. **2.** Mast (fodder obtained from acorns, beechnuts, etc.).

Mast (of ship, etc.) = *der Mast*

materiell Material, but in some contexts "financial" is a clearer translation. *Ich hätte es nie geschafft, wenn meine Eltern mich nicht materiell unterstützt hätten.* I'd never have made it if my parents hadn't supported me financially. Applied to persons, it is best translated by "materialistic." *Für mich ist er zu materiell—er interessiert sich nur für teure Autos und dergleichen.* He's too materialistic for my taste—he's only interested in expensive cars and that sort of thing.

Material (very important) = *wesentlich*

Matrize, die Matrix (in typesetting, record pressing), but also a stencil, as used in a typewriter. *Ich verwende lieber Fotokopien als Matrizen.* I prefer to use photocopies rather than stencils.

Matrix (math.) = *die Matrix*

Mattress = *die Matratze*

Matsch, der **1.** Slush (i.e., snow that has begun to thaw). **2.** Mud, sludge. **3.** A general "mush," e.g., of things that have been pulped. *Aus den schönen Pflaumen, die sie mitgebracht hatten, war ein klebriger Matsch geworden.* The beautiful plums they had brought with them had turned into a sticky pulp.

Match (game) = *das Spiel*

(for producing fire) = *das Streichholz, das Zündholz*

Other uses: They're a good match (i.e., they fit well together): *Sie passen gut zusammen;* You'll never find a match for that paint: *Du wirst nie genau die gleiche Farbe finden;* Jim was always a match for anybody: *Jim konnte es schon immer mit jedem aufnehmen.*

matt   **1.** Mat(t) (of colors, paper, photographic prints), but the German word has several other uses.   **2.** Weak, feeble. *Ich fühle mich heute ein bißchen matt.* I feel a bit run-down.   **3.** Dim, dull (light, etc.).   **4.** (Check)mate (chess).

maturieren   The Austrian and Swiss term for passing the final examination at secondary school (the *Matura*), which gives one the right to study at university (the equivalent of the German *Abitur,* or high school graduation in the U.S.A.). *Sie hat erst mit 21 maturiert.* She didn't pass her *Matura* till she was 21.

To mature (person) = *reifer werden*
        (wine, etc.) = *reifen*

Maus, die   **1.** Mouse (also for computer).   **2.** (coll. in the plural) Money. *Wo hast du die Mäuse versteckt?* Where have you hidden the dough?

Mechanik, die   **1.** Mechanics, as a subject of study.   **2.** (fig.) Mechanical nature of, for example, a monotonous activity. *Die Mechanik der Fließbandarbeit langweilte ihn zu Tode.* The mechanical nature of assembly line work bored him to death.

Mechanic = *der Mechaniker*

Medaillon, das   Not only a medallion, but also a locket. *Sie öffnete das Medaillon und zeigte das Bild ihres Mannes.* She opened the locket and showed her husband's picture.

Mediziner, der   S.o. who has studied medicine (i.e., a doctor) or is studying it (i.e., a medical student, a medic).

Medicine (science) = *die Medizin*
        (particular drug) = *das Medikament*

meinen   **1.** Mean. *So habe ich das nicht gemeint.* I didn't mean it like that.   **2.** Esp. common is the sense of "to have an opinion," "to think." *Ich meine, wir sollten die finanzielle Seite ihm überlassen.* I think we ought to leave the financial side to him. *Was meinst du, Hans?* What do you think, Hans?

To mean (word) = *bedeuten*
        (intend) = *beabsichtigen, vorhaben*
        (result in) = *zur Folge haben, bedeuten*

Meinung, die   Opinion, view. *Dieser Bericht hat mich gezwungen, meine Meinung zu ändern.* This report has forced me to change my opinion. *meiner Meinung nach* In my opinion.

Meaning = *die Bedeutung*

Meister, der Master, in the sense of an expert or brilliant exponent. In the context of manual skills, the concept of the master craftsman is stronger in Germany than in the U.S.A. or Britain, and many German *Handwerker* (skilled craftsmen, skilled manual workers) strive to pass the *Meisterprüfung* (examination for master craftsman's certificate). As *Meister* they are then often in a position of authority, hence the extension of the term to mean "foreman." *Frag' mal den Meister, ob du früher gehen darfst.* Ask the foreman if you can leave early. Informally, it is also used as a casual mode of address toward a male person, often an unknown one. It may be used humorously or indicate lack of education in the speaker. *Hallo, Meister! Zur Berliner Straße?* Hey, mac (BrE guv), how do you get to Berliner Strasse?

Master (schoolteacher) = *der Lehrer*

Melodie, die Both "melody" and "tune." *Den Text konnte ich nicht verstehen, aber die Melodie war schön.* I couldn't understand the words, but the tune was nice.

Melone, die 1. Melon. 2. Derby, BrE bowler (hat). *Es stimmt gar nicht, daß der Durchschnittsengländer eine Melone trägt.* It's quite untrue that the average Englishman wears a bowler.

Mentor, der As well as denoting a mentor in the general sense of the word, this also indicates an experienced teacher who supervises and advises a student doing an internship (*Praktikum*) at a school.

Menü, das 1. In modern German this normally denotes a set *table d'hôte* meal of several courses. *Ich entschied mich für das Menü 2: Tomatensuppe, Rumpsteak und anschließend Pfirsich Melba.* I decided on the second set meal: tomato soup, rump steak, and, to follow, peach melba. 2. (computers) Menu.

Menu (in restaurant) = *die Speisekarte*

Messe, die 1. Mess (army or navy). 2. Mass (Catholic). 3. Trade fair. *die Frankfurter Buchmesse* the Frankfurt Book Fair.

Mess (disorganized) = *das Durcheinander*
    (untidy) = *die Unordnung*
    (dirty) = *die Schweinerei*
    (awkward situation) = *der* or *das Schlamassel*

Milan, der Kite (bird of prey).

Milan (Italian city) = *Mailand*

mild 1. Mild, in a variety of contexts (weather, coffee, soap, etc.). 2. Lenient. *Bei einem weniger milden Richter wäre er bestimmt im Gefängnis gelandet.* A less lenient judge would certainly have sent him to prison. *milde Gabe(n)* Alms.

Militär, der   A (high-ranking) officer in the armed forces. *Die politische Macht liegt bei den Militärs.* Political power resides with the high-ranking officers.

The military = *das Militär*

Milliarde, die   Billion. SEE **BILLION**. *fünf Milliarden Mark* five billion (i.e., 5,000,000,000) marks.

Mime, der   A humorous or dated word to denote an actor: a "thespian."

Mime (person) = *der (die) Pantomime(-in)*

(activity) = *die Pantomime*

mimen   **1.** To mime.   **2.** To play-act, to pretend. *Er mimte ein gewisses Interesse.* He feigned a certain interest. *Er mimt in letzter Zeit den Umweltschützer.* Recently he's been playing the conservationist.

Mimik, die   Facial expression. *Sie sagte, sie habe nichts dagegen, aber ihre ganze Mimik zeigte Enttäuschung.* She said she didn't object, but her whole (facial) expression showed disappointment.

Mimic (noun) = *der Imitator* (or the verbs *nachahmen* or *nachmachen* are used)

To mimic (verb) = *nachahmen, imitieren*

mimisch   Relating to facial expression. SEE **MIMIK**. *Der gute Schauspieler kann auch ohne Worte—und zwar mimisch—eine ganze Reihe verschiedener Gefühle ausdrücken.* A good actor can express a whole range of different emotions without words, namely by using facial expression.

Mine, die   **1.** Underground mines for extracting gold or other metals.   **2.** Mine (weapon).   **3.** Lead in a pencil.   **4.** (Refill) cartridge for a pen or ballpoint.

Minus, das   Often denotes a negative feature or disadvantage. *Daß Sie kein Englisch können, ist natürlich ein Minus.* Of course, the fact that you don't speak English counts against you. *Die Handelsbilanz weist ein Minus von 2 Milliarden Dollar auf.* The trade balance shows a deficit of 2 billion dollars.

Misere, die   Expresses a thoroughly bad or desperate situation, rather than the intense and usually protracted unhappiness of English "misery." *Die gegenwärtige Bildungsmisere ist nicht nur auf fehlende Investitionen zurückzuführen.* The present crisis in education is not only due to a lack of investment. *Die finanzielle Misere des Landes scheint den Durchschnittsbürger nicht zu tangieren.* The deplorable state of the country's finances does not appear to affect the average citizen.

Misery = *das Elend, der Kummer*

missen   To do without, to be without, normally used in the negative. *Meinen Geschirrspüler möchte ich nicht mehr missen.* I wouldn't like to be without my dishwasher. In certain contexts "miss" may be the idiomatic translation. *Es ist ein Erlebnis, das ich nicht missen möchte.* It's an experience I wouldn't like to miss.

To miss (train, appointment, etc.) = *versäumen, verpassen*
(target) = *verfehlen*
(person, thing, now absent) = *vermissen*
(overlook) = *übersehen*
(omit) = *auslassen*

Mist, der   **1.** Dung, manure, droppings. *Der Bauer hat gestern den Mist auf den Wagen geladen.* The farmer loaded the manure on to the cart yesterday. **2.** By extension, "trash," "rubbish." *Reden Sie doch nicht so einen Mist!* Oh, don't talk such rubbish! **3.** An expression of annoyance. *Mist! Da fährt unser Bus.* Damn! There goes our bus.

Mist = *(dünner) Nebel*

Mittag, der   Midday, noon, but also—colloquially—the lunch break, lunch hour. *Es ist schon 12.30 Uhr—wir wollen jetzt Mittag machen.* It's already 12:30—let's take our lunch break now.

Mittag, das   Lunch (coll.) *Kommt zum Mittag!* Come to lunch!

Midday = *der Mittag*

Mittel, das   **1.** "Middle," "central" in compounds. *Mitteleuropa* Central Europe; *Mittelweg* middle course. But as a separate word it has other meanings: **2.** Way, method, means. *Ich kenne kein besseres Mittel, die Inflation zu bekämpfen.* I know no better way of combating inflation. **3.** Medicine, drug, preparation, remedy, etc. *Ich kenne ein gutes Mittel gegen Heuschnupfen.* I know a good remedy for hay fever. **4.** (pl.) Funds, resources. *Wir würden gern mehrere solche Kliniken gründen, aber uns fehlen die Mittel.* We'd like to establish several clinics of this type, but we don't have the resources. **5.** (math.) Mean, average. *Ich zeige euch jetzt, wie man das geometrische Mittel ausrechnet.* I'll show you now how to work out the geometrical mean.

Middle = *die Mitte*

Mittelalter, das   The Middle Ages. *Das Manuskript stammt aus dem Mittelalter.* The manuscript dates back to the Middle Ages.

Middle age = *das mittlere (Lebens)alter*

mittelalterlich   Medieval. *Er wohnt in einem mittelalterlichen Schloß.* He lives in a medieval castle.

Middle-aged = *mittleren Alters, in den mittleren Jahren*

Mixer, der   **1.** A mixer or blender (as used in the kitchen). **2.** The technician (i.e., sound mixer). **3.** A short form of *Barmixer,* meaning "cocktail waiter." *Er erzählte dem Mixer seine ganzen Sorgen.* He related all his troubles to the cocktail waiter.

He's a good mixer (i.e., sociable) = *Er ist kontaktfreudig*

Modalität, die   **1.** (philosophy, logic) Modality. **2.** Usually, a way of doing s.t., a procedure. *Diese Prüfungsmodalität hat den Vorteil, daß sich der Kandidat gezielt vorbereiten kann.* This examination procedure has the advantage that the candidate knows specifically what to prepare for.

Mode, die   Fashion, with regard to clothes and other things. *Diese neue Mode ist für die vollschlanke Frau weniger günstig.* This new fashion is not so good for the woman with the fuller figure. *Das ist jetzt Mode.* That's the fashion now.

Mode = *die Art, die Art und Weise*

Moderation, die   Presentation, of a radio or TV program. *Die Moderation im "Report" hat heute abend Franz Alt.* Franz Alt will be presenting "Report" this evening.

Moderation = *die Mäßigung*

Moderator, der   Presenter, of a radio or TV program.

Moderator: Most uses of this word are culture-specific and real translation equivalents rarely exist.

moderieren   To present (a radio or TV program). *Weißt du, wer das "Auslandsjournal" normalerweise moderiert?* Do you know who normally presents the "Auslandsjournal"?

To moderate = *mäßigen*

Moment, das   1. Factor, element. *Psychologische Momente spielen eine große Rolle in solchen Entscheidungen.* Psychological factors play a great part in such decisions.   2. (phys.) Moment.

Moment (of time) = *der Moment, der Augenblick*

momentan   Not "momentous," but "momentary" or "present." *Die momentane Lage ist unklar.* The present situation is unclear. *Wir befinden uns momentan mitten in einer Rezession.* At present we are in the middle of a recession.

Momentous = *bedeutsam*

mondän   Sophisticated, elegant. *Diese mondäne Frau konnte mit dem einfachen Leben im Dorf nichts anfangen.* This sophisticated woman could find no satisfaction in the simple life of the village.

Mundane = *profan, alltäglich*

Montage, die   Montage, in art and filmmaking, but more frequently "assembly," as part of the manufacturing process. *Die Montage haben wir nach Taiwan verlagert.* We've transferred the assembly to Taiwan. The concept of "assembly" may be extended to major building operations, when it means in effect "erection," "building." *auf Montage sein* To be away on a (building) job.

Montan-   Refers not to mountains, but to coal and steel (as industries). *die Montanindustrie* the coal and steel industry.

Mountain = *der Berg*

montan   1. Relating to the coal and steel industry. *die montane Industrie* the coal and steel industry. SEE **MONTAN-**.   2. Occasionally a technical term meaning "relating to mountain areas." *montane Vegetation* mountain vegetation.

montieren   To assemble or install (a structure, piece of machinery, etc.). *Die einzelnen Teile werden in Deutschland hergestellt und die Maschinen dann in Spanien montiert.* The individual parts are produced in Germany and the machines are then assembled in Spain. *Unsere Handwerker brauchen nur zwei Stunden, um die Alarmanlage zu montieren.* It takes our workmen only two hours to install the alarm system.

To mount (climb on to) = *besteigen*

Monumentalfilm, der   Not a film that represents any memorial or monument, but a cast-of-thousands "epic," such as *Ben Hur* or *The Ten Commandments*.

Moor, das   This may mean "moor," esp. in the compounds *Hochmoor* and *Heidemoor,* but often it indicates what in English would be termed a "bog."

Moorhuhn, das   Not a "moorhen," but a "grouse."

Moorhen = *das Teichhuhn*

Mops, der   Pug (dog). Also slang for a short, fat person and, in the plural, "money," though this latter usage is rather dated.

Mop (for cleaning floor) = *der Mop*

Moral, die   1. Moral (of a story or a fable). But more commonly: 2. Morality. *Die heutige Moral nimmt an solchem egoistischen Verhalten anscheinend keinen Anstoß mehr.* Apparently present-day morality no longer takes offence at this sort of selfish behavior.   3. Morale. *Unseren Truppen fehlt es vor allem an Moral.* Above all our troops lack morale.

Mörder, der   Murderer.

Murder = *der Mord*

Moskito, der   Mosquito, but the German word will normally be taken to denote the tropical variety that transmits such diseases as malaria. It is not normally applied to the irritatingly bloodthirsty, but essentially harmless "mosquito" of temperate climes: this is normally referred to as *die Mücke.*

Motiv, das   1. Motive (i.e., reason for doing s.t.).   2. (art, music, etc.) Theme, subject, motif. *Ich fotografiere gern—ich interessiere mich vor allem für menschliche Motive.* I like taking photos—I'm especially interested in human subjects. *Das ist ein Hauptmotiv in seinen Gedichten.* This is a major theme in his poems.

Motor, der   1. Most commonly used to indicate an internal combustion engine, where BrE in particular prefers "engine." *Nach 150.000 Kilometern half nur noch ein neuer Motor.* After 150,000 kilometers there was nothing to do but install a new engine.   2. (fig.) Driving force behind some undertaking. *Er hatte nur die Funktion einer Galionsfigur—der eigentliche Motor des ganzen Unterfangens war sein ältester Sohn Heinz.*

His role was merely that of a figurehead—his eldest son Heinz was the real driving force behind the whole venture.

Motto, das   Motto. *nach dem Motto* Used to indicate a precept according to which people behave. *Ich habe die Zahlen selbst geprüft—nach dem Motto: Vertrauen ist gut, Kontrolle ist besser.* I've checked the figures myself, on the principle that it's better to be safe than sorry.

Muff, der   There are two homonyms here, one of which means "muff" (item of clothing). The other (North German dialect, but familiar outside the region) means a "musty smell," "fustiness." Found in the celebrated phrase used during the student rebellion of the late 1960s: *Unter den Talaren der Muff von tausend Jahren* (*Talar* indicates the academic gown).

Muffe, die   A technical expression for a "sleeve" (e.g., encasing the shaft of a machine). But also used in several colloquial expressions denoting craven fear, "funk," e.g., *Muffe haben* = to be in a funk.

Muff = *der Muff*

Muffel, der   On its own this denotes a person who is unfriendly and complaining—a "grouch," "grump." But it is especially common in compounds, where it denotes a lack of interest or enthusiasm for the matter concerned. Thus a *Morgenmuffel* is someone who is at his or her worst in the mornings, while a *Sexmuffel* displays indifference to sex. It may also indicate an old-fashioned or unimaginative attitude to s.t. Thus a *Krawattenmuffel* is uninterested in neckties to the point of being quite impervious to the demands of fashion when it comes to selecting one.

To muffle (sound) = *dämpfen*

Muffler (scarf) = *der Schal*

(of car exhaust) = *der Schalldämpfer*

muffeln   **1.** To be grumpy.   **2.** To mutter (esp. in a grumpy manner).

To muffle (sound) = *dämpfen*

Mühle, die   **1.** Mill.   **2.** A board game: (nine men's) morris.   **3.** (coll.) An old aircraft, car, or bicycle. *Sollen wir mit dieser Mühle nach Madeira fliegen?* Are we supposed to fly to Madeira in this old crate?

Murmel, die   Marble (children's toy).

Murmur = *das Murmeln, das Gemurmel*

murmeln   To murmur, mutter.

But there is also a homonym meaning "to play marbles." SEE **MURMEL.**

Mus, das   A mash or purée obtained by boiling fruit. *Apfelmus* apple purée, apple sauce.

Moose = *der Elch*

Mousse = *die Creme(speise), die Mousse*

Muschel, die   Mussel (the shellfish). Also a short form for a "mouth-piece" (*Sprechmuschel*) or "earpiece" (*Hörmuschel*) on a telephone, etc.

Muscle = *der Muskel*

Musikbox, die   Jukebox. *Seitdem wir die Musikbox haben, bekommen wir mehr junge Gäste.* We've been getting more young customers since we've had the jukebox.

Music box = *die Spieluhr, die Spieldose*

musisch   Connected with the (fine) arts. *In solchen Schulen werden die musischen Fächer vernachlässigt.* Art and music are neglected in such schools. *ein Kind mit einer musischen Begabung* an artistically gifted child.

Musical = *musikalisch*

müssen   It is important to remember that in the negative this verb normally expresses lack of obligation ("don't have to") rather than prohibition ("must not"). *Diesen Artikel können Sie natürlich auch lesen, aber Sie müssen nicht.* Of course you can read this article too, but you don't have to.

Must not = *nicht dürfen*. *Hier darfst du nicht rauchen.* You mustn't smoke here.

Muster, das   **1.** Pattern. *Mein Pullover hatte ein ganz anderes Muster.* My pullover had a completely different pattern.   **2.** Sample. *Der Vertreter brachte einige Muster mit.* The sales representative brought some samples.   **3.** (Ideal) model. *Sie ist ein Muster an Hilfsbereitschaft.* She is a model of helpfulness.

Muster (mil.) = *der Appell*

mustern   **1.** To look at carefully and critically. *Das Mädchen musterte ihn kühl.* The girl coolly scrutinized him.   **2.** To inspect (troops, e.g., at a parade).   **3.** To give prospective servicemen their medical.

To muster (soldiers) = *(zum Appell) antreten lassen*

　　　　　　　　　(courage, etc.) = *aufbringen*

Mutter, die   **1.** Mother (pl.: *Mütter*).   **2.** Nut of a bolt (pl.: *Muttern*). *Vergiß nicht, die Muttern anzuziehen.* Don't forget to tighten the nuts.

N

nächst- Not only "next," but also "nearest." *Wo ist das nächste Postamt?* Where's the nearest post office?

Nacken, der Not the whole of the neck, but specifically the "nape," "back of the neck." *Nach dem Tippen habe ich immer Schmerzen im Nacken.* I always have pains in the back of my neck after typing.

Neck (whole of) = *der Hals*

Nadel, die **1.** Needle (also "stylus," for a phonograph). But it is occasionally found as a short form for *Stecknadel* = pin. **2.** A brooch (esp. one that is long and thin in form).

nagen To gnaw. *Ratten hatten am Seil genagt.* Rats had been gnawing at the rope.

To nag = *herumnörgeln*

namentlich **1.** (adj.) By name. *eine namentliche Liste* a list of names. **2.** Adverbially, it also has the meaning of "especially." *Die neue Regelung hat viele hart getroffen, namentlich die Arbeitslosen.* The new ruling has hit many people hard, especially the unemployed.

Namely = *nämlich, und zwar*

nämlich **1.** This can be used like English "namely." **2.** It is also used as a causal adverb, giving the reason for a previous statement. It is frequently unnecessary to translate it explicitly. *Ihr könnt heute keinen Fußball spielen, der Boden ist nämlich hartgefroren.* You can't play soccer today—(because) the ground's frozen hard. **3.** (adj.) Same (this is no longer a common use). *die nämlichen Leute* the same people.

Nassauer, der May indicate an inhabitant of Nassau, but colloquially it is also used by some speakers to denote a "sponger," "scrounger," i.e., a parasite who lives off other people's generosity.

national National, but also "nationalist(ic)," i.e., subject to strong or even excessive feelings of national identity. *Mein Vater war sehr national eingestellt.* My father had a strongly nationalist outlook.

National- In certain compounds this corresponds to "international" rather than "national." *ein Nationalspieler* an international player; *die amerikanische Nationalmannschaft* the American (international) team.

nationalisieren **1.** To nationalize (an industry, etc.). **2.** To naturalize (i.e., give s.o. citizenship).

Natur, die **1.** This usually corresponds to "nature." There are exceptions: **2.** It sometimes indicates "countryside," "scenery," rather than nature generally. *Vor allem die Natur zieht die Touristen scharenweise in diese Gegend.* It is above all the scenery that attracts the tourists to this area in droves. **3.** A person's disposition. *Sie ist eine etwas komplizierte Natur, launisch und unberechenbar.* She's a rather complicated type, moody and unpredictable. **4.** Not artificial—where English would not normally use the noun "nature." *Wir haben uns für einen Eßtisch in Eiche Natur entschieden.* We decided on a dining table in natural oak. *Ihre Haarfarbe ist fast zu blond—das ist bestimmt nicht Natur.* Her hair's almost too blond—it's certainly not her real color.

Naturalien (pl.)   Natural produce, goods (rather than money). *in Naturalien bezahlen* To pay in kind.

She's a natural = *Sie ist ein Naturtalent*

Naturell, das   Disposition, temperament. *Eine solche Handlung entspräche nicht seinem Naturell.* An action of that sort wouldn't be compatible with his temperament.

She's a natural = *Sie ist ein Naturtalent*

Necessaire, das   A small bag or case for manicure equipment: manicure case. The compound form *Nagelnecessaire* is often used.

Necessary = *notwendig, nötig*

"The necessary" (i.e., money) = *das nötige Kleingeld*

necken   A now perhaps slightly dated verb meaning "to tease." *Jetzt hör' auf, deine kleine Schwester zu necken!* Now, stop teasing your little sister!

To neck = *schmusen, knutschen*

Nektar, der   Nectar, in the context of mythology and botany. But it has also been introduced as one of the official classifications of fruit drinks, to denote a drink that is not pure juice, but diluted to some extent. *Orangennektar* orange fruit drink.

nerven   To get on s.o.'s nerves, pester. *Dein Onkel nervt mich, wie er ständig die gleiche Melodie pfeift.* Your uncle gets on my nerves, the way he keeps whistling the same tune. *Meine kleine Tochter hat mich genervt, ihr einen Fußball zu kaufen.* My little daughter pestered me to buy her a football.

BrE to nerve oneself (to do s.t.) = *sich Mut machen, sich vorbereiten (etwas zu tun)*

nervig   Sinewy, wiry. *Er war eine kleine, untersetzte aber unheimlich nervige Gestalt.* He was a small, stocky, but extremely sinewy figure.

Nervy (bold) = *frech*

(BrE: tense) = *nervös, unruhig*

nervös   Nervous, but in some contexts "jumpy" or "on edge" may be better translations. Sometimes the word virtually means "irritable." *Schrei mich nicht so an! Du bist heute verdammt nervös!* Don't shout at me like that! You're damned irritable today!

Nest, das   Nest, though one important metaphorical usage is not shared by the English word: a small, dull town. *In dem Nest wäre ich verrückt geworden.* I would have gone mad in that dump.

nett   Nice. *Sie findet ihn zwar sehr nett, aber sie liebt ihn nicht.* Although she thinks he's very nice, she doesn't love him.

Net (weight, salary, etc.) = *netto*

Netz, das   **1.** Net, but also "network." *Das Straßennetz ist sehr gut.* The road network is very good.   **2.** Spider's web (the full form *Spinnennetz* is normally used).

Netzball, der   Not the British game of netball, but a net ball, a ball that (in tennis, volleyball, etc.) strikes the top of the net and then falls in the opponent's side of the court: a "let" in tennis.

BrE Netball = *der Korbball*

neulich   Recently, a short time ago. *Ich bin ihr neulich im Supermarkt begegnet.* I met her the other day in the supermarket.

Newly = *neu-, frisch* new(ly) mown *frisch gemäht*

nicken   To nod. *Er nickte beifällig.* He nodded in approval.

To nick (e.g., a piece of wood) = *einkerben*
(of a bullet) = *streifen*
(BrE coll., = steal) = *klauen*
(BrE catch, arrest) = *schnappen*

nippen   To sip. *Er nippte nur an dem billigen süßen Wein.* He just sipped at the cheap sweet wine.

To nip (pinch) = *zwicken, kneifen*

nobel/Nobel-   **1.** Most commonly used colloquially to indicate luxury, elegance, etc. *Ich esse nicht gern in solchen noblen Restaurants [Nobelrestaurants].* I don't like eating in that sort of posh restaurant.   **2.** It may also be used colloquially to denote generosity. *Das ist ja ausgesprochen nobel von dir, mir eine Flasche Malt-Whisky zu schenken.* It's very generous of you to give me a bottle of malt whiskey.

Noble (quality of character) = *edel(mütig)*
(aristocratic) = *adlig*

Nomenklatura, die   Used as a collective term to denote the ruling élite in a communist system.

Nomenclature = *die Nomenklatur*

Nordlicht, das   The Northern Lights, Aurora Borealis. But in the plural *Nordlichter* the word is used ironically, especially by South Germans, to denote North German personalities (usually political) who have an exaggerated idea of their abilities and importance.

Note, die   **1.** Grade, BrE mark. *Meine Noten in Spanisch sind nicht besonders gut.* My grades in Spanish are not especially good.   **2.** (Special) quality, touch, "trademark." *Diese ausgefallenen Hüte sind ihre besondere Note.* These weird hats are her trademark.   **3.** (pl.) (Sheet) music, score. *Die Noten für die Sonate liegen irgendwo im Schrank.* The score for the sonata is somewhere in the closet.

Note (informal letter, etc.) = *der Zettel, der kurze Brief, die Notiz*
(on a text) = *die Anmerkung*
Notes (for a lecture) = *das Manuskript*
(of a lecture) = *die Notizen, die Aufzeichnungen*

notieren **1.** To note (down). **2.** (stock exchange) To quote, to be quoted. *Händler notieren diese Aktie mit 80 Mark.* Dealers quote this share at 80 marks. *Diese Aktie notiert mit 80 Mark.* This share is quoted at 80 marks.

Notiz, die **1.** (Written) note. *Nur wenige Studenten haben während der Vorlesung Notizen gemacht.* Only a few students took notes during the lecture. **2.** Item, in a newspaper, etc. *Einige Zeitungen brachten eine kurze Notiz über die Sache.* Some newspapers had a short item about the matter. *Notiz nehmen* To take notice.

Notice (on a board, etc.) = *der Anschlag, die Bekanntmachung*
(of dismissal, etc.) = *die Kündigung*

notorisch This may mean "notorious," but frequently means "habitual" (with reference to bad habits). *Ihr Vater ist ein notorischer Trinker.* Her father is a habitual drinker.

Notorious = *berüchtigt*

Nougat, der or **das** This denotes a soft substance used as a filling in chocolates, generally consisting of powdered nuts, sugar, and cocoa: there is no ready English translation.

Nougat: No real German equivalent, though the candy known as *türkischer Honig* is similar.

Novelle, die **1.** A particular type of short story well represented in German literature—the novella. **2.** Amendment (to a law). *Eine Novelle zu diesem Gesetz ist dringend erforderlich.* An amendment to this law is needed urgently.

Novel = *der Roman*

Nuance, die Nuance, but the German word is broader in meaning than the English, sometimes meaning simply "a bit," "a shade." *Tja, das Bild hängt um eine Nuance zu hoch.* Hm, the picture's a bit too high.

Nummer, die Number, but also size in shoes, etc. *Haben Sie diesen Rock eine Nummer größer?* Have you got this skirt one size larger?

Nut, die A term in carpentry, etc., for a type of groove. *Nut und Feder* tongue and groove; *Nut und Zapfen* mortise and tenon.

Nut = *die Nuß*

Nutte, die Slang term for a prostitute: hooker, BrE tart.

Nut = *die Nuß*

Objekt, das   Object, but also commonly used in real estate contexts to denote a house, piece of property, etc. *Es handelt sich um ein sehr günstiges Objekt in einer schönen Wohngegend.* It's a very reasonably priced (piece of) property in a very attractive residential area.
Object (aim) = *das Ziel*

Objektiv, das   There is an important frequency difference here: *Objektiv* is the normal word for the "lens" of a camera, telescope, etc., whereas English "objective" is a technical term scarcely used by the layperson. *Mit meinem neuen Teleobjektiv kann ich tolle Vogelbilder machen.* With my new telephoto lens I can take great bird pictures.
Objective (aim) = *das Ziel*

Obligation, die   A financial term for a fixed-interest security or bond, often issued by a public body.
Obligation = *die Verpflichtung*

Occasion, die   (Sw.) Something (very often a car) sold second-hand (often as a bargain). *Hansruedi hat seinen Fiat als Occasion gekauft.* Hansruedi bought his Fiat second-hand.
Occasion (special occasion, etc.) = *der Anlaß*

Ofen, der   This may denote an oven for cooking food or baking pottery, but more commonly refers to a stove in a heating system. *Solche Ölöfen findet man oft in Altbauwohnungen.* One often finds this type of oil stove in older apartments. *heißer Ofen* (coll.) Motorcycle.

offensiv   Not "offensive" in the sense of "abusive," but rather "on the offensive." *offensiver Fußball* soccer offense (BrE attacking soccer).
Offensive (abusive) = *ausfallend, beleidigend*

offiziös   Semiofficial. *Es hat kein Kommuniqué gegeben, nur die offiziöse Nachricht, daß die Verhandlungen gescheitert seien.* There was no communiqué—only the semiofficial news that the negotiations had failed.
Officious = *übereifrig, dienstbeflissen*

Ohr, das   Ear.
Oar = *das Ruder*
Ore = *das Erz*

Öhr, das   The umlaut makes all the difference—this means the eye of a needle.
Ear = *das Ohr*

Oldtimer, der   This may very occasionally refer to a person, more or less as in English, but much more commonly denotes a vintage or veteran car. *Der 1925er Rolls-Royce ist das Kernstück seiner Oldtimer-Sammlung.* The 1925 Rolls-Royce is the centerpiece of his collection of vintage cars.

ominös   A typical example of a *Fremdwort* adjective whose meaning is often difficult to pin down. "Ominous" is an accurate translation in many instances, but in others the meaning seems to be "dubious," "suspicious," "sinister," or even "notorious." Duden's example of *die ominöse 7. Runde* (in boxing) would correspond to "the notorious 7th round," while *ein ominöser Beigeschmack* (a further Duden example) would be "a suspicious aftertaste." A recent TV program talked of *ominöse Firmen* listed in address books: here the meaning was "dubious firms." Each case must be judged according to its context.

operativ   Normally refers to a medical operation. *operative Behandlung* surgical treatment. May also mean "operational," in a military context. Operative (law, etc.) = *in Kraft, (rechts)wirksam, geltend* The operative word = *das wichtigste Wort* (or paraphrase)

ordinär   Vulgar, common, coarse. *Seine Schwester? Eine ganz ordinäre Person!* His sister? She's very common! *Warum mußt du dich immer so ordinär ausdrücken?* Why do you always have to express yourself in such a vulgar way? Ordinary = *normal, gewöhnlich*

Organ, das   Used in most senses of the English word (though not for the musical instrument). Also used to denote the voice. *Dieses Kind hat ein furchtbar schrilles Organ.* That child's got a terribly piercing voice. Organ (musical) = *die Orgel*

organisieren   To organize, but colloquially the word frequently has the connotation of obtaining things by perhaps dubious methods. *Der Heiner konnte immer einen Kasten Bier in einer Viertelstunde organisieren.* Heiner could always lay his hands on a case of beer within a quarter of an hour.

orientieren   **1.** To orient, but often the German word means little more than "to inform." *Anhand von diesem Buch habe ich mich schnell über das Grundproblem orientiert.* With the help of this book I soon got an idea of the basic problem.   **2.** To find one's bearings. *Es dauert lange, bis man sich in dieser Stadt orientieren kann.* It takes a long time to find one's way around this city.

Orientierung, die   **1.** Orientation.   **2.** Information. *Dieses Heft gibt Ihnen eine erste Orientierung.* This leaflet will give you the basic information. *Er hat keinen Orientierungssinn.* He has no sense of direction.

Original, das   Original, but can also denote an unconventional, eccentric person. *Lutz ist ein Original, und Sie sollten sich von seinen Marotten nicht stören lassen.* Lutz is a character, and you shouldn't let his funny ways worry you.

originell **1.** Original, in the sense of "fresh," "novel." **2.** In some contexts the German word may mean "witty," and the exact meaning may not always be absolutely clear. *Diese Erzählungen sind alle höchst originell.* All these stories are extremely original/witty. **3.** (coll.) Strange, weird. *Der Manfred ist ein origineller Typ.* Manfred is a strange guy.

Otter, die Viper, adder (usually in the compound *Kreuzotter*).
Otter = *der Otter*

P

Paar, das/paar, ein In its capitalized spelling *Paar* corresponds to "pair," though "couple" will normally be required in relation to people. *Sie sind ein nettes Paar—ich kenne sie schon lange.* They're a nice couple—I've known them for a long time. *ein paar* (with the lower case *p*) corresponds to "a few," "a couple of." *Abends gibt es wenig zu tun: es gibt ein paar Kinos und sonst nichts.* There's not much to do in the evenings: there are a few movie houses and nothing else.

Pack, das A pejorative term applied to a group of people. *Ich will mit diesem Pack nichts mehr zu tun haben.* I don't want to have any more to do with that rabble.
Pack (of cigarettes, etc.) = *die Packung*
(of cards) = *das Kartenspiel*
(of wolves) = *das Rudel*

packen **1.** To pack (suitcase, etc.), but there are many other uses. **2.** To seize, grab. *Er packte den Jungen am Kragen.* He grabbed the boy by the collar. **3.** To enthrall, thrill. *Seine Kriegsgeschichten hatten uns Kinder immer gepackt.* His war stories had always thrilled us children. **4.** (coll.) To go, particularly in the phrase (esp. common in South Germany) *Packen wir's!* Let's go! **5.** (coll.) To understand. *Das hat der Manfred nie gepackt.* Manfred just didn't get it. **6.** (coll.) To manage. *All das in vier Wochen lernen? Ich pack' das nie!* Learn all that in four weeks? I'll never manage that!

Pädagoge(-gin) der (die) Used much more frequently than English "pedagog(ue)," and free of the pejorative connotations the latter sometimes has. It may denote: **1.** A teacher. *Ein guter Pädagoge will seine Schüler am Unterricht aktiv beteiligen.* A good teacher wants to involve his pupils actively in the lesson. **2.** An educational theorist, education(al)-ist. *Die Pädagogin Montessori hat ihn stark beeinflußt.* The educationalist Montessori influenced him greatly.

Pedagog (pejorative: pedantic teacher) = *der Schulmeister* (The noun is not very common, and the pejorative idea is more usually conveyed by the adjective *schulmeisterlich.*)

Pädagogik, die More frequently used than English "pedagogy." SEE PÄDAGOGE. As such corresponds more closely to "educational theory," "education" (as a subject of study).

Paket, das There is a good deal of overlap between this and English "packet," but the following uses should be noted. **1.** Parcel. *Bei Paketen ins Ausland kostet das Porto mehr als der Inhalt.* When you send a parcel abroad the postage costs more than the contents. **2.** Package, in the abstract sense of a number of proposals, etc. *Das neue Steuerreformpaket ist auf wenig Resonanz gestoßen.* The new tax reform package has met with little response.

Packet (of tea, etc.) = *die Packung*

Palette, die **1.** Palette (for painting). **2.** (fig.) Range, variety. *Unsere Firma bietet eine breite Palette von Lebensversicherungen.* Our firm offers a wide range of life insurance policies. **3.** (industry) Pallet. *Mit dem Gabelstapler lassen sich diese Paletten sehr schnell wegräumen.* These pallets can be moved quickly with a forklift truck.

Pamphlet, das Unlike the neutral English word, this is always pejorative, denoting a defamatory piece of writing, a lampoon.

Pamphlet = *die Broschüre*

(political, distributed by hand) = *das Flugblatt*

Panne, die Breakdown (e.g., of car). *Hoffentlich haben wir auf der Autobahn keine Panne.* I hope we don't have a breakdown on the highway. *eine technische Panne* a technical hitch. May also refer generally to things going wrong. *Beim Versand hat es zu viele Pannen gegeben.* There have been too many slip-ups in the dispatch department.

Pan = *die (Brat)pfanne*

Pantomime(-min) der (die) Mime (i.e., person performing this). *Marcel Marceau ist wohl der berühmteste Pantomime.* Marcel Marceau is probably the most famous mime.

Pantomime, die Mime (the art). *Die Kunst der Pantomime findet in unserem Land kein großes Publikum.* There is no great interest in the art of mime in our country.

Pantomime: No real cultural equivalent in German-speaking countries.

Panzer, der **1.** A German word familiar to English ears in its modern military sense of "tank," or, collectively, "armor." **2.** The armor plating used on various military vehicles. **3.** Armor in the context of earlier military techniques—a "suit of armor." *Der Ritter trug einen Panzer.* The knight wore a suit of armor. (*Die Rüstung* is the more usual term.) **4.** (zool.) The shell of a turtle, armadillo, etc., or of certain insects.

Papier, das 1. Paper. **2.** (fin.) Security (*Wertpapier*). *Ich habe meine ganzen Papiere verkaufen müssen.* I've had to sell all my securities.
Paper (i.e., newspaper) = *die Zeitung*

Pappe, die 1. Cardboard. *Ich habe die Zeitungsbilder auf Pappe montiert.* I mounted the newspaper pictures on cardboard. **2.** Roofing felt (in *Dachpappe*).
Pap (insipid food) = *der Brei*
> (low-level entertainment, etc.): A paraphrase with the adjective *seicht* ("shallow") can be used.

Parabel, die 1. Parable. **2.** (math.) Parabola.

Parade, die 1. Parade. **2.** (Dramatic) "save" by a goalkeeper in soccer, or a "parry" in fencing. *Nur glänzende Paraden durch den Torhüter verhinderten eine deutsche Niederlage.* Only brilliant saves by the goalkeeper prevented a German defeat.

paradox Paradox*ical*.
Paradox = *das Paradox, das Paradoxon*

Paragraph, der A section in a document, esp. in a law, denoted by the symbol §. *Diese Frage ist jetzt in § (Paragraph) 65 geregelt.* This question is now dealt with in Section 65. By extension, the complications of bureaucracy. *Da mußt du die ganzen Paragraphen kennen.* You have to know the regulations inside out.
Paragraph = *der Absatz*

Pardon, der or **das** The showing of mercy; the word is normally employed in the negative. *Die Partisanen kannten kein Pardon.* The partisans showed no quarter. *Wenn es ums Geschäft geht, kennt er kein Pardon.* If it's a matter of business, he's quite ruthless.
Pardon (legal) = *die Begnadigung*

parieren 1. To parry (in fencing, etc.). **2.** To rein in (a horse). **3.** To clear (a ball in soccer).
There is also a colloquial homonym meaning "to obey." *Wenn du nicht parierst, gibt's Ärger, Freund!* If you don't do what you're told, there'll be trouble, my friend!

Pariser, der 1. A Parisian. **2.** (coll.) Condom, rubber.

Park, der In addition to the common meaning of "park," the word is also used in various compounds to indicate collectively machinery, vehicles, equipment, etc., owned by a firm or institution. *Fuhrpark* fleet (of vehicles), motor pool; *Maschinenpark* (industrial) plant.

parken Unlike the English verb "to park," *parken* can be used with the vehicle as the grammatical subject, meaning "to be parked." *In letzter Zeit parkt diese Rostlaube direkt vor meiner Haustür.* Recently that heap of rust has been parked right in front of my front door. *ein parkendes Auto* a parked car.

Parkett, das   **1.** Parquet (patterned flooring).   **2.** Main floor, orchestra seats in a theater, BrE stalls. *Ich sitze nicht gern im Parkett.* I don't like sitting in the main floor.

Parkstudent(in), der (die), Parkstudium, das   None of these words is connected with outdoor studies or the science of landscape gardening. Instead they refer to a peculiarity of higher education in Germany. For certain particularly popular subjects students may find themselves on a waiting list (e.g., if the grades they obtain in their high school graduation examination, the *Abitur,* are not high enough to give them immediate admission), and in such cases many students study another subject until they are admitted to the course they really want to take. Such students are *Parkstudenten,* and the studies they pursue in the meantime are their *Parkstudium.*

Parole, die   **1.** Slogan, motto. *Unsere Parole lautet: dem Volk die Macht zurückgeben.* Our slogan is: give the power back to the people.   **2.** Password. *Die Parole sollten Sie sich merken und nicht aufschreiben.* You should remember the password and not write it down.

Parole (release for good behavior, etc.) = *die Bewährung*
(temporary release only) = *der Kurzurlaub*
(word of honor, of prisoner-of-war, etc.) = *das Ehrenwort*

Partei, die   Party (esp. political), but in certain phrases denotes bias, partisan feeling. *Man sollte bei diesen Ehestreiten lieber nicht Partei ergreifen.* One shouldn't take sides in these marital disputes.

Party (celebration) = *die Party, die Fete, das Fest*
(group) = *die Gruppe*

Partie, die   **1.** (jur.) Party.   **2.** Game. *Ich versuche, jede Woche eine Partie Tennis zu spielen.* I try to play a game of tennis every week.   **3.** (theater, etc.) Role, part. *Er spezialisierte sich auf die Partie des Hamlet.* He made the role of Hamlet his specialty.   **4.** Part (of s.t.). *Die linke Partie des Bildes wurde beschädigt.* The left part of the picture was damaged.   **5.** A potential marriage partner, a "catch." *Als Alleinerbe ist er natürlich eine gute Partie.* Of course, as the sole heir he's a good catch.   **6.** *mit von der Partie sein* To be in on s.t., present at s.t.

Party (celebration) = *die Party, die Fete, das Fest*
(group) = *die Gruppe*

Paß, der   **1.** Pass, in relation to mountains and to ball games.   **2.** Passport. *Ich habe meinen Paß verloren.* I've lost my passport.

Pass (military document) = *der Passierschein*

Passage, die   **1.** Passage.   **2.** Arcade, shopping mall. *Die neue Einkaufspassage bietet fast alle Geschäftstypen unter einem Dach.* The new shopping arcade offers practically every type of shop under one roof.

passen **1.** To pass, as in soccer, etc. **2.** To be unable to answer. *Da muß ich passen.* I'll have to pass on that one.

But there is a homonym meaning "to fit," "to suit" (i.e., to be convenient). *Diese Schuhe passen ihm nicht mehr.* Those shoes don't fit him any more. *Morgen um 10 Uhr paßt mir gut.* Tomorrow at 10 suits me fine.

To pass (an examination) = *bestehen*
(food at table) = *reichen*
(overtake) = *überholen*

passieren **1.** To pass, in the sense of "go past" or "go over." **2.** To happen. *In diesem Kaff passiert überhaupt nichts.* Nothing at all happens in this hole. **3.** (cul.) To strain.

To pass (a test) = *bestehen*
(food at table) = *reichen*
(overtake) = *überholen*

Passiva (pl.)   Liabilities, in the phrase AKTIVA UND PASSIVA (Q.V.).

Patent, das   **1.** Patent. **2.** (coll.) S.t. that, however ingenious it may be, does not really work. *Dieser Thermostat ist vielleicht ein blödes Patent!* This thermostat's a damn silly thing. **3.** Document certifying a professional qualification, esp. for ship's officers. *Kapitänspatent* master's certificate. **4.** (Sw.) More generally, a permit or license to practice a particular profession.

Patent leather = *das Lackleder*

patent   An informal adjective, applied to s.o. who is generally capable, resourceful, etc. *Wir haben in Herrn Brinkmann einen ganz patenten Chef.* We have a great boss in Herr Brinkmann.

Patent (protected by patent) = *patentiert*
(obvious) = *offensichtlich*

pathetisch   Denotes the presence of strong, passionate emotion, sometimes with a negative connotation of undue solemnity. It is a difficult word to translate: context is all-important. *Diese pathetische Rede fesselte die 20.000 Zuhörer.* This passionate speech gripped the audience of 20,000. *Sein pathetischer Stil spricht uns heutzutage wenig an.* His solemn/high-flown style has little appeal for us today. *Mit pathetischen Worten läßt sich die Situation nicht ändern.* The situation can't be changed by means of emotional/dramatic words.

Pathetic (arousing pity) = *mitleiderregend*
(BrE coll., = of poor quality) = *miserabel, kläglich, jämmerlich*

Pathos, das   Strong emotion, sometimes with the suggestion that it is inappropriate. SEE **PATHETISCH.** *Das Pathos dieser Tragödien sollte das Publikum erschüttern.* The strong/fervent emotion of these tragedies was meant to shock the audience. *Er war ein einfacher Mensch und ich finde* *solches Pathos im Nachruf fehl am Platz.* He was a simple man, and I think this sort of dramatic emotion is out of place in the obituary.

Pathos: Translating the English word into German is equally difficult. In its meaning of the power of arousing a feeling of pity, a nominalized adjective such as *das Mitleiderregende* or *das Rührende* may be most suitable. If the word is meant to suggest sentimentality, then *die Sentimentalität* or *die Rührseligkeit* are accurate, if rather direct, translations.

Patron, der   1. Patron saint. *Christophorus ist der Patron der Reisenden.* St. Christopher is the patron saint of travelers.   2. (rather dated, coll.) Man. *Was, den Meier hast du eingeladen—diesen langweiligen Patron?* What—you've invited Meier? That boring old devil?

Patron (customer) = *der Kunde, der Gast, der Besucher*
(of the arts, etc.) = *der Gönner, der Mäzen*

Patrone, die   A cartridge, for a fountain pen or a gun or to contain film.

Patron (customer) = *der Kunde, der Gast, der Besucher*
(of the arts, etc.) = *der Gönner, der Mäzen*

Patsch, der   An onomatopoeic word, denoting a "slap," "smack."

Patch (for mending) = *der Flicken*
(over eye) = *die Augenklappe*

Patt, das/patt   Stalemate. *Auch nach dieser zweiten Wahl gab es ein politisches Patt.* Even after this second election there was a political stalemate. *Das Schachspiel endete patt.* The game of chess ended in a stalemate.

Pat (light smack, etc.) = *der Klaps*
To pat (animal, etc.) = *tätscheln*

Pause, die   1. A break, from some other activity. *"Zehn Minuten Pause!" rief der Trainer.* "Ten-minute break!" shouted the coach. *Während der Pause sprach er mit den anderen Schülern darüber.* He spoke to the other pupils about it during the break.   2. Intermission, BrE also interval (at a theater, etc.); rest (mus.).

There is also a dated homonym denoting a photocopy (*die Fotokopie* is now the usual word), or (still current) a tracing in drawing. *Blaupause* blueprint.

Pause (in conversation) = *das Schweigen*

pausieren   To have/take a break. SEE **PAUSE**. *Auch der beste Spieler muß gelegentlich pausieren.* Even the best player has to have a break occasionally.

To pause (i.e., be silent for a moment) = *innehalten, schweigen*

pedantisch   Denotes general fussiness, not merely with regard to academic matters. *Was seine Kleidung betrifft, ist er sehr pedantisch.* He's very fussy about his clothes.

Pedantic = *haarspalterisch*

Pendant, das   Counterpart, opposite number. *Vergeblich sucht man in der westlichen Gesellschaft ein Pendant zur japanischen Geisha.* One looks in vain for a counterpart in western society for the Japanese geisha.

Pendant = *der Anhänger*

penetrant   Can mean "penetrating" (or "pungent," "overpowering") with relation to smells, tastes, etc. But it may also be applied to persons, when it indicates an unpleasantly insistent, pushy, or aggressive character. *Es dauerte eine Viertelstunde, bis er den penetranten Vertreter loswurde.* It took him a quarter of an hour to get rid of the pushy sales rep.

Penne, die   (sl.) School.

Pen (fountain) = *der Füller, der Füllfederhalter*
     (ballpoint) = *der Kugelschreiber*

pennen   (coll.) To sleep. *Sie hat während der ganzen Vorlesung gepennt.* She was snoozing (BrE kipping) during the whole lecture.

To pen (i.e., write) = *schreiben, verfassen*

Pension, die   **1.** A pension, though the German word denotes one specifically paid to civil servants. *in Pension gehen* To retire (of a civil servant). **2.** Guest house, boarding house. *Diese Pension in Vermont war toll.* That guest house in Vermont was great. **3.** The "board" one receives at a hotel, etc. *Vollpension kostet DM 98, Halbpension DM 84.* Full board costs 98 marks, half board 84 marks.

Pension (general) = *die Rente*

per   "By" rather than "per." *Die Ware wird immer per Bahn geschickt.* The goods are always sent by rail. *per Luftpost* by airmail. *per Du sein* This indicates that two (or more) people address each other with the informal pronoun *du* rather than the formal *Sie*.

Per = *pro*

perfekt   **1.** Perfect. **2.** Complete, settled. *Mit der Ankunft von Onkel Heinz war die Überraschung perfekt.* Uncle Heinz's arrival made the surprise complete. *Wir haben die Lieferfrist geändert und der Vertrag ist jetzt perfekt.* We've changed the delivery time and the contract is now all tied up.

Perle, die   **1.** Pearl. **2.** Bead, of such materials as wood, glass, etc. *Schweißperlen* Beads of sweat.

perplex   The German word is stronger than English "perplexed," and corresponds rather to "dumbfounded," "thunderstruck," "astounded." *Als wir hörten, daß Ingrid die Englischprüfung bestanden hatte, waren wir völlig perplex.* We were quite dumbfounded when we heard that Ingrid had passed the English test.

To perplex (baffle, puzzle) = *vor ein Rätsel stellen*

Person, die   **1.** Person. **2.** (play or film) Character. *Alle Personen in diesem Film sind frei erfunden.* All the characters in this film are fictional. **3.** Also used to refer emotively—and usually pejoratively—to a woman.

Diese eingebildete Person meint, daß sie über alles zu entscheiden hat. That conceited woman thinks that she should make all the decisions.

Personal, das Staff, personnel. *Wir brauchen dringend mehr Personal, um diese ganzen Aufträge zu bearbeiten.* We urgently need more staff to process all these orders. Care should be taken not to equate it with "personal" in such compounds as *Personalfrage. Das ist eine Personalfrage.* That's a staffing matter. (Compare: *Das ist eine persönliche Frage:* That's a personal matter.) *Personalien* (pl.) Particulars (for an identity card, etc.) *Ich muß Ihre Personalien aufnehmen—dann dürfen Sie weiterfahren.* I have to take down your particulars—and then you can continue your journey.

Personal (adj.) = *persönlich*

personell Relating to staff or personnel. *Wir hatten mit personellen Problemen zu kämpfen.* We had to cope with staffing problems.

Personal = *persönlich*

Perspektive, die 1. Perspective, both in the technical sense and with the meaning of "point of view." 2. Prospect. *Die Perspektiven für die chemische Industrie sind zur Zeit etwas düster.* The prospects for the chemicals industry are rather gloomy at the moment.

Pest, die The disease known in English as "plague." *Die Pest ist eine Krankheit, die in Europa kaum noch vorkommt.* The plague is a disease that is hardly found in Europe any more.

Pest (insect, etc.) = *der Schädling*
(irritating thing) = *die Plage*
(irritating person) = *die Nervensäge*

Petroleum, das No longer used to denote crude oil, but one of the fuels produced therefrom: kerosene, BrE paraffin.

Petroleum = *das Erdöl*

Pfannkuchen, der According to regional usage, this may denote either a pancake or a doughnut.

Pflaster, das 1. A bandage (BrE: plaster) to protect a wound. *Schnell! Hol' mir ein Pflaster! Ich habe mich geschnitten.* Quick! Fetch me a bandage! I've cut myself. 2. A type of cobbled surface formerly used a great deal in Germany and other parts of Europe, consisting of small, regular paving stones. *Das Auto ist sehr laut, wenn es über Pflaster fährt.* The car is very noisy when it is traveling over cobbles. 3. (fig.) A locality. *München ist vielleicht ein teures Pflaster geworden.* Munich's become a really expensive place.

Plaster (for walls) = *der Putz*
(for broken legs, etc.) = *der Gips*

pflastern 1. To cover (a road surface) with cobbles, paving stones. SEE **PFLASTER**. *Warum hat man den Platz gepflastert und nicht asphaltiert?* Why did they use cobbles for the surface of the square, rather than asphalt? **2.** (coll.) To hit. *Wenn du dich weiter so benimmst, pflastere ich dir eine!* If you go on behaving like that I'll sock you one!

To plaster (a wall) = *verputzen*

Phantasie, die **1.** Imagination, rather than "fantasy." *Im Aufsatzschreiben ist er schlecht, weil er überhaupt keine Phantasie hat.* He's bad at essay writing because he has absolutely no imagination. **2.** In some contexts, however, *Phantasie* may correspond to "fantasy," when it suggests imagination that goes beyond the normal limits into a world of unreality. *Ingrid nimmt Rauschgift, meidet andere Leute, und lebt in einer Phantasiewelt.* Ingrid takes drugs, avoids people, and lives in a fantasy world. SEE **FANTASIE.**

Fantasy (erotic, etc.) = *der Tagtraum*

phantasieren **1.** To fantasize. **2.** (med.) To be delirious. **3.** (mus.) To improvise. *Oft phantasierte er stundenlang auf dem Klavier.* He would often improvise for hours on the piano.

Phantom, das **1.** Phantom. **2.** (med.) Anatomy model. **3.** (fencing) Dummy for practice. *Phantombild* Photofit (I.D.) picture used in criminal investigations.

Photograph, der. SEE **FOTOGRAF.**

Photographie, die. SEE **FOTOGRAFIE.**

Phrase, die **1.** Normally pejorative, so that "phrase" is not a suitable translation unless accompanied by a suitable adjective. *Seine Rede bestand nur aus Phrasen.* His speech only consisted of empty phrases. *Phrasen dreschen* To blather (on), to talk in clichés. **2.** Also used as a technical term in grammar and music.

Phrase (set expression) = *die Redewendung*

Physiker, der "Physicist," not "physician."

Physician = *der Arzt, der Mediziner*

Pickel, der A pimple, zit, BrE spot. *Es ist doch normal, daß du in deinem Alter Pickel hast.* It's only normal to have zits at your age.

There is also a homonym meaning "pickaxe."

Pickle (pickled cucumber) = *die Essiggurke*
      (brine solution) = *die Salzlake, der Pökel*
      (vinegar solution) = *die Essigsoße, die Marinade*
      (mixture of vegetables, e.g., onions, cucumber, corn, pickled in vinegar) = *Mixed Pickles* (pl.)

British pickle, a type of relish made out of vegetables, vinegar and other ingredients and used as an accompaniment to cold meat and other dishes, is unknown in German cuisine.

picken **1.** To pick, colloquially, in the sense of extracting s.t. with one's fingers, a fork, etc. *Mit seiner Gabel pickte er Kirschen aus dem Glas.* He used his fork to pick cherries out of the jar. **2.** To peck (of birds). *Ein* *paar Hühner pickten nach den Weizenkörnern, die im Staub lagen.* A few hens were pecking at the grains of wheat lying in the dust.

To pick (select) = *(aus)wählen*

(fruit, flowers, etc.) = *pflücken*

Pietät, die   Usually more general than "piety": respect, reverence. *Eine Leiche so zu behandeln, zeugt von mangelnder Pietät.* It shows a lack of respect to treat a dead body in this way.

Piety = *die Frömmigkeit*

pikant   Piquant (taste), though the German word is used more frequently than the English and "spicy" may be a closer translation in view of this. May also be used of jokes and stories verging on the indecent without being blatantly so: risqué, racy, spicy.

Pikkolo, der   **1.** a quarter bottle (of champagne). Some speakers (and Duden) feel the correct gender for this meaning is feminine, but there is considerable uncertainty.   **2.** A now rather dated and unfamiliar term for a "trainee waiter."

Piccolo (instrument) = *die Pikkoloflöte*

Pimpf, der   Still used in certain areas (e.g., Austria) to denote a young, inexperienced boy, a "whippersnapper." But it is now probably most familiar in historical contexts, particularly as a term used to denote a member of the Nazi *Jungvolk* organization (for 10- to 14-year-olds): as such it cannot really be translated and the original term should be kept.

Pimp = *der Zuhälter*

pink; Pink, das   "Shocking pink," rather than simply "pink."

Pink = *rosa*

Pinte, die   (coll.) A drinking establishment: a pub, bar.

Pint: If not converting to metric system, *das Pint* can be used, with English pronunciation.

Plage, die   S.t. close to being intolerable, a nuisance, pest. *Diese Tauben sind zur Plage geworden.* These pigeons have become a (real) nuisance.

Plague (disease) = *die Pest*

plagen   To plague, though other translations (e.g., to bother, worry, pester) may be more appropriate in some contexts. The reflexive *sich plagen* can mean, colloquially, "to work hard," "to slave away." *Er muß sich richtig plagen, um das bißchen Geld zu verdienen.* He really has to slave (away) to earn that little bit of money. It may also be used in the context of persistent illness. *Seit vier Wochen plage ich mich mit dieser Bronchitis.* This bronchitis has been troubling me for four weeks now.

Plaid, das or **der**   Normally denotes a tartan traveling rug.

Plaid (adj.: pattern) = *kariert*

A plaid skirt = *ein karierter Rock*

Plakat, das   May mean "placard," but the German word is more general and also extends to flimsier items: poster, bill. *Die Plakate wurden von* *den Litfaßsäulen entfernt.* The posters were removed from the advertisement pillars. *die Plakatwand* billboard.

Plane, die   Tarpaulin. *Er wollte wissen, was unter der Plane versteckt war.* He wanted to know what was hidden under the tarpaulin.

Plane (level, plane surface, etc.) = *die Ebene*

   (tool) = *der Hobel*

   (tree) = *die Platane*

   (airplane) = *das Flugzeug*

planieren   To level (off) (a piece of ground, etc.). *Mit einer Raupe können wir das Gelände schnell planieren.* We can level the site quickly with a bulldozer.

To plane (wood, etc.) = *hobeln*

Planke, die   Plank (esp. in ship construction), but the word is also used as a shortened form of *Leitplanke* to denote a crash barrier such as that often found running along the center of a highway.

Plank: The more usual and general word is *das Brett.*

Plastik, die   **1.** Sculpture. *Eine moderne Plastik stand vor dem Eingang.* A modern sculpture stood at the entrance. *Der größte deutsche Meister der Plastik war Riemenschneider.* Riemenschneider was the supreme German master of sculpture.   **2.** Vividness. *Sein Erzählstil zeichnet sich durch Energie und Plastik aus.* His narrative style is distinguished by energy and vividness.   **3.** Plastic surgery, in certain compounds such as *Nasenplastik.*

Plastic (substance) = *das Plastik*

Platte, die   Plate, in the sense of "serving-dish," though it may also denote what is served up. *kalte Platte* cold dish. Otherwise it is used to denote a large number of things that have the general quality of flatness, e.g., a slab (of concrete, etc.), a table (for ping-pong), a hotplate on a cooking stove. One other important use is to denote a phonograph record (or CD: *CD-Platte*). *Von den Rolling Stones habe ich sämtliche Platten.* I have all the Rolling Stones' records.

Plate (for food) = *der Teller*

Platz, der   **1.** Place, in a few contexts. *Studienplatz* university place. In most cases, different translations are needed: **2.** Space, room. *In dieser Wohnung ist kein Platz für einen Hund.* There's no room for a dog in this apartment.   **3.** Square (in a town). *Seitdem es hier keine Autos mehr gibt, sieht man, wie schön dieser Platz ist.* Ever since they got rid of the cars you can see what a beautiful square this is.   **4.** Ground, course, court, BrE pitch, etc. (for various sports): *Sportplatz, Fußballplatz, Golfplatz, Tennisplatz. Spielplatz* Playground (for children).   **5.** Seat. *Ihr Platz ist in Reihe B.* Your seat is in row B. *Bitte, nehmen Sie Platz.* Please take a seat.

Place (general) = *die Stelle, der Ort*

plausibel Plausible, though the German word is largely free of the connotation of "convincing, even if not actually true" that the English word sometimes has. *Plausibel* is also not used of people as "plausible" is in English in such expressions as "a plausible liar." *jdm. etwas plausibel machen* To explain s.t. to s.o., make s.t. clear to s.o.

Plausible (skillful, of liar, etc.) = *geschickt*

Playback, das The use of recorded music to accompany a singer, dubbing; also lip-synching, the use of a recording of a singer to which he or she mimes. *Wenn ich zu Playback singe, fehlt mir das persönliche Verhältnis zum Orchester.* If I sing to a background recording (BrE backing track), I miss the personal rapport with the orchestra. *Der Sänger ist live nicht so gut, und wir halten es für besser, wenn wir Playback benutzen.* This singer's not so good live, and we think it's better if he lip-synchs.

Playback = *die Wiedergabe*

plump Clumsy, awkward. *Es war ein plumper Versuch, sich bei seinen Kollegen anzubiedern.* It was a clumsy attempt to ingratiate himself with his colleagues.

Plump (persons) = *pummelig, mollig*

　　　　　(animals for eating) = *fett*

Plunder, der Things no longer wanted—"trash," "junk." *Ich gebe Ihnen 50 Mark, wenn Sie den ganzen Plunder vom Boden mitnehmen.* I'll give you 50 marks if you take all that junk from the attic.

Plunder (loot) = *die Beute*

Plüsch, der Plush (the material), but this is not a suitable translation in the context of soft toys. *Plüschbär* (furry) teddy bear; *Plüschtier* (cuddly) soft toy. *Plüschaugen* (coll.) Big, gentle, rather innocent eyes.

Poesiealbum, das An autograph book, esp. one in which schoolchildren collect autographs from friends, teachers, etc. The autographs are accompanied by pieces of verse, proverbs, aphorisms, etc.

Pointe, die **1.** The final line or punch line in a joke or story. *Die Pointe kam so schnell, daß ich sie nicht mitbekommen habe.* The punch line was delivered so quickly that I didn't catch it. **2.** It may also denote the "point" of a story—i.e., the sense behind it, its significance.

Point (dot, place, argument, etc.) = *der Punkt*

　　　　(purpose) = *der Zweck, der Sinn*

　　　　(sharp end) = *die Spitze*

pointiert Concisely effective: trenchant, pithy. *eine pointierte Bemerkung* a pithy comment.

Pointed = *spitz*

Police, die (Insurance) policy. *Die Police für die Lebensversicherung erhalten Sie in den nächsten Tagen.* You'll receive the life insurance policy in the next few days.

Police = *die Polizei*

polieren 1. To polish (up). 2. (coll., in expressions of personal violence) To smash, etc. *Dem werde ich die Fresse polieren, wenn er sich weiterhin so benimmt.* I'll smash his face in if he goes on behaving like that.

Politik, die Politics, but also the normal word for "policy." *In der Politik haben Idealisten nichts zu suchen.* There's no room for idealists in politics. *Wir brauchen eine Politik, die den Hausbau fördert.* We need a policy that encourages house building.

pompös Unlike "pompous," this does not refer to people, though it can refer to a style of writing, when it is equivalent to the English word. But most commonly it refers to things that are designed or made to impress: grand, grandiose. *Ich hatte es inzwischen satt, jeden Tag pompöse Schlösser zu besichtigen.* By now I was fed up with visiting grandiose châteaux every day.
Pompous (person) = *aufgeblasen, wichtigtuerisch*

Pony, der Bangs, BrE fringe, with reference to hair. *Christine? Ist das die Blonde mit dem Pony?* Christine? Is that the blonde with the bangs?
Pony (animal) = ***das Pony***
Ponytail (hair style) = *der Pferdeschwanz*

Porto, das Postage. *Was kostet das Porto für einen Luftpostbrief nach Neuseeland?* How much is the postage for an airmail letter to New Zealand?
Port (harbor) = *der Hafen*
(wine) = *der Portwein*
(nautical: opposite of starboard) = *das Backbord*

Porzellan, der More general than English "porcelain": it can also denote ordinary "china." *Nehmen Sie am besten Blechgeschirr mit—Porzellan geht so leicht kaputt.* It's best if you take metal cooking utensils—china breaks so easily. *Diese Ming-Vase ist aus fast durchsichtigem Porzellan.* This Ming vase is made of almost transparent porcelain.

positiv "Positive" in most contexts, but the sense may sometimes be "definite," "certain." *Über seinen Verbleib wissen wir nichts Positives.* We don't know anything definite about his whereabouts. *eine positive Antwort* an answer in the affirmative.

Posse, die A traditional form of popular, often crude comedy: a farce. Posse: No real German equivalent for this American term, but paraphrases with *das Aufgebot, der Suchtrupp,* or *die Schar* are possible.

Post, die Indicates a post office as well as actual mail. *Wenn du zur Post gehst, kannst du bitte dieses Paket aufgeben?* If you're going to the post office, can you mail this parcel?
Post (job) = *die Stelle*
(mil.) = *der Posten*
(of wood, etc.) = *der Pfosten, der Pfahl*

Posten, der   1. Post (i.e., job).   2. Item (on bill, etc.). *Die Hypotheken-zinsen sind ein besonders großer Posten.* The mortgage interest is an especially big item.   3. Guard, sentry (mil.). *Posten aufstellen* to mount a guard.   4. Picket (i.e., *Streikposten*).   5. (comm.) Amount, quantity (ordered).

auf dem Posten sein To be fit (and well); to be alert, awake.

Post (job) = *die Stelle*

　　　(mil.) = *der Posten*

　　　(of wood, etc.) = *der Pfosten, der Pfahl*

potent   Used in the sexual sense, but also with regard to financial or economic strength, when English "potent" is not a happy translation and "strong" is to be preferred. *Wir suchen potente Partner, die bereit sind, in diesem lukrativen Geschäft Geld zu investieren.* We are looking for (financially) strong partners who are prepared to invest money in this lucrative business.

Potenz, die   Potency, power. SEE **POTENT**. Also "power" in the mathematical sense. *Wenn man 8 in die vierte Potenz erhebt, bekommt man 4096.* If you raise 8 to the power of four, you get 4,096.

Power, die   A vogue word with reference to stereos, ghetto-blasters, high-performance engines, etc. This has led to usages that do not translate directly into English. *Mach' mal Power!* Turn it all the way up/full on (e.g., a stereo).

Power (political) = *die Macht*

　　　(physical) = *die Kraft*

Prädikat, das   1. Predicate (grammatical, etc.).   2. Rating, judgment. *Der Film erhielt das Prädikat "wertvoll."* The film was awarded a high quality rating.   3. The word is also used in the German system of wine classification. A *Qualitätswein* can be awarded further *Prädikate* to indicate higher quality, namely, in ascending order (at least of price): *Kabinett, Spätlese, Auslese, Beerenauslese, Trockenbeerenauslese,* and *Eiswein*.

prägnant   Concise, succinct. *Er hat den Kern des Problems prägnant formuliert.* He has expressed the heart of the problem concisely.

Pregnant (woman) = *schwanger*

　　　(animal) = *trächtig*

　　　(pause, etc.) = *bedeutungsvoll*

Prägnanz, die   Concision, succinctness. SEE **PRÄGNANT**.

Pregnancy (woman) = *die Schwangerschaft*

Praktikum, das   This normally refers to a period of work experience as part of a course of study or training: placement, practical training. *Im dritten Studienjahr muß man ein Praktikum bei einer Firma absolvieren.* In the third year you have to do an internship (BrE placement) with a firm.

Practice (doctor's; practice as opposed to theory) = *die Praxis*
    (custom) = *der Brauch*
    (repetition of action, etc., to acquire skill) = *die Übung*
Practice makes perfect = *Übung macht den Meister*

Praline, die   A chocolate, as in a box of chocolates, i.e., with a center (of flavored cream, liqueur, nut, etc.). *Kein Wunder, daß er Übergewicht hat—jedes Wochenende ißt er eine Schachtel Pralinen.* It's no wonder he's overweight—he eats a box of chocolates every weekend.
BrE Praline: Various German confectioners will have various names for this particular type of chocolate, but *Praline mit Nuß- und Karamelfüllung* would be a general description.

Prämie, die   **1.** Premium (as for an insurance policy).   **2.** A bonus payment. *Wenn diese Stückzahl übertroffen wird, erhält jeder Arbeiter eine entsprechende Prämie.* Every worker receives an appropriate bonus if more items than this are produced.   **3.** A prize, e.g., in a lottery. *Bei dieser Lotterie gibt es am Monatsende zusätzliche Prämien.* In this lottery there are additional prizes at the end of the month.

Pranke, die   Paw (of large animal: lion, bear, etc.).
Prank = *der Streich*

präparieren   To preserve organs, etc., for scientific study; also "to dissect" the same. Very occasionally used to mean "to prepare."
To prepare (general) = *vorbereiten*
    (food) = *zubereiten*

Präservativ, das   A contraceptive, and—nowadays—nearly always specifically a condom. *Präservative dienen nicht nur der Empfängnisverhütung, sondern beugen auch der Verbreitung von Geschlechtskrankheiten vor.* Condoms not only serve as contraceptives, but also prevent the spread of sexually transmitted diseases.
Preservative = *das Konservierungsmittel*

Praxis, die   **1.** Practice, as opposed to theory.   **2.** Practice of a doctor or attorney.   **3.** Also, the premises themselves: doctor's office, BrE surgery. *Am besten kommen Sie gleich in die Praxis.* You'd better come to the doctor's office right away.
Practice (custom) = *der Brauch*
    (repetition of action, etc., to acquire skill) = *die Übung*
Practice makes perfect = *Übung macht den Meister*

Preis, der   **1.** Price.   **2.** Prize. *Überraschenderweise erhielt er den zweiten Preis.* Surprisingly, he was awarded second prize.

prekär   A good example of a *Fremdwort* whose exact meaning is often difficult to pin down. It is frequently applied to situations posing problems that are difficult to solve: thus *eine prekäre Lage/Situation* may denote an "awkward" (rather than "precarious") situation. Context is all-important, and other translations may be required. *Wir müssen dis-*

kret sein—es handelt sich um eine sehr prekäre Sache. We must be discreet—this is a very delicate matter. *Niemand kann diesen prekären Frieden noch retten.* No one can save this uneasy peace.

Precarious (dangerous) = *gefährlich*

Presse, die 1. Press (mechanical; journalism). 2. (rather dated, coll.) A private school that prepares pupils intensively for examinations: BrE a crammer.

Press (cupboard) = *der Wandschrank*

prickeln 1. To tingle, tickle (skin, etc.). *Nach der Dusche verspürte er ein angenehmes Prickeln auf der Haut.* The shower made his skin tingle in a pleasant way. 2. To sparkle, bubble (of liquids).

To prickle (of thorns, etc.) = *stechen*

Pricktest, der An alarming medical expression, from an English-speaking point of view, but it is simply one term to denote the "skin test" patients undergo to determine their allergies.

primitiv Sometimes means "primitive," but more often the German word is applied pejoratively to persons to denote intellectual, educational, or cultural deficiencies. *Wie konnte ein so intelligentes Mädchen diesen primitiven Kerl heiraten?* How could such an intelligent girl marry that philistine? *primitiver Fehler* basic/rudimentary error.

prinzipiell Used in a variety of ways, none of them corresponding to English "principal(ly)." 1. On principle, as a matter of principle. *Ich kaufe prinzipiell kein Obst aus diesem Land.* I don't buy any fruit from that country as a matter of principle. 2. Without exception, always. *Wir verwenden prinzipiell nur diese Art Kleister.* We always use this type of paste. 3. Relating to a principle in the sense of a basic rule. *Ein solches Vorgehen wäre prinzipiell möglich.* In principle, action of this sort would be possible. *Es handelt sich hier um einen prinzipiellen Unterschied, den man nicht außer acht lassen darf.* This is a difference of principle/a basic difference, which must not be ignored.

Principal(ly) = *hauptsächlich*

Prise, die 1. Pinch (of salt, snuff, etc.). 2. (hist.) Prize, in the sense of a captured ship.

Price = *der Preis*

Prize (in competition, etc.) = *der Preis*

probat Tried and tested, reliable, suitable. *Geldstrafen sind anscheinend kein probates Mittel, das Falschparken zu verhindern.* Fines are apparently not a suitable method for preventing illegal parking.

Probate = *gerichtliche Testamentsbestätigung*

Probe, die 1. Test. *Wir haben das Trinkwasser einer Reihe von Proben unterzogen.* We have subjected the drinking water to a number of tests. *die Probefahrt* Test drive. 2. Probationary period, trial period (for a job, etc.). *Diese Sekretärin ist auf Probe angestellt worden.* This secretary has been engaged for a probationary period. **3. Sample.** *Die Proben aus der Flußmündung ergaben besorgniserregende Radioaktivitätswerte.* The samples taken from the estuary produced alarming radioactivity levels. **4. Rehearsal.** *Die Probe lief nicht gut, weil Hamlet ständig in seinem Text steckenblieb.* The rehearsal did not go well because Hamlet kept forgetting his lines.

Probe (medical, space, etc.) = *die Sonde*

proben To rehearse. *Wir probten bis 11 Uhr, bis der Regisseur endlich zufrieden war.* We rehearsed till 11 o'clock, till the director was finally satisfied.

To probe (into) = *untersuchen*

probieren To try (s.t. to see what it is like). *Du solltest Kaffee mal ohne Zucker probieren.* You should try coffee without sugar some time.

To probe (into) = *untersuchen*

produzieren **1.** To produce. **2.** (coll.) To create s.t. undesirable or run-of-the-mill. *Solche dummen Romane könnte jeder produzieren.* Anyone could turn out this sort of stupid novel. **3.** *sich produzieren* To show off. *Es ist doch normal, wenn sich deine Kinder bei Besuch ein bißchen produzieren.* It's only normal for your children to show off a bit when there are visitors.

profan **1.** Can mean "profane," though in the sense of "not concerned with religion," "secular" (rather than indicating any lack of respect for religion). *profane Kunst* secular art. **2.** Everyday, not unusual. *Er bediente sich ziemlich profaner Formulierungen, um dieses weltbewegende Ereignis zu beschreiben.* He used quite mundane expressions to describe this world-shaking event.

Profane (blasphemous) = *gotteslästerlich*

Professor(in), der (die) In contrast to AmE, this is not a title accorded to all academic teachers. It designates those at the top of the academic hierarchy, in particular those who have a *Lehrstuhl* (chair).

Professor (AmE) = *der (die) Dozent(in)*
         (BrE) = *der (die) Professor(in)*

Profil, das **1.** Profile, in the sense of a side view, esp. of the head. But there are several other uses: **2.** A distinctive image that sets s.o. apart from others. *Durch solche Aktionen versuchte der Politiker, an Profil zu gewinnen.* The politician tried to use such campaigns to improve his image. **3.** Tread, grip (on tires and shoes). *Der Wagen mußte wegen fehlenden Profils an allen vier Reifen aus dem Verkehr gezogen werden.* The car had to be taken off the road because of bad treads on all four tires. **4.** Cross section (of a building in architectural plans).

Profile (i.e., short account, description) = *die Kurzbeschreibung, das Kurzporträt*

To keep a low profile = *sich im Hintergrund halten*

To keep a high profile = *sich in den Vordergrund drängen*

profilieren   **1.** Usually reflexive: to give oneself a distinctive image, to make a name for oneself. *Bei diesen Prozessen profilierte er sich als hervorragender Verteidiger.* In these trials he made a name for himself as a brilliant defender.   **2.** To put a tread on (the surface of a tire, etc.). *Es empfiehlt sich nicht, alte Reifen neu zu profilieren.* It is not advisable to retread old tires.

To profile (describe) = *kurz beschreiben, skizzieren*

Programm, das   Sometimes used to denote an individual broadcast. But it may also indicate the totality of TV or radio broadcasts in a particular period, or an actual TV channel. *Das Nachmittagsprogramm bietet kaum anspruchsvolle Sendungen.* The afternoon's viewing hardly contains any sophisticated programs. *Im zweiten Programm kommt auch nichts Besonderes.* There's nothing special on channel 2 either.

Program (individual broadcast) = *die Sendung*

Prominenz, die   **1.** Prominence, in the sense of the abstract quality of being in the public eye.   **2.** Prominent people, usually, though not always, as a collective noun. *Durch diese Party gewann ich Zugang zur Münchener Prominenz.* This party gave me access to Munich's VIPs. *Professor Bleike war dabei und andere Prominenzen aus der Welt der Wissenschaft.* Professor Bleike was there, as were other prominent figures from the world of science.

Promotion, die   **1.** With German pronunciation this denotes the gaining or awarding of a doctoral degree. *Er möchte bereits mit 25 die Promotion in der Tasche haben.* He'd like to have his doctorate in the bag by the time he's 25.   **2.** With English pronunciation, promotion in the context of marketing.

Promotion (to higher job) = *die Beförderung, der Aufstieg*

promovieren   To obtain, be awarded a doctorate. SEE **PROMOTION.** *Worüber haben Sie promoviert?* What subject did you do your doctorate in?

To promote (to higher job) = *befördern*

Propaganda, die   Propaganda. But the word may occasionally be encountered in business contexts in the sense of "publicity." *Wenn wir ein bißchen mehr Propaganda für Ihr nächstes Buch machen, wird es sich bestimmt besser verkaufen.* If we have a bit more publicity for your next book it's sure to sell better.

proper   Neat, tidy, clean, trim. This is a rather dated adjective, often applied to women and girls and, nowadays, having sexist connotations for many. *Propere Kellnerinnen runden das Bild eines gepflegten Lokals ab.* Trim waitresses complete the picture of a well-run restaurant.

Proper = *richtig*

Prospekt, der   Printed matter to advertise s.t.: brochure, leaflet, prospectus. *Wir bieten allerlei Pauschalreisen—am besten schicke ich Ihnen unseren Prospekt.* We offer all sorts of package tours—the best thing is if I send you our brochure.

Prospect = *die Aussicht*

Protokoll, das   1. Protocol, in the sense of diplomatic etiquette, etc.   2. The written record of a meeting, interrogation, etc.: minutes (or "statement" in certain police contexts). *Das Protokoll der letzten Sitzung liegt inzwischen vor.* The minutes of the last meeting are now available. *Über alle besonderen Vorkommnisse müssen Sie Protokoll führen.* You must keep a record of all unusual events.

Provinz, die   Province, but the word is also used collectively (and often pejoratively) where English needs a plural. *Hier in der [tiefsten] Provinz ist ein Theaterabend ein ganz bedeutendes Ereignis.* An evening at the theater is a very important event out here in the provinces/boondocks/sticks.

Provision, die   Commission, on sales, etc. *Das Gehalt eines Versicherungsvertreters ist nicht sehr hoch: der Hauptteil des Verdienstes kommt von der Provision.* An insurance agent's salary is not very high: most of the earnings come from commission.

Provision (i.e., supplying) = *die Bereitstellung, die Versorgung*
(stipulation) = *die Bestimmung*

Provisions (food) = *die Lebensmittel* (pl.), *der Proviant*

Prozent, das   Percentage, but the plural form *Prozente* can also mean "discount." *Wenn ich es hier kaufe, kriege ich Prozente.* I get a discount if I buy it here.

Prozeß, der   This can mean "process," but another major meaning refers to judicial matters: a trial, court case, lawsuit. It is a very general word in this latter sense, applying to civil and criminal matters. *Der Prozeß gegen den Mörder Charles Manson erregte weltweites Aufsehen.* The trial of the murderer Charles Manson caused a worldwide sensation. *Er führt schon wieder einen Prozeß gegen seinen Nachbarn.* He's taking his neighbor to court again.

prozessieren   To take legal action, go to court. *Wir haben nicht vor, gegen die beiden Politiker zu prozessieren.* We do not intend to take legal action against the two politicians.

To process = *verarbeiten, bearbeiten*

prüfen   1. To check, see. *Der Leutnant ging vor, um zu prüfen, ob die Straße noch befahrbar sei.* The lieutenant went on ahead to see if the road was still passable. **2.** To test. *Der Fahrlehrer hat mein Reaktionsvermögen geprüft.* The driving instructor tested my reactions.

To prove (that s.t. is true, etc.) = *beweisen*

To prove to be (i.e., turn out) = *sich erweisen als*

psychisch Mental, psychological. *Der Mißbrauch solcher Medikamente führt zu physischen und psychischen Nebenwirkungen.* The abuse of such drugs leads to physical and mental side effects.

Psychic (having a sixth sense): No single translation equivalent. Paraphrases with expressions like *übersinnliche Kräfte* can be used.

Publikum, das Normally a less general word than English "public": audience (theater, etc.), crowd (sport), customers, clientele (of a business); also specific groups of fans, admirers, readers. *Als das Stück zu Ende war, applaudierte das Publikum begeistert.* When the play was over the audience applauded enthusiastically. *Das Publikum in diesem Restaurant besteht fast ausschließlich aus Geschäftsleuten.* The clientele in this restaurant consists almost exclusively of business people. *Der Autor hat sein Publikum enttäuscht.* The author disappointed his readers.

Public = *die Öffentlichkeit*

Pudding, der This corresponds to BrE "pudding" only in the sense of a type of cold, sweet dessert made with milk.

BrE Pudding (blood sausage) = *die Blutwurst*

BrE Pudding (general term for dessert) = *der Nachtisch, das Dessert*

Puff, der There are several homonyms here. **1.** Blow, prod, nudge, thump, etc. *Sie gab ihm einen leichten Puff mit dem Ellenbogen.* She gave him a nudge with her elbow. *Knuff* is the more usual word. **2.** Brothel: a colloquial, though not vulgar, expression. *Auf dem Stadtplan hatte jemand den Puff markiert.* Someone had marked the brothel on the town map. **3.** In the compound *Wäschepuff*, a "linen basket" (for washing).

Puff of smoke = *die Rauchwolke*

Puff of air = *der Luftstoß*

Puff, das A board game similar to backgammon.

Puff of smoke = *die Rauchwolke*

Puff of air = *der Luftstoß*

puffen **1.** To puff (e.g., of a locomotive, or of smoke from a chimney). **2.** To hit, to nudge, to prod. *Sie puffte ihm in den Rücken.* She prodded him in the back. *Knuffen* is the more usual word.

To puff (a cigarette, etc.) = *paffen*

Puffer, der **1.** Not s.o. or s.t. that puffs, but a "buffer" (on railroad rolling stock). *der Pufferstaat* buffer state. **2.** A shortened form of *Kartoffelpuffer* = potato fritter.

Pulli, der A colloquial shortening of *Pullover.* *Ich ziehe meinen blauen Pulli an.* I'll put my blue pullover/sweater on.

Pulley (i.e., block and tackle) = *der Flaschenzug*
    (wheel only) = *die Rolle*

Pump, der *auf Pump* (coll.) Purchased on credit. *Meiers haben schon immer auf Pump gelebt.* The Meiers have always lived on credit (BrE on tick).

Pump = *die Pumpe*

pumpen **1.** To pump. **2.** (coll.) To lend, to borrow. *Kannst du mir 10 Mark pumpen?* Can you lend me 10 marks?

Punkt, der As a punctuation term, this corresponds to "period," BrE "full stop." *Hier sollte kein Komma, sondern ein Punkt stehen.* There should be a period here, not a comma.

punktuell **1.** Of a selective nature, dealing only with certain cases or points. *Punktuelle Promille-Tests sind bei vielen Autofahrern unbeliebt.* Random breath tests are unpopular with many drivers. *Bei dieser Diskussion sollten wir nicht punktuell, sondern global vorgehen.* We should consider general issues rather than selective points in this discussion. **2.** In the context of assessment procedures, *punktuell* indicates a single examination rather than continuous assessment. *Eine punktuelle Prüfung kann über ein vierjähriges Studium keinen Aufschluß geben.* A single examination cannot give adequate information about a four-year course of study.

Punctual = *pünktlich*

Puppe, die **1.** Marionette, puppet. **2.** Doll. *Sind Puppen nur für Mädchen geeignet?* Are dolls only suitable for girls? **3.** Dummy (for clothes). *Die nackten Puppen im Schaufenster wirkten grotesk.* The naked dummies in the shop window seemed grotesque. **4.** Pupa (of insect). **5.** (coll.) Girl—sexist in tone.

Puppet (i.e., s.o. without real power) = *die Marionette*

pur Occasionally means "pure" in the sense of "sheer," "utter." *purer Neid* pure/sheer envy. Usually means "undiluted," "straight," "neat" with reference to drinks. *Ich trinke meinen Whisky lieber pur.* I prefer to drink my whiskey straight.

Purpur, der Crimson (except in fixed phrases like *den Purpur tragen* = to wear the purple).

Purple (adj.) = *violett, lila*

puzzeln To work a jigsaw puzzle. *Ich puzzle nur, wenn ich krank bin.* I only work jigsaws when I'm ill.

To puzzle = *(herum)rätseln*

Puzzle, das Jigsaw puzzle.

Puzzle (s.t. difficult to understand) = *das Rätsel*
    (game) = *das Rätselspiel, das Geduldsspiel*

Q

quaken Onomatopoeic word, applied in particular to frogs ("to croak") and ducks ("to quack"), and also, pejoratively, to people ("to squawk").

To quake = *beben, zittern*

quäken Onomatopoeic word to denote an unpleasantly shrill sound: to screech, squawk.

To quake = *beben, zittern*

qualifiziert Qualified, of a worker, but also of the work itself: professional, expert. *Für qualifizierte Arbeit muß man eben mehr bezahlen.* You simply have to pay more for professional work.

Qualm, der (Dense, thick) smoke. *Der Qualm von den brennenden Reifen war unerträglich.* The dense smoke from the burning tires was unbearable.

Qualm (misgiving) = *das Bedenken*

Qualms of conscience = *Gewissensbisse* (pl.)

qualmen To (give off) smoke (of a thick, dense nature). SEE **QUALM**.

Quartier, das Like English "quarters," this can refer to military accommodations. It is also, however, found in more general contexts, and also with reference to holiday accommodations. *Innerhalb von 24 Stunden hatte ich ein neues Quartier bezogen.* Within 24 hours I had moved into new accommodations.

Quarter (one-fourth; town district) = *das Viertel*

quellen 1. To stream, well, spring, pour (from). *Klares Wasser quoll aus der Spalte im Gestein.* Clear water poured out of the crack in the rocks. **2.** To soak (of beans, etc., left in water). *Diese Bohnen muß man mindestens zwei Stunden quellen lassen.* You have to leave these beans to soak for at least two hours.

To quell (rebellion, etc.) = *unterdrücken, niederschlagen*

Queue, das (Billiard) cue.

BrE Queue (line of people) = *die Schlange*

quitt 1. Quits, even (with s.o.). *Ich habe ihm beim Umzug geholfen, wie er mir vor zwei Jahren, und jetzt sind wir quitt.* I helped him move, as he helped me two years ago, and now we're quits. **2.** It may also denote that a relationship has been severed. *Mit Angelika bin ich jetzt quitt, und ich habe seit zwei Wochen eine neue Freundin.* Angelika and I are through, and I've had a new girlfriend for two weeks.

quittieren 1. To quit, resign (esp. in the phrase *den Dienst quittieren*). More commonly: **2.** To give a receipt for or sign for s.t. *Ich habe den Empfang der eingeschriebenen Sendung quittiert.* I signed for the registered letter.   **3.** To react to. *Er quittierte diese Vorwürfe mit einem müden Lächeln.* He reacted to these criticisms with a weary smile.

To quit (give up) = *aufgeben*

     (stop) = *aufhören*

Quote, die   **1.** Quota. *Einwanderungsquote* immigration quota.   **2.** (statistics) More commonly, rate, proportion, percentage. *Die Arbeitslosenquote beträgt zur Zeit 8%.* The unemployment rate is 8% at the moment.

Quota (of goods) = *das Kontingent*

R

raffiniert   **1.** Refined, with reference to sugar or oil. But far more often it is an adjective denoting: **2.** Cleverness or even cunning. *Er ist ein raffinierter Taktiker, dem du auf keinen Fall trauen solltest.* He's a cunning tactician whom you should on no account trust.   **3.** Attractiveness, stylishness. *Das Restaurant ist wegen seiner raffinierten Ausstattung berühmt.* The restaurant is famous for its stylish decor.

Refined (i.e., genteel, distinguished) = *vornehm*

ragen   To stand out as taller against a background: to tower, project, loom, etc. *Aus den Wolken ragten einzelne Berggipfel.* Isolated mountain peaks jutted out of the clouds.

To rage = *toben, wüten*

Rakete, die   **1.** A rocket, whether a firework, a weapon, or a space vehicle.   **2.** Missile, esp. of the nuclear kind. *1962 entdeckten die Amerikaner, daß es sowjetische Raketen auf Kuba gab.* In 1962 the Americans discovered that there were Soviet missiles in Cuba.

Rampe, die   **1.** Ramp.   **2.** (theat.) Forestage, apron.

rangieren   **1.** To rank (of relative order). *Er rangiert bestimmt unter den drei besten Schriftstellern der Nachkriegszeit.* He certainly ranks among the three best writers of the postwar era.   **2.** To shunt (of trains). *Der Unfall ist beim Rangieren geschehen.* The accident occurred during shunting.

To range (extend from . . . to) = *gehen, reichen (von . . . bis)*

rank   Normally used in the doublet *rank und schlank* = slim (and supple).

Rank (vegetation) = *üppig*

    (rancid) = *ranzig*

Ranke, die   A tendril, shoot (e.g., of a vine, strawberry plant, etc.).

Rank (mil.) = *der Rang*

    (status) = *der Stand, der Status*

ranken To entwine itself (around), of climbing plants. *Um den Baum-stamm rankte sich dichter Efeu.* Dense ivy was entwined round the tree-trunk.

To rank (among) = *rangieren (unter), zählen (zu)*

rasch Indicates speed, promptness. *Rasch kam ihre Antwort.* Her reply arrived promptly.

Rash (action) = *voreilig, überstürzt*

(person) = *unbesonnen*

Rasse, die 1. Race (ethnic). 2. Breed (of animals). *Einen Hund dieser Rasse würde ich nie kaufen.* I would never buy that breed of dog. 3. "Spirit," as an exciting quality of wine, certain animals (notably horses)—and, with sexist connotations, women. *Die Frau hat Rasse.* That woman has spirit/is hot-blooded.

rassig Fiery, hot-blooded, spirited. SEE **RASSE** 3.

Racy (risqué) = *gewagt*

Rat, der 1. Advice. 2. Council. *Stadtrat* town council, city council. 3. Councilor. Thus *Stadtrat* may also mean "town/city councilor." There are also a number of special titles that are essentially untranslatable, though approximate equivalents can be supplied: thus the academic *wissenschaftlicher Rat* corresponds roughly to an "assistant professor" in the U.S.A. or a "lecturer" in Britain.

Rat = *die Ratte*

Rate, die Rate, in certain statistical contexts, but more commonly an "installment" of payment. *Die Anzahlung beträgt 200 Mark: den Rest zahlen Sie in zehn monatlichen Raten.* The deposit is 200 marks—you pay the rest in ten monthly installments.

Rathaus, das Not a rat-infested house, but a "town hall," "city hall."

Ratio, die (The faculty of) reason. *Durch die Ratio allein kann man die Leute nicht überzeugen.* You cannot convince people by reason alone.

Ratio = *das Verhältnis*

rationell A term normally used in economic contexts, corresponding to "efficient" rather than "rational." *Der rationellere Einsatz der Maschinen würde den Gewinn steigern.* The more efficient use of the machines would increase profits.

Rational = *rational, vernünftig*

Real- (lexikon/politik/schule) In compound nouns *Real-* may well correspond to "real" (as in *Realeinkommen* = real income), but there are some well-established exceptions. *Realenzyklopädie, Reallexikon* = (specialist) encyclopedia or dictionary; *Realpolitik* = political realism, pragmatism (the German word is sometimes used in English); a *Realschule* is a type of secondary school, occupying the middle rung of the tripartite ladder, "above" the *Hauptschule,* but "below" the *Gymnasium.*

Realisation, die Realization (in the sense of "making real"), but also "production" in the context of the performing arts (esp. TV and film). Realization (awareness) = *die Erkenntnis*

realisieren **1.** To realize (in the sense of "to make real"), to carry out, etc. **2.** To produce (TV, film, etc.). SEE **REALISATION**. To realize (become aware) = *erkennen, einsehen*

rechnen **1.** To reckon, in a variety of contexts, though other translations may be preferable. *Mit solchem Wetter haben wir nicht gerechnet.* We didn't expect this sort of weather. **2.** (math.) To calculate, do calculations, work out. *Moment mal—so schnell kann ich nicht rechnen.* Just a moment—I can't do calculations that quickly.

Rechnung, die Bill, check, invoice. Reckoning: by my reckoning *meiner Schätzung nach;* the day of reckoning *der Tag der Abrechnung*

Recorder, der The context will make it clear whether it denotes a tape recorder, cassette recorder, or video recorder: unlike English, German quite often uses the word as a shortened form for *Kassettenrecorder, Videorecorder, Radiorecorder* (the latter corresponding to English radio/cassette recorder). Recorder (musical instrument) = *die Blockflöte*

reell **1.** Real, actual. **2.** Honest, respectable, sound. *Ein reeller Geschäftsmann würde so etwas nicht tun.* A respectable businessman wouldn't do something like that. *Das sind hier ganz reelle Preise.* They've very reasonable prices here.

Referent, der This may be used in the technical linguistic sense of the English "referent" (i.e., a thing referred to), but its normal meaning indicates s.o. who can give an expert opinion on s.t. This could be a speaker giving a paper on a particular subject or a person giving an opinion on a piece of scholarly work. It could also be s.o. in charge of a *Referat*, i.e., an administrative department dealing with a particular area. *Unser Thema heute abend ist die Schaffung von Biotopen, unser Referent Herr Dr. Martens.* Our subject this evening is the creation of biotopes and our speaker is Dr. Martens. *Unser Referent für Umweltfragen hat starke Bedenken gemeldet.* Our expert in charge of environmental issues has voiced serious doubts.

referieren. SEE **REFERENT**. **1.** To give a (scholarly) paper on a subject. *Herr Dr. Martens hat über die Schaffung von Biotopen referiert.* Dr. Martens gave a paper on the creation of biotopes. **2.** To give a report or summary on a particular field (e.g., research developments). *In diesem Artikel referiert er über die neuesten Forschungsergebnisse.* In this article he gives a summary of the latest research findings. To refer (to s.t.) = *sich beziehen (auf eine Sache)*

Reformhaus, das   Not a corrective establishment for wayward young people, but a shop that caters to the health-conscious: a health food shop (though these shops have a longer history than most health food establishments in the U.S.A. or Britain, and the movement that produced them dates back to around 1890).

Reform house/school = *die Erziehungsanstalt, die Besserungsanstalt.* Both terms are no longer in use.

Reformkost, die   Not the cost of reform, but "health food." SEE RE-FORMHAUS; KOST.

Regal, das   (A set of) shelves. *Wir haben jetzt so viele Bücher, daß wir unbedingt ein neues Regal kaufen müssen.* We have so many books now that we simply must buy a new bookcase.

Regal (adj.) = *königlich*

Regiment, das   **1.** (mil.) Regiment.   **2.** System of discipline, rule. *Er klagte über das harte Regiment der Offiziersschule.* He complained about the hard discipline at the military academy. *Unser neuer Chef führt ein strenges Regiment.* Our new boss is very strict.

Register, das   Register, in the sense of certain official lists, or in the technical musical sense. But most commonly an "index" (at the back of a book, etc.). *Es ist ein tolles Buch—aber ohne Register fast völlig unbrauchbar.* It's a great book, but almost totally useless without an index.

reif   Ripe, but also "mature" (esp. of people). *Für sein Alter ist er sehr reif.* He's very mature for his age.

Reklamation, die   Complaint, esp. in business and retailing contexts. *Es liegen viele Reklamationen wegen unsachgemäßer Verpackung vor.* There have been a lot of complaints regarding unsuitable packaging.

Reclamation (of land) = *die Wiedergewinnung*

Reklame, die   Advertising; also an individual advertisement or commercial. *Inzwischen geben wir über 10 Millionen Mark im Jahr für Reklame aus.* We now spend over 10 million marks a year on advertising. *Ich finde die Reklame für dieses neue Waschpulver ziemlich blöd.* I think the advertisement for this new washing powder is pretty stupid.

Reclaim (noun), baggage reclaim = *die Gepäckausgabe*

reklamieren.   SEE REKLAMATION. To complain. *Sie müssen innerhalb von 14 Tagen reklamieren.* You must complain within 14 days. *Er hat die Versandkosten reklamiert.* He queried the transport costs.

To reclaim   (land) = *(zurück)gewinnen*
(baggage) = *abholen*
(claim back, tax, etc.) = *zurückfordern*

Rektor, der   **1.** This normally indicates the principal of various educational institutions, in particular of an elementary/primary school (*Grundschule*) or the secondary schools *Realschule* and *Hauptschule,* or the (elected) head of some tertiary establishments, both of the university and *Fachhochschule* (polytechnic) types. Nomenclature varies considerably, however, in particular in the case of universities. **2.** The holder of an ecclesiastical office in the Roman Catholic church.

rentabel Profitable. *Diese Bahnstrecke ist nicht mehr rentabel.* This section of railroad is no longer profitable.

Rente, die Pension (in particular that paid to those who are not *Beamte*, i.e., not civil servants). *Er bezieht eine monatliche Rente von über 3.000 Mark.* He receives a pension of over 3,000 marks a month. *in Rente gehen* To retire.

Rent = *die Miete*

rentieren (sich) To be profitable, worthwhile. *Das neue Geschäft beginnt sich zu rentieren.* The new business is beginning to show a profit. *Es rentiert sich nicht, dieses alte Radio noch einmal zu reparieren.* It's not worth repairing that old radio again.

To rent = *mieten*

repetieren This is an essentially dated expression to denote the rereading and learning of notes, etc., for a test: to study, to review, BrE to revise.

To repeat = *wiederholen*

Repetition, die Study (for a test), BrE revision. SEE **REPETIEREN**.

Repetition = *die Wiederholung*

Repräsentation, die This word and the associated adjective **repräsentativ** and verb **repräsentieren** have two basic meanings. The first is equivalent to English "representation," "representative," and "to represent." The second is peculiar to German and concerns the idea of creating a favorable impression on other people, sometimes in the specific context of diplomatic or ceremonial duties, but also quite generally when the aim is to demonstrate one's status (or status symbols) —in effect, to show off. Neat translation equivalents do not exist, and paraphrases are often needed. *Kein Diplomat braucht einen solchen Wagen im überfüllten Singapur—er dient ausschließlich der Repräsentation.* No diplomat needs such a car in overcrowded Singapore—it is there exclusively to create the right impression. *Eine repräsentative Villa mit Swimming-Pool gehört zum Lebensstil eines Topmanagers.* A prestigious villa with swimming pool is part of a top executive's lifestyle. *Ich kaufe mir einen Rolls-Royce—wir müssen auch ein bißchen repräsentieren.* I'm buying a Rolls-Royce—we've got to put on a bit of a show too. *Selbstverständlich muß die Frau eines Botschafters ihm beim Repräsentieren helfen.* Of course an ambassador's wife must help him with his official (and social) duties.

repräsentativ. SEE **REPRÄSENTATION**.

repräsentieren. SEE **REPRÄSENTATION**.

requirieren To requisition, commandeer. *Auch solche kleinen Boote wurden von der Marine requiriert.* Even such small boats were requisitioned by the Navy.

To require = *benötigen, verlangen*

Requisit, das Occasionally found in the sense of English "requisite," meaning an accessory needed for a particular purpose, but much more common in the plural in the sense of "props" (properties) in the context of the theater and filmmaking. *Herr Klein ist für die Requisiten zuständig.* Herr Klein is in charge of the props.

BrE Toilet requisites = *Toilettenartikel* (pl.)

Requisite (adj.) = *erforderlich*

Residenz, die This may denote the residence, i.e., palace, of a reigning prince, or the capital of a state ruled by a prince, i.e., royal seat. It is not used to denote the place where ordinary people live, though it is sometimes applied to people holding high office, such as ambassadors, governors, etc.

Residence = *der Wohnsitz*

resignieren To give up, in the sense of surrendering to discouragement and abandoning one's endeavors. *Er resignierte, nachdem seine hundertste Bewerbung keinen Erfolg gehabt hatte.* He gave up when his hundredth application met with no success.

To resign (job, as employee) = *kündigen*

(from public office, committee, etc.) = *zurücktreten*

resolut Like "resolute," this denotes firmness of purpose and strength of will in achieving that purpose, but the German word tends to indicate a permanent trait of character, rather than an attitude in a particular situation. There is also a tendency for it to be applied to women. *Die Ministerin war eine äußerst resolute Frau, vor der er Angst hatte.* The minister was an extremely determined woman and he was afraid of her.

Resolute = *(fest) entschlossen*

Resonanz, die 1. Response, in the sense of the reaction to s.t. by means of discussion (and often agreement). *Sein neuester Vorschlag ist auf wenig Resonanz gestoßen.* His latest proposal has met with little response. 2. Resonance, in the context of sound waves, music, etc.

respektive 1. This is the stylistically rather elevated *Fremdwort* equivalent of *beziehungsweise (bzw.)*, and, like that word and English "respectively," may be used to make clear the relations between groups containing an equal number of elements. *Klaus und Heinrich wohnen in Göttingen respektive Kassel.* Klaus and Heinrich live in Göttingen and Kassel respectively. 2. Like *beziehungsweise* and unlike "respectively," it is also used to make a previous statement more accurate, corresponding to "or rather," "to be more precise." *Sie wohnt in Ham-*

burg, respektive in einem Vorort von Hamburg. She lives in Hamburg, or rather in a suburb of Hamburg.

Ressort, das   Department, in the sense of a (concrete or abstract) sphere of responsibility. *Herr Dr. Thewes leitet das Ressort "Forschung und Entwicklung."* Dr. Thewes is in charge of the research and development department. *Das fällt nicht in mein Ressort.* That's not my department.

Resort (tourist) = *der Ferienort,* or specifically *der Skiort, das Seebad,* etc.

As a last resort, in the last resort = *wenn alle Stricke reißen, im schlimmsten Fall, schlimmstenfalls*

Rest, der   Rest (remainder), in some contexts. *Ich behalte 40 Prozent und du bekommst den Rest.* I keep 40 percent and you get the rest. But in other contexts more appropriate translations like "remainder," "remnant(s)," "leftovers," "remains" will be needed (and the very common plural *Reste* can, of course, never be translated by "rests"). *Diese riesigen Steine sind die einzigen Reste dieser Zivilisation.* These enormous stones are the sole remnants of this civilization. *Diese Reste kannst du der Katze geben.* You can give these leftovers to the cat. *Wenn du 30 durch 7 dividierst, bekommst du einen Rest von 2.* If you divide 30 by 7 you get a remainder of 2.

restlos   Complete, total. *Cato verlangte die restlose Zerstörung von Karthago.* Cato demanded the complete destruction of Carthage.

Restless = *unruhig, rastlos*

resümieren   To give a summary of; to recapitulate. *Die Theorie ist zu komplex, als daß ich sie in ein paar Sätzen resümieren könnte.* The theory is too complex for me to summarize in a few sentences. *Zum Schluß darf ich die Hauptpunkte resümieren.* Finally, let me recapitulate the main points.

To resume (start again) = *wiederaufnehmen, fortsetzen*

(seat) = *wieder einnehmen*

Retorte, die   1. (chem.) Retort.   **2.** (fig.) But the word is also used nontechnically with reference to the creation of s.t. synthetically, by "unnatural" means. *aus der Retorte* Synthetic. *Ich mag diese Ferienorte aus der Retorte nicht, mit ihren Riesenhotels und Souvenirläden.* I don't like these synthetic resorts with their huge hotels and souvenir shops. *Retortenbaby* Test-tube baby.

Retort (sharp answer) = *scharfe Antwort, Erwiderung*

Revanche, die   1. May denote revenge, but also in the less bitter context of sports and games: a rematch, return match, return game. *OK—wir haben verloren. Aber gebt ihr uns Revanche?* OK—we've lost. But will you give us a return match?   **2.** The returning of a favor or reciprocation of help given. *Ulli hat mir beim Radwechsel geholfen und als Revanche* *habe ich ihn zum Abendessen eingeladen.* Ulli helped me change the wheel and I've invited him to dinner to reciprocate.

Revenge = *die Rache*

revanchieren, sich. SEE **REVANCHE.** *Mit diesem Sieg haben wir uns für die Niederlage von letzter Woche revanchiert.* This victory has made up for last week's defeat. *Danke, daß du uns beim Umzug so geholfen hast: wir werden uns bestimmt revanchieren!* Thanks for helping us so much with the move: we will certainly return the favor.

To revenge oneself = *sich rächen*

Revers, das Lapel, revers. The German word is applied to both men's and women's clothing. *Er trug eine seltsame Medaille am Revers.* He wore a strange medal on his lapel.

Reverse (opposite) = *das Gegenteil*

(back) = *die Rückseite*

revidieren **1.** To revise (one's opinion, a text, etc.). **2.** To audit. **3.** To review, to check. SEE **REVISION.**

Revision, die Has various uses, all with the basic idea of checking. **1.** (jur.) Appeal. *Wir haben verloren, aber wir gehen in die Revision.* We've lost, but we shall appeal. **2.** (comm.) Audit(ing). *Die große Revision findet nächsten Monat statt.* The big audit takes place next month. **3.** (print.) Final proofread(ing). **4.** Change, revision (of policy, opinion, etc.).

Rezept, das **1.** (Medical) prescription. *Kannst du bitte dieses Rezept bei der Apotheke abgeben?* Could you hand in this prescription at the pharmacy, please? **2.** Recipe. *Ich kenne ein wunderbares Curry-Rezept.* I know a wonderful curry recipe.

Receipt (written confirmation of payment) = *die Quittung*

(at supermarket checkout, etc.) = *der (Kassen)bon*

(act of receiving) = *der Erhalt, der Empfang*

rigoros Adamant, firm. Indicates a strict or even ruthless approach to s.t., whereas English "rigorous" may denote care and precision (e.g., in analysis and study). Context is the all-important factor in deciding where the two words are equivalent and where not. *Was die Frage der Rückerstattung betrifft, ist er ganz rigoros.* He's quite adamant about the question of reimbursement.

Rigorous (i.e., careful, thorough) = *gründlich*

Rind, das Cow; (pl.) cattle. *Wir hatten früher 50 Rinder.* We used to have 50 head of cattle.

Rind (of cheese) = *die Rinde*

(of fruit) = *die Schale*

(of bacon) = *die Schwarte*

Rinde, die   Rind (on cheese), but also bark (of a tree) or crust (of a loaf). In anatomical contexts it denotes the cortex of certain organs (e.g., kidney).

ringen   To wrestle, struggle. *Auf dem Bild rangen zwei Dinosaurier miteinander.* The picture showed two dinosaurs engaged in a struggle. *die Hände ringen* To wring one's hands; *jdm. etwas aus der Hand ringen* To wrest s.t. out of s.o.'s hand.

To ring (bell) = *klingeln, läuten*
          (to telephone) = *anrufen, telefonieren*

Ringer, der   A wrestler. *Ich konnte es nicht verstehen, daß sich diese Ringer anscheinend nie ernsthaft verletzten.* I couldn't understand why these wrestlers apparently never got seriously hurt.

(Bell-)ringer = *der Glöckner*

Dead ringer: He's a dead ringer for the senator. *Er sieht dem Senator verblüffend ähnlich.*

Rippe, die   Rib. *Beim Unfall habe ich mir zwei Rippen gebrochen.* I broke two ribs in the accident.

Rip (tear) = *der Riß*

Rist, der   **1.** A term most commonly used in the context of sport, sports injuries, etc., and denoting the "instep" of the foot or, less usually, the "back" of the hand.   **2.** Withers of a horse.

Wrist = *das Handgelenk*

Roastbeef, das   May denote either roast beef or (uncooked) beef. It corresponds to English "roast beef" when cooked meat is being referred to, though it should be noted that the German word very often applies to *cold* roast beef, rather than hot. Unlike the English word, however, *Roastbeef* can also denote a particular cut of raw beef. *Ich habe ein sehr zartes Roastbeef gekauft, das wir am Sonntag braten können.* I've bought a very tender beef roast that we can cook on Sunday.

(Hot) roast beef = *der Rinderbraten*

Robbe, die   Seal (animal).

Robber = *der Räuber*

robben   To crawl (on one's stomach). *Die Soldaten robbten bis zur Umzäunung.* The soldiers crawled as far as the perimeter fence.

To rob (person) = *bestehlen*
          (bank, house, etc.) = *ausrauben*

Rock, der   **1.** Skirt. *Ich finde, der Rock ist etwas zu kurz.* I think the skirt is a bit too short.   **2.** In older contexts or in dialect it may also denote a man's jacket.

There is also a modern homonym meaning "rock" in the musical sense.

Rock = *der Fels*

Roller, der Roller (high wave). But most commonly a "scooter," as used by children or, as a motor vehicle, by adults (*Motorroller*).
(Road-)roller = *die (Straßen)walze*
(for applying paint) = *die Rolle*
(for hair) = *der Lockenwickler*

Roman, der Novel. *Ich habe alle Romane von Henry James gelesen.* I've read all Henry James's novels.
Roman = *der Römer*

Romancier, der Novelist.
Romancer = *der Phantast*

Romanist, der Denotes a student or scholar not of ancient Rome, but of Romance languages (and literature).

rosa Pink. *Sie trug eine rosa Bluse.* She was wearing a pink blouse.
Rose(-colored) = *rosarot* To see the world through rose-colored glasses (BrE spectacles) *die Welt durch eine rosarote Brille sehen*

Rosine, die Raisin.
Rosin/resin (substance) = *das Harz*
(specifically for violin bow, etc.) = *das Kolophonium*

Routine, die 1. Routine, with the rather negative connotation of the English word. 2. Experience. *Bei solchen Aufträgen zählt die langjährige Routine.* It's long experience that counts with this type of order.

routiniert Experienced. *Natürlich braucht die Mannschaft frisches Blut— aber die routinierten Spieler dürfen auch nicht fehlen.* Of course the team needs new blood, but we need the experienced players too.
Routine (adj.) = *routinemäßig*

Rowdy, der (pl.: *Rowdys* or *Rowdies*) The German word is more general in application than English "rowdy," which primarily denotes noisy and uncouth behavior. A *Rowdy* may engage in violence (= "hooligan") or senseless destruction (= "vandal"). *Im Fußballstadion machten sich die Rowdys wieder bemerkbar.* The hooligans were making their presence felt again in the soccer stadium. *Rowdies hatten das Wartehäuschen demoliert.* Vandals had smashed up the bus shelter. *Straßenrowdy, Verkehrsrowdy* road hog.

Rubrik, die This corresponds to English "rubric" in various specialist senses, but not in the commonest use of the German word, namely to denote a (usually regular) section or column in a newspaper or magazine. *Ab nächster Woche gibt es eine neue Rubrik "Männermode."* From next week we shall be featuring a section on men's fashion.
BrE Rubric (examination instructions) = *Prüfungsanweisungen* (pl.)

rüde There is considerable overlap between this and English "rude," but generally it can be said that *rüde* tends to denote behavior that is coarsely insensitive or excessively brusque, whereas English "rude" indicates more the idea of breaking the accepted rules of courtesy.

Certain contexts may thus require translations such as "uncouth" or "brusque," rather than "rude."

Ruder, das   **1.** Rudder, helm.   **2.** Oar.

Rüffel, der   Telling-off. *jdm. einen Rüffel erteilen* To give s.o. a telling-off.

Ruffle (frill on dress, etc.) = *die Rüsche*

(ripple on surface of water, etc.) = *das Kräuseln*

rüffeln (coll.)   To tell off (i.e., to reprimand). SEE **RÜFFEL.** (The verb is relatively uncommon.)

To ruffle (feathers, etc.) = *zerzausen*

(annoy) = *verärgern*

Ruhr, die   The River Ruhr, but also a word for "dysentery." *Die meisten Soldaten hatten die Ruhr.* Most of the soldiers had dysentery.

The Ruhr (as a geographical area, not just the river) = *das Ruhrgebiet*

rumoren   **1.** To make a noise, often "to rumble" (stomach, etc.). *Seitdem ich die Äpfel gegessen hatte, rumorte es in meinem Magen.* My stomach had been rumbling ever since I had eaten the apples.   **2.** May also be applied to (civil) unrest. *Seit November rumorte es in Bukarest.* There had been unrest in Bucharest since November.   **3.** Also used of (recurring) thoughts. *In meinem Kopf rumorte nur der Gedanke an ihre Untreue.* The thought of her unfaithfulness kept going round and round in my head.

Rumor (noun) = *das Gerücht*

rumpeln   To make a noise, specifically "to rumble" or "to clatter" (sound words rarely correspond exactly in any two languages). *Das Rumpeln der Straßenbahnen weckte ihn jeden Morgen um fünf Uhr.* The rumbling of the streetcars woke him at five every morning.

To rumple (clothes, sheets, paper) = *zerknittern, zerknüllen*

(hair) = *verwuscheln, zerzausen*

Rumpf, der   **1.** Body of human being or animal, usually without arms, legs, or head: torso, carcass.   **2.** Trunk, body, when referring to a living person (e.g., in descriptions of fitness exercises).   **3.** Hull (of ship).   **4.** Fuselage (of aircraft).

Rump (of animal) = *Hinterbacken* (pl.)

(of bird) = *der Bürzel*

(humorous, of person) = *der Hintern, der Hinterteil*

Runde, die   **1.** Round, in several contexts, e.g., stage in a sporting competition or in negotiations, or as an order of drinks for a group of people.   **2.** Lap, circuit (in races). *Bei der zehnten Runde kam sein Wagen von der Piste ab.* In the tenth lap his car left the track.   **3.** Company, group of people meeting socially. *Die ganze Runde sang die Nationalhymne.* The assembled company sang the national anthem.   **4.** A walk (for recreational purposes). *So, ich mache schnell eine Runde—ich* *brauche frische Luft.* Well, I'm going for a quick stroll—I need some fresh air.   **5.** Beat, rounds (of policeman, night watchman, etc.).

rüsten   To arm (mil.). *Ihre Armee ist schlecht gerüstet.* Their army is poorly equipped.   *sich rüsten* (fig.) To prepare, to get ready. (This usage is largely confined to rather formal or literary style.) *Wir müssen uns für diese neue Herausforderung rüsten.* We must prepare for this new challenge.

To rust = *rosten*

rüstig   Used of old people who are still fit and active: sprightly. *Sie hat immer noch zwei ganz rüstige Großeltern.* She still has two very sprightly grandparents.

Rusty = *rostig*

Rüstung, die   **1.** Armament; arms, weapons. *Wir geben viel zu viel für Rüstung aus.* We are spending much too much on arms.   **2.** (hist.) (Suit of) armor.

To rust = *rosten*

S

Sakko, der or **das**   Sport coat, BrE sports jacket. *Bei diesem warmen Wetter brauchst du doch keinen Sakko!* You certainly don't need a sport coat in this hot weather!

Sack = *der Sack*

Salat, der   Salad, though different countries have of course different ideas about what belongs in a salad. Also, specifically, a (head of) lettuce (also referred to as *Kopfsalat*). *Ich möchte ein Pfund Tomaten und zwei Kopf Salat bitte.* I'd like a pound of tomatoes and two heads of lettuce (BrE lettuces), please. *Da haben wir den Salat!* We're in a fine mess!

Saline, die   Salt works. *In dieser Saline wird Süßwasser aus Meerwasser gewonnen.* Fresh water is obtained from sea water in these salt works.

Saline solution = *die Salzlösung*

Salon, der   **1.** Salon, with reference to hairdressing, fashion, etc., and also in historical contexts (e.g., the literary salon).   **2.** Drawing room, i.e., a large room for receiving guests, etc.   **3.** Saloon on board ship.   **4.** Stand (at a trade fair, etc.). *Haben Sie unseren Salon auf der Möbelmesse gefunden?* Did you find our stand at the furniture trade fair?

Same, der   An elevated variant of the more usual *Samen.*   **1.** Seed (of plant).   **2.** Semen, sperm.

(The) same (one and the same) = *derselbe/dieselbe/dasselbe*
(of the same type) = *der (die, das) gleiche*

sanieren   Nothing to do with sanitation, or making people sane: it means "to redevelop," "to renovate," "to modernize," etc. The basic concept is one of carrying out changes so that s.t. can meet the modern demands placed upon it. It is used especially of town planning, urban renewal, etc., and can refer both to renovation of existing buildings and to thoroughgoing redevelopment involving large-scale demolition. *Das ganze Zentrum muß saniert werden.* The whole center must be redeveloped. It is also used in economic contexts, e.g., of firms and industries that have fallen behind and need to be brought up to date and made viable. *Die Stahlindustrie mußte zuerst saniert werden, was Massenentlassungen zur Folge hatte.* The steel industry had to be made efficient first, which resulted in mass redundancies.

Sanierung, die   Redevelopment, renovation, making efficient, etc. SEE SANIEREN.

Sanität, die   An Austrian and Swiss term for the (military) medical service and, colloquially, for an ambulance.

Sanity = *der Verstand, die Vernunft*

saturieren   To satisfy, meet (demand, wishes, etc.). *Der Bedarf an 4-Zimmer-Wohnungen ist kaum zu saturieren.* It is hardly possible to satisfy the demand for 3-bedroom apartments. *saturiert* Excessively (and smugly) prosperous. *Er konnte den Anblick dieser saturierten Geschäftsleute nicht mehr ertragen.* He could no longer stand the sight of these smug and prosperous businessmen.

To saturate = *sättigen*

sauer   1. Sour, indicating a taste that is contrary to sweet (also "tart" with reference to fruit).   2. (chem.) Acid(ic). *Das Lackmuspapier wird zeigen, ob die Lösung sauer oder alkalisch ist.* The litmus paper will show whether the solution is acid or alkaline.   3. Pickled. *saure Gurke* pickled gherkin.   4. (coll.) Very commonly "annoyed," "mad," "cross." *Ich war vielleicht sauer, als ich den Brief las.* I was really mad when I read the letter.

Schal, der   Scarf. *Wenn das Wetter kalt ist, braucht man beim Radfahren unbedingt einen dicken Schal.* When the weather is cold it is essential to wear a thick scarf when cycling.

Shawl = *das Umhängetuch, Schultertuch*

Schale, die   Shell (of eggs, nuts, etc.). But the German word is wider in application and may also correspond to "peel," "skin" (of fruit, vegetables, etc.).

There is also a homonym meaning "bowl." *Nur noch eine kleine Banane lag in der Schale.* There was only one small banana left in the bowl.

scharf **1.** Sharp (knife, etc.). **2.** Hot (= highly spiced). *Ich kann diese Gulaschsuppe nicht essen—sie ist mir zu scharf.* I can't eat this goulash soup—it's too spicy for me. **3.** (coll.) Keen (on). *Anne ist nicht so scharf auf Knoblauch.* Anne isn't so keen on garlic. **4.** In focus, sharp. *Die Belichtung stimmt, aber das Foto ist nicht ganz scharf.* The exposure's right, but the photo isn't quite in focus. There are quite a number of combinations where "sharp" will not provide the correct translation: *scharfe Munition* Live ammunition; *scharfe Maßnahmen* Drastic measures.

Schauer, der **1.** Shower (of rain). **2.** Shudder (owing to fear, cold, etc.). *Als er die Leiche sah, überlief ihn ein Schauer.* A shudder went through him when he saw the body.

Schein, der **1.** The shining of a light: gleam, glow, etc. **2.** Appearance, particularly with the suggestion that appearance and reality are not the same. *Dem Schein nach interessiert er sich sehr für Umweltfragen.* On the face of it he is very interested in environmental issues. *Schein und Sein* Appearance and reality.

Shine (of bright surface) = *der Glanz*

scheinen **1.** To shine (of light; esp. sun, moon). **2.** To seem, to appear. *Er scheint uns nicht mehr kennen zu wollen.* He doesn't seem to want to know us any more. *Wie es scheint, haben wir in der Sache keine Wahl.* As it seems, we have no choice in the matter.

To shine (of bright surface) = *glänzen, leuchten*

Schelle, die **1.** (Small) bell. *Er trug Schellen an seiner Jeans.* He wore bells on his jeans. **2.** Handcuff (*Handschelle*). **3.** (tech.) Clamp.

Shell (of egg, nut, etc.) = *die Schale*
    (found on beach) = *die Muschel*
    (of turtle, etc.) = *der Panzer*
    (mil. projectile) = *die Granate*

schellen To ring (of bell)—a common dialect equivalent for *klingeln* or *läuten*.

To shell (nuts) = *schälen*
    (peas) = *enthülsen* (though regional/dialect terms are often preferred)
    (mil.) = *beschießen*

Schellfisch, der Haddock (fish).

Shellfish = *Meeresfrüchte* (pl.)

Schema, das More common than the formal English "schema." Most frequent uses: **1.** Pattern (= familiar conceptual framework). *Wenn Sie Geschäftsbriefe schreiben, sollten Sie sich an dieses Schema halten.* When you write business letters you should follow this pattern. **2.** Diagram. *Man kann diesen Teufelskreis durch ein Schema veranschaulichen.* This vicious circle can be illustrated by means of a diagram.

Scheme = *der Plan, das Programm*

Schere, die   **1.** This may denote "shears," as used in the garden. But it is also the normal word for "(a pair of) scissors." *Ich kann diese Packungen nur mit einer Schere aufmachen.* I can open these packs only with a pair of scissors.   **2.** Claw, pincer (of a crab, lobster, etc.).

scheu   May refer to a person who is shy, timid, but *schüchtern* is the normal word in such contexts. *Scheu* tends to be applied more readily to animals. *Die Rehe sind viel zu scheu, als daß man sie streicheln könnte.* The deer are much too timid to be stroked.

schick   **1.** Chic, as applied, for example, to women or women's fashion. But the word is applied in many other contexts, meaning "stylish," "elegant." *Für diese schicken Möbel hat sie 20.000 Mark ausgegeben.* She spent 20,000 marks on that stylish furniture.   **2.** (coll.) It may denote nothing more than enthusiastic appreciation on the part of the speaker. *So ein schickes Auto möchte ich auch haben!* I'd like to have a fantastic car like that! Thus *ein schickes Mädchen* may not necessarily refer to a stylishly dressed girl, but to a girl who is "great," "neat," etc. This usage appears to be becoming dated.

Schikane, die   Not "chicanery," though it may mean "chicane" in motor racing. Most commonly it denotes a worldwide phenomenon for which English, however, has no neat single-word translation: the attempt to make life difficult for people, in particular through the abuse of a position of authority or the narrow-minded application of regulations. *Hinter diesem Verbot steckt nur Schikane.* The ban has only been imposed to mess people up/harass people. *Die Zollbeamten durchsuchen alles— aus reiner Schikane.* The customs officials search everything—just to make life difficult/out of sheer bloody-mindedness. *mit allen Schikanen* With all the trimmings.

Chicanery (hair-splitting) = *die Haarspalterei*
(with intent to deceive) = *Machenschaften* (pl.)

Schimmer, der   As so often with words denoting sensory perception, the terms in two languages do not correspond exactly: "shimmer" may be the correct translation in some contexts (e.g., moonlight on water), but in others (e.g., gold, candlelight) "gleam" or "glimmer" is more accurate. *keinen (blassen) Schimmer (von etwas) haben* (coll.) Not to have the faintest idea (about s.t.).

schizophren   Schizophrenic, as a term in clinical psychology, but the word is also used frequently in the much more general sense of "absurd" (i.e., going against common sense). *Das ist doch völlig schizophren, wenn sie vom Energiesparen reden, aber gleichzeitig die Steuer für Benzin senken.* It's quite absurd when they talk about saving energy and lower the tax on gas at the same time.

Schleim, der 1. Slime. 2. The normal word for "mucus," "phlegm." *Dieser Hustensaft wird den Schleim lösen.* This cough mixture will loosen the mucus. 3. Gruel, as prepared for those with digestive problems, for example.

schlimm Bad, nasty.
Slim = *schlank*

schmal Narrow, slender, thin.
Small = *klein*

Schmalz, das (Animal) fat, lard; dripping (as spread on bread). *Meine Mutter hat immer Schmalz verwendet, um Krapfen zu backen.* My mother always used lard to fry doughnuts. *Frisches Brot und Gänseschmalz—das schmeckt vielleicht!* Fresh bread and goose fat—that's really fantastic!
Schmal(t)z (sentimental) = *der Schmalz.* The word has passed into American through Yiddish.

schmieren 1. To smear (grease, etc.), but the word is used in a variety of contexts to denote the application of soft, viscous substances to a surface—without the negative connotation that English "smear" generally has. *Mutter schmierte Marmelade auf die Brötchen.* Mother spread jam on the rolls. *Du mußt dir jeden Abend diese Salbe ins Gesicht schmieren.* You must rub this ointment into your face every night. 2. To lubricate, to grease. *Ich muß nur noch schnell die Scharniere schmieren.* I've just got to lubricate the hinges. 3. (coll.) To scrawl. *Anarchistische Parolen waren auf die Mauer geschmiert worden.* Anarchist slogans had been scrawled on the wall. 4. (coll.) To bribe (hence the noun *Schmiergeld*). *Wir müssen den Wächter schmieren.* We'll have to bribe the guard.

Schnake, die Denotes different insects in different areas, but refers most commonly to the crane fly (BrE also: daddy-longlegs).
Snake = *die Schlange*

schnappen 1. To snap (as of a dog, etc.). 2. To snatch, to grab. *Einer der vielen Diebe hatte seinen Koffer geschnappt.* One of the many thieves had snatched his suitcase. 3. (inform.) To catch (criminal, etc.). *Die Polizei hat ihn geschnappt.* The police have caught him. 4. To click shut, to snap shut, of such mechanisms as locks. *(frische) Luft schnappen* To get some fresh air; *nach Luft schnappen* To gasp for breath.
To snap (break) = *entzweibrechen, zerbrechen*

Schnecke, die Snail; slug.
Snake = *die Schlange*

schnippen 1. To flick (with the fingers). *Er schnippte die Zigarettenstummel vom Tisch.* He flicked the cigarette ends off the table. 2. To click, snap (one's fingers). *Du meinst, wenn du mit den Fingern schnippst, kommt jeder gelaufen.* You think you just have to snap your fingers for everyone to come running.
To snip = *schnippeln*

Schnörkel, der   A flourish or embellishment, usually curved in form, in handwriting, furniture, architecture, etc.

Snorkel = *der Schnorchel*

Schokoladenseite, die   **1.** Chocolate side of a cookie (BrE biscuit), for example, but much more commonly used metaphorically to indicate: **2.** Generally, the most attractive side of s.t. *Bei solchen Staatsbesuchen sieht man nur die Schokoladenseite.* You only see the best side of things during such state visits.   **3.** Specifically, a person's "best side" (i.e., better profile), when being photographed or drawn.

Schulmeister, der   No longer a usual term for a schoolmaster: it is now humorous or pejorative, or both. It may also be used to denote a pedant who enjoys lecturing people. The adjective *schulmeisterlich* is more commonly used than the noun.

Schoolmaster = *der Lehrer*

Schulung, die   Training (in a particular skill, etc.; not general vocational training, which = *die Ausbildung*). *Die Schulung des Hörverstehens ist besonders wichtig.* It is particularly important to train listening comprehension.

Schooling (education at school) = *die Schulbildung, die Ausbildung, der (Schul)unterricht*

Compulsory schooling = *die Schulpflicht*

schwanken   Unsteadiness is the basic concept behind this verb.   **1.** To sway, rock, shake. *Als er in das kleine Boot stieg, schwankte es auf eine alarmierende Art und Weise.* When he got into the little boat it rocked alarmingly.   **2.** To stagger, totter. *Sein Vater schwankte betrunken nach Hause.* His father staggered home drunk.   **3.** To vary, fluctuate. *Der Wechselkurs schwankt zwischen 3 und 4 Mark.* The exchange rate varies between 3 and 4 marks.   **4.** To waver, vacillate, hesitate (rather literary in style). *Du darfst nicht länger schwanken—du mußt handeln!* You mustn't hesitate any longer—you must act!   **5.** To oscillate (of measuring instruments, etc.).

BrE To swank (boast) = *angeben*

Schwarm, der   **1.** Swarm (of bees, insects, etc.).   **2.** (coll.) A person with whom one is infatuated, on whom one has a crush: heart-throb, (pop singer, etc.) idol. *Manfred ist ihr neuester Schwarm.* Manfred is her latest heart-throb.

schwärmen   **1.** To swarm (bees, etc.).   **2.** To be very enthusiastic or talk very enthusiastically about s.o. or s.t., often with reference to an infatuation. *Bernd schwärmt schon immer für Motorräder.* Bernd's always been crazy about motorcycles. *Er schwärmt schon wieder von seinem neuen Computer.* He's going on about his new computer again. *Doris schwärmt für den neuen Sportlehrer.* Doris has a crush on the new PE teacher.

schwarze Star, der. SEE **STAR.**

schwimmen **1.** To swim. **2.** To float, of objects on the surface of a liquid. *Auf dem Wasser schwammen leere Cola-Dosen.* Empty cola cans were floating on the water. **3.** Also expresses confusion and uncertainty in a situation with which one cannot apparently cope: to flounder. *Bei den vielen Fragen begann der Politiker zu schwimmen—er beherrschte den Stoff nicht.* The politician began to flounder under all the questions—he had not mastered the subject.

Schwindel, der **1.** Swindle, fraud, etc. **2.** The physical feeling of dizziness, giddiness. *Schwindel allein ist kein besonders aufschlußreiches Symptom.* Dizziness on its own is not a very revealing symptom. *Ich bin schwindelfrei.* I don't suffer from vertigo.

schwindeln **1.** To feel dizzy (impersonal construction). *Mir schwindelte, als ich vom Balkon heruntersah.* I felt dizzy when I looked down from the balcony. **2.** (coll.) To tell lies, to fib. *Du schwindelst! Du warst gar nicht da.* You're lying! You weren't there at all.

To swindle (s.o.) = *(jdn.) beschwindeln, betrügen*

schwingen **1.** To swing, wave, brandish, etc. **2.** (phys.) To vibrate. *Wenn man diese Saite berührt, fängt sie an zu schwingen.* If you touch this string it starts to vibrate. **3.** (refl.) *sich schwingen* To jump, to leap (onto s.t.). *Es war ein wunderschöner Tag. Ich schwang mich aufs Fahrrad und fuhr zum Strand.* It was a wonderful day. I jumped onto my bicycle and rode to the beach.

See, der Lake. *Der See ist klein, aber sehr tief.* The lake is small, but very deep.

Sea = *die See, das Meer*

Seide, die Silk.

Side = *die Seite*

Seite, die **1.** Side. **2.** Page. *Das Diagramm finden Sie auf Seite 145.* You'll find the diagram on page 145.

Sekret, das Secretion (physiological). *Ein solches Sekret deutet auf eine ernsthafte Erkrankung hin.* This sort of secretion indicates a serious illness.

Secret = *das Geheimnis*

Sekretär, der **1.** (Male) secretary. **2.** A type of writing desk with a slant top (BrE bureau). *Ein gut erhaltener Sekretär aus dem 18. Jahrhundert wird natürlich seinen Preis haben.* Of course a well-preserved eighteenth-century writing desk (BrE bureau) won't be cheap.

Sekt, der Sparkling wine, champagne. The word tends not to be used to refer to genuine French champagne (*der Champagner*). A great deal of *Sekt* is produced (and drunk) in Germany.

Sect = *die Sekte*

Sektion, die 1. Section, department. 2. Occasionally, dissection of animals. *Die Sektion dieser kleinen Nagetiere erfordert viel Geschick.* The dissection of these small rodents requires a great deal of skill. 3. Autopsy—though this is hardly a normal or common usage. *Bei der Sektion wurde festgestellt, daß der Fahrer kurz vor dem Unfall einen Herzinfarkt erlitten hatte.* The autopsy showed that the driver had suffered a heart attack just before the accident.

Sektor, der Sector, but also "field," "area" in the abstract sense. *Auf dem Sektor der Quantenphysik ist er einer der führenden Experten.* He's one of the leading experts in the field of quantum physics.

selbstbewußt Although *bewußt* corresponds to "conscious," it is important to remember that *selbstbewußt* means "self-confident" and not "self-conscious."

Self-conscious = *befangen, gehemmt*

Selbstbewußtsein, das Self-confidence. SEE SELBSTBEWUSST.

Self-consciousness = *die Befangenheit, die Gehemmtheit*

Selbstkontrolle, die May denote self-control, but more usually denotes keeping a check on oneself, self-monitoring. *Ein Buch mit Schlüssel bietet die Möglichkeit der Selbstkontrolle.* A book with a key means the user can monitor his or her own progress.

Self-control = *die Selbstbeherrschung*

selbstgemacht Self-made in the sense of "made by oneself," "homemade." *Jeden Monat bringt er mir ein Glas von seiner verdammten selbstgemachten Marmelade.* Every month he brings me a jar of his damned homemade jam.

Self-made man = *der Selfmademan*

Sellerie, der 1. Celery, when it refers to *Stangensellerie* (or *Staudensellerie*), with its long stalks. 2. Celeriac, when it refers to *Knollensellerie,* with its large turniplike root.

Semester, das 1. Semester, i.e., one of the two half-yearly terms of the university year. 2. Also used to refer to students who are "in" a certain semester (i.e., have completed a certain number of terms). *Diese Vorlesung ist nur für Zweitsemester.* This lecture is only for second-semester students. This application to people is found colloquially outside of the university context in the phrase *(ein) ältere(s) Semester. Solche Musik ist eher für ältere Semester interessant.* This type of music is of more interest to older people.

Seminar, das 1. Seminar (type of class). 2. (University) department. *Entschuldigung, wo finde ich das Seminar für Geschichte?* Excuse me, where can I find the history department? 3. Seminary (for the training of priests). *Nach einem halben Jahr verließ er das Priesterseminar, weil ihm die Motivation fehlte.* After six months he left the seminary because he did not feel sufficiently motivated.

senden 1. To send. 2. To broadcast, to transmit. *Wir haben beschlossen, das Interview doch nicht zu senden.* We have decided not to broadcast the interview after all.

To send = *schicken, senden*

Sender, der Transmitter, (radio/TV) station. *Mit diesem Radio kann ich auch chinesische Sender empfangen.* With this radio I can even pick up Chinese stations.

Sender (of letter) = *der Absender*

Senior, der The word "senior" on its own does not normally provide an adequate translation. 1. Senior citizen, old-age pensioner. *Senioren können mittwochs zum halben Preis fahren.* Senior citizens can travel at half-fare on Wednesdays. 2. Senior partner. *Wir müssen die Sache erst einmal mit unserem Senior besprechen.* We shall have to discuss the matter with our senior partner first. 3. Senior player, veteran (sport). *die Seniorenmeisterschaft* the veterans' championships.

Senior (college student in final year) = *Student(in) im letzten Studienjahr*

Seniors (BrE, = older pupils) = *ältere Schüler*

Sense, die Scythe. *Er benutzt eine Sense, wenn er seinen Rasen mäht.* He uses a scythe to cut his lawn. *Jetzt ist Sense!* That's the end!

Sense (physical; also understanding of s.t.) = *der Sinn*

(feeling) = *das Gefühl*

(common sense) = *der gesunde Menschenverstand*

(meaning) = *der Sinn, die Bedeutung*

sensibel Sensitive. *Für ein so sensibles Mädchen war es ein großer Schock.* It was a great shock for such a sensitive girl. *Ich habe eine sehr sensible Haut.* I've got very sensitive skin.

Sensible = *vernünftig*

Sentenz, die Aphorism, maxim.

Sentence (grammar) = *der Satz*

(judicial) = *das Urteil, die Strafe*

Serie, die Series, serial. The word is also used with reference to mass production, often denoting a particular type or "run" of a model. There is no English equivalent that suits all contexts. *Solche Möbel können gar nicht in Serie hergestellt werden.* This sort of furniture simply cannot be mass-produced. *Die erste Serie von diesem Auto zeichnete sich durch ihre Rostanfälligkeit aus.* The first cars of this type were notable for their tendency to rust quickly. *Ich weiß nicht, ob wir ein Regal der gleichen Serie auftreiben können.* I don't know if we can get hold of a shelf of the same type. *serienmäßig* Standard (of fittings on a mass-produced item). *Bei diesem Auto sind die Nebelscheinwerfer serienmäßig.* Fog lamps are standard on this car.

seriös **1.** Denotes respectability in a variety of contexts—moral decency, sober dress or behavior, legality, financial soundness, etc. *Es war eins von jenen Restaurants, wo die Gäste immer sehr seriös wirken.* It was one of those restaurants where the guests always seem to be very respectable. *Er trug grundsätzlich nur seriöse Anzüge.* He made a point of only wearing conservative suits. *Ich halte sie für keine seriöse Firma.* I don't think it's a reputable firm. **2.** Sincere, i.e., not meant in jest. *Nicht alle Zuschriften, die man auf eine Heiratsannonce erhält, sind seriös.* Not all the replies one receives to an advertisement for a marriage partner are serious.

Serious = *ernst, ernsthaft*

(accident, etc.) = *schwer*

Serpentine, die A double or hairpin bend in a road, or a road that contains many such bends. Normally refers to mountain roads, where such bends are inevitable. *Bei solchen Serpentinen werde ich immer reisekrank.* I always get carsick on this type of winding road.

Serpentine (mineral) = *der Serpentin*

Set, das **1.** Place mat, BrE tablemat. *Ich habe meiner Mutter Sets aus Bast zum Geburtstag geschenkt.* I gave my mother raffia place mats for her birthday. **2.** Set, kit, in the sense of a group of units serving a common purpose. *Unser neues Reinigungsset enthält alles, was man für die Schallplattenpflege braucht.* Our new cleaning kit contains everything you need to take care of your records.

setzen **1.** To set, put, place: a key verb with a large number of uses. **2.** (sports) To seed. *Bei den Wimbledon-Meisterschaften wurde sie mehrfach als Nummer eins gesetzt.* She was seeded number 1 several times for the Wimbledon championships.

Showmaster, der A pseudo-anglicism meaning the "host," "emcee" of a show.

Sieg, der Victory.

Siege = *die Belagerung*

Signatur, die **1.** Has a variety of technical meanings, the commonest being the call number (BrE shelf-mark) of a library book. *Unter welcher Signatur findet man Bücher über Selbstverteidigung?* What's the call number for books on self-defense? **2.** Occasionally, a person's signature (e.g., at the end of a letter, on a check, etc.).

Signature (of person) = *die Unterschrift*

signieren **1.** To sign (one's name): this is more commonly used than the noun **SIGNATUR** (Q.V.). **2.** To initial. *Das Bild war mit einem rätselhaften 'NN' signiert.* The painting had been initialed with the mysterious letters "NN." **3.** To designate with a (library) call number (BrE shelfmark). *Selbstverständlich müssen die Bücher signiert werden, bevor sie in* *die Regale kommen.* Naturally the books have to be given call numbers before they are put on the shelves. SEE **SIGNATUR.**

To sign (one's name) = *unterschreiben, unterzeichnen*

simulieren 1. To simulate (as in experiments, etc.). 2. To pretend to be ill, to malinger. *Er ist gar nicht krank—er simuliert nur.* He's not ill at all—he's just malingering. *Jedesmal wenn es harte Arbeit gibt, simuliert er Rückenschmerzen.* Whenever there's hard work to be done he pretends he's got a backache.

To simulate (i.e., feign: emotion, etc.) = *vortäuschen*

sinnvoll Meaningful; sensible.

Sinful = *sündhaft*

Sinus, der 1. (anat.) Sinus. 2. (math.) Sine.

situiert Does not normally denote location, but combines with *gut* or *schlecht* to denote a person's financial circumstances. *gut situiert* (or *gutsituiert*) well-off; *schlecht situiert* badly off.

To be situated (location) = *sich befinden, liegen*

sitzen 1. To sit. There are various idiomatic usages, the most important of which are: 2. To hit home (of a remark, etc.). *Diese Bemerkung hat vielleicht gesessen!* That comment really hit home! 3. To sink in/have sunk in (of material to be learned). *Die Grammatik habe ich schnell gelernt, aber der Wortschatz sitzt nicht.* I learned the grammar quickly, but the vocabulary won't sink in. 4. (coll.) To be in prison, BrE inside. *Der hat schon mehrfach gesessen.* He's been in prison quite a few times.

Skala, die 1. Scale (mus.; also on measuring instrument). 2. Dial from which readings can be taken, e.g., values on a pressure gauge, or the tuning frequency on a radio. 3. (fig.) Range, gamut. *Die Skala der Reklamationen reicht von elektrischen Störungen bis hin zu sich lösenden Tapeten.* The range of complaints extends from electrical faults to peeling wallpaper.

Scale (mus.) also = *die Tonleiter*
    (extent) = *der Umfang, das Ausmaß*
    (of map) = *der Maßstab*
    (of fish) = *die Schuppe*
    (pair of) scales (for weighing) = *die Waage*

Skooter, der Longer form: *Autoskooter.* Bumper car, dodgem.

Scooter = *der (Motor)roller*

skrupellos Unscrupulous. *Er entpuppte sich bald als skrupelloser Killer.* He soon revealed himself to be an unscrupulous killer.

Scrupulous = *gewissenhaft, mit Skrupeln*
(cleanliness, etc.) = *peinlich*

skurril Bizarre, odd, droll, even "ridiculous." *Er war ein überaus skurriler Mensch: er hatte z.B. die seltsame Gewohnheit, ein eigenes Messer mitzu-*

nehmen, wenn er ins Restaurant ging. He was an exceptionally droll person: for example, he had the strange habit of taking his own knife with him when he went to a restaurant. *Er stieß mit seinen skurrilen Ideen auf wenig Verständnis.* His bizarre ideas met with little understanding.

Scurrilous (libelous) = *verleumderisch*
(indecent) = *unflätig, unanständig, obszön*

Slip, der Legless undergarment: briefs, panties, BrE (under)pants, BrE knickers. (The German word refers to both men's and women's clothing.)

Slip (i.e., underskirt) = *der Unterrock*
(error) = *das Versehen, der (Flüchtigkeits)fehler*

Slipper, der Slip-on shoe, loafer. *Schuh-Schmidt hat diese Woche Slipper im Angebot.* Smith's Shoes have a special offer on loafers this week.

Slipper (i.e., light, soft footwear worn around the house) = *der Hausschuh, der Pantoffel*

Smoking, der Tuxedo, dinner jacket. *Wenn du bei uns zum Abendessen eingeladen bist, brauchst du wirklich keinen Smoking zu tragen.* If we invite you to dinner you really don't need to wear a dinner jacket.

Smoking = *das Rauchen*

so **1.** So (before adj.; also *so daß* = so that). But, there are other uses for which "so" does not provide a translation. **2.** In this way, like this/that. *Wir haben es immer so gemacht.* We've always done it like this. **3.** Before the indefinite article: like this/that; (exclamation) What a . . . !; (emphatic) such a. *So ein Haus hatten wir auch einmal.* We had a house like that once too. *So ein Idiot!* What an idiot! *Ihr Vater war immer ein so hilfreicher Mann.* Your father was always such a helpful man. **4.** About (i.e., approximately). *Ich fahre so 15.000 Kilometer im Jahr.* I drive about 15,000 kilometers a year. **5.** As a vague interjection it corresponds to "OK," BrE "right," or "well," when beginning a sentence; and to "Oh" or "Really" as a surprised reaction. *So, wir fangen auf Seite 15 an.* OK, we'll start on page 15. *"Mein Onkel spricht kein Englisch."—"So."* "My uncle doesn't speak English." "Oh, doesn't he?" *Ach so!* (Ah) I see!

So etwas. SEE **SO WAS.** *oder so* Or something like that. *Ich glaube, der Ort heißt Pommelsbrunn oder so.* I think the place is called Pommelsbrunn or something like that.

So (therefore) = *also*

so was **1.** A shorter form of *so etwas:* something like this/that. *So was würde ich nie sagen.* I'd never say something like that. **2.** An exclamation of surprise, etc. *Marianne heiratet einen Siebzigjährigen? Na so was!* Marianne's going to marry a seventy-year-old? Good Lord!

So what? = *Na und?*

Sole, die   Saltwater, brine.

Sole (of shoe) = *die Sohle*

(fish) = *die Seezunge*

solid(e)   In some cases "solid" will provide a suitable translation. *solider Fels* solid rock. Yet the sense is often that of "solid" meaning "sturdy" rather than "not hollow." *ein solides Haus* a sturdy/well-built house. The main exception is the application of the word to people or places they frequent, when the meaning is that of respectability. *Ein solider Mensch steht für seine Fehler gerade.* A decent person answers for his mistakes. *Sie sucht ein solides Mädchen für ihren Sohn.* She's looking for a respectable girl for her son. *Ich meine, wir sollten uns ein solides Lokal suchen, wo man in Ruhe gut essen kann.* I think we ought to look for a respectable restaurant where you can eat a good meal in peace. *Eine solide Firma tut so etwas nicht.* A reputable firm doesn't do that sort of thing.

Solid (not hollow) = *massiv*

Sonne, die   **1.** Sun or sunlight.   **2.** Also a short form for *Heizsonne* (an electric fire) or *Höhensonne* (a sunlamp).   **3.** One word for the fireworks known in BrE as a catherine wheel.

Sonnyboy, der   A (normally young) man who enjoys general popularity through his charming and cheerful nature. The term is perhaps now used most often ironically. *Wenn sie sich nicht in diesen Sonnyboy verliebt hätte, wäre sie mit Manfred bestimmt sehr glücklich gewesen.* If she hadn't fallen in love with that Prince Charming she would certainly have been very happy with Manfred.

Sonny boy (as mode of address) = *mein Junge*

Sorten (pl.)   Foreign currency. *Sorten bestellt man am besten eine Woche im voraus.* It's best to order foreign currency a week in advance.

Sort (type) = *die Art, die Sorte*

sortieren   To sort, but note the use of the participle *sortiert* to indicate the range of selection that, for example, a shop has. *Gehen Sie am besten zu Elektro-Schmidt—die sind gut sortiert.* Your best bet is to go to Elektro-Schmidt—they have a good selection.

Soße, die   May denote a sauce used in cooking (though the spelling *Sauce* is often preferred in this sense), but may also indicate straightforward "gravy," i.e., the juice from cooked meat thickened with flour, etc. *Es geht nichts über einen handfesten Rinderbraten mit schmackhafter Soße.* There's nothing like good solid roast beef with tasty gravy.

souverän   **1.** Sovereign (i.e., having jurisdiction, autonomy, etc.).   **2.** Displaying confident, even effortless superiority—there is no obvious single English equivalent for this. *Er hat die Lage souverän beherrscht, das muß man ihm lassen.* He was in full command of the situation, you've got to give him that. *Die deutsche Mannschaft spielte souverän und siegte souverän.* The German team were in full command of the game and won an effortless victory. *Sie wollten ihn natürlich verunsichern, aber er blieb ganz souverän.* They wanted to unnerve him, of course, but he remained quite unruffled. *Es gibt keinen Zweifel—in einem Mercedes fährt man ganz souverän.* There's no doubt about it—nothing handles like a Mercedes.

sozial **1.** Social, in the neutral sense of "relating to society." **2.** The word is more difficult to translate in its other main meaning, when it carries a value judgment. Here it refers to people or things that promote public welfare, cement the cohesion of a society, and in particular protect the interests of those less well able to stand up for themselves: socially conscious/aware, public-spirited. The exact translation depends very much on the context. *Er handelt immer sozial.* He always acts in a socially responsible manner. *Er ist ein sehr sozialer Mensch.* He's a very public-spirited/socially conscious person. *Diese neue Steuerpolitik ist nicht sozial.* This new tax policy is socially divisive. *Ich habe heute meinen sozialen Tag.* (coll.) I'm feeling charitable/generous today.

spannen "Making taut" is the basic meaning. **1.** To tighten, tauten, tense. *Er spannte die Muskeln.* He tensed his muscles. **2.** To stretch (and fasten). *Ich spannte etwas Plastikfolie über die Tomaten.* I stretched some plastic film over the tomatoes. **3.** To cock (rifle, etc.). **4.** To hitch up, harness (e.g., a horse to a cart). **5.** (coll.) To listen for, to watch out for. *Immer spannt sie auf die Gespräche anderer Leute.* She's always eavesdropping. Also denotes the activities of a voyeur. *Im Park versteckt er sich hinter Büschen und spannt.* He's a peeping Tom, who hides behind bushes in the park. **6.** *sich spannen über* To span (bridge, etc.). *Eine Riesenbrücke spannt sich über den Rhein.* A huge bridge spans the Rhine. **7.** *ich bin gespannt* I wonder. *Ich bin gespannt, ob er die Rechnung irgendwann zahlt.* I wonder if he'll pay that bill one day. *spannend* Exciting, tense (film, etc.).

To span (time) = *sich erstrecken über*

Spanner, der **1.** Denotes various devices for keeping things stretched or taut, e.g., a shoe tree, a hanger (for trousers), a press (for a tennis racquet). **2.** (coll.) Voyeur, peeping Tom.

Spanner (BrE, = wrench) = *der (Schrauben)schlüssel*

sparen **1.** To save (money, time, etc.). *Dein Großvater sparte sein Leben lang.* Your grandfather saved all his life. *Ich spare auf einen Sportwagen.* I'm saving up for a sports car. *Der neue Computer spart mir viel Zeit.* The new computer saves me a lot of time. **2.** To be economical with. *Frau Drexler versuchte, am Haushaltsgeld zu sparen.* Mrs. Drexler tried to economize on her housekeeping money. *Er spart am falschen Ort.* He's making false economies. *Er sparte nicht mit seinem Kognak.* He wasn't sparing with his cognac. **3.** To save, spare, in the sense of avoiding bother, etc. *Ich spare mir viel Ärger, wenn ich ihr aus dem Weg gehe.* I'll save myself a lot of trouble if I keep out of her way.

To spare (do without) = *entbehren*
(not kill, etc.) = *(ver)schonen*
(have available) = *übrig (haben)* Can you spare me five minutes? *Hast du fünf Minuten Zeit für mich?*

Speck, der   1. Bacon (fat), though the German word embraces a wider range than English "bacon," and some pieces of *Speck* may look more like lumps of fat than bacon to American or British eyes.   2. (coll.) Fat, flab (on a person).

Speck (of dust) = *das (Staub)korn*
(of paint, etc.) = *der Spritzer*

Spedition, die   Various specific meanings, all concerned with transportation of goods, etc. *Die Spedition kostet mehr als die Waren selbst.* The freight (BrE carriage) costs more than the goods themselves. *Herr Brandt arbeitet in der Spedition.* Herr Brandt works in the shipping (BrE dispatch) department. *Wir brauchen eine gute Spedition für solche empfindlichen Geräte.* We need a good shipping (BrE haulage) firm for such delicate equipment. *Wir ziehen in zwei Wochen um—kennst du eine gute Spedition?* We're moving in two weeks' time—do you know a good moving company (BrE removal firm)?

Expedition = *die Expedition*

Speer, der   Spear, but "javelin" in sporting contexts. *Im Speerwerfen hat er schlecht abgeschnitten.* He did badly in the javelin.

Spektakel, der   (coll.) Loud noise, general fuss and bother. *Die Nachbarn machen immer so einen Spektakel im Flur.* The neighbors are always making such a racket in the hall. *Wenn mein Vater das erfährt, gibt es einen großen Spektakel.* If my father finds out about this there'll be a dreadful fuss.

Spectacle (impressive) = *das Schauspiel*
To make a spectacle of oneself = *unangenehm auffallen, sich unangenehm zur Schau stellen.* That drunken girl is making an unpleasant spectacle of herself. *Dieses betrunkene Mädchen fällt unangenehm auf/stellt sich unangenehm zur Schau.*

spendabel   (coll.) Generous. *Du bist heute aber recht spendabel!* You're extremely generous today!

Spendable: This money isn't spendable yet. *Dieses Geld kann noch nicht ausgegeben werden.*

spenden   1. To donate, contribute. *Er weigert sich, Geld für die Heilsarmee zu spenden.* He refuses to contribute to the Salvation Army. *Blut spenden* to donate blood.   2. Give off, emit (heat, etc.). *Unsere neuen Heizkörper spenden eine behagliche Wärme.* Our new radiators give off a cosy warmth. *Schatten spenden* to give/offer shade.   3. Various collocations, with the vague general sense of "give": *Beifall spenden* to applaud; *Lob spenden* to praise.

To spend (money) = *ausgeben*

(time) = *verbringen*

Spender, der   Donator, contributor; donor (blood). SEE **SPENDEN.**

Spender: She's a big spender. *Bei ihr sitzt das Geld locker.*

spendieren   To buy (s.t. for s.o. else); BrE stand (s.o. s.t.), treat (s.o. to s.t.). *Onkel Hans spendierte den Kindern ein Eis.* Uncle Hans treated the children to an ice cream. *So, ich spendiere eine Runde.* All right, this round's on me.

To spend (money) = *ausgeben*

(time) = *verbringen*

Spiel, das   Match, game, play. Not used like English "spiel" to denote glib talk. *das Kartenspiel* Card game; deck of cards; *das Schachspiel* Chess game; chess set.

Spiel = *Sprüche* (pl.)

Spieler, der   Player; gambler. SEE **SPIEL.**

Spieler (glib talker) = *der Sprücheklopfer*

(cheat) = *der Schwindler*

Spikes (pl.)   **1.** Spikes (on running shoes).   **2.** Studs on winter tires, or such tires themselves. *Mit Spikes hätte ich den Berg geschafft.* I'd have managed the hill if I'd had studded tires.

Spike (on railing, etc.) = *die Spitze*

spinnen   **1.** To spin (wool, etc.).   **2.** (coll.—extremely common) To be crazy, to talk nonsense, to tell tall stories. *Ausgerechnet dieses Auto willst du kaufen? Du spinnst wohl!* You want to buy this car of all cars? You must be out of your mind! *Das ist doch alles gesponnen!* That's a pack of lies!

To spin (revolve) = *(sich) drehen*

Spinner, der   **1.** Spinner (of cloth, etc.).   **2.** Screwball, nut, etc. SEE **SPINNEN.**

Spirale, die   **1.** Spiral.   **2.** The intrauterine contraceptive device (IUD) known in BrE as the coil. *Die Spirale eignet sich nicht für Frauen, die noch keine Kinder bekommen haben.* The IUD is unsuitable for women who have not had any children.

Spleen, der   A strange or crazy notion, an eccentricity. *Sie hat den Spleen, immer nur Lederhosen zu tragen.* She has an obsession about always wearing leather trousers. *Er hat doch einen Spleen!* He's out of his mind!

Spleen (bad temper) = *schlechte Laune*

To vent one's spleen (on s.o.) = *seine Wut (an jdm.) auslassen*

(organ) = *die Milz*

Sporen (pl.)   This may be the plural of *die Spore* = spore (bot., biol.). But it is also the plural of *der Sporn* = spur (horse riding).

Spot, der   Commercial, advertisement (*Werbespot*). *Zwischen den beiden Sendungen werden wir fünf Spots von jeweils 30 bis 40 Sekunden einblenden.* Between the two programs we'll slot in five commercials, each 30 to 40 seconds in length.

Spot (place) = *die Stelle*

(stain; also of leopard, etc.) = *der Fleck*

(point) = *der Punkt*

Spott, der   Mockery, derision.

Spot (place) = *die Stelle*

(stain; also of leopard, etc.) = *der Fleck*

(point) = *der Punkt*

spotten   To mock, poke fun.

To spot (see) = *sehen*

(find) = *finden*

Spötter, der   S.o. who mocks, mocker.

Spotter (spotter plane) = *der Aufklärer, das Aufklärungsflugzeug*

springen   1. The normal word for "to jump" (though certain contexts may make more dramatic words like "spring" or "leap" more appropriate translations).   2. To break, to crack (intrans.). *Eine der Saiten ist gesprungen.* One of the strings has snapped. *Diese Art Porzellan springt leicht.* This type of china cracks very easily.

Sprit, der   1. Not a "sprite," but a colloquial term for gasoline: "gas," "juice."   2. (coll.) Juice (alcohol, spirits).

Sprite (elf) = *der Elf, die Elfe*

(goblin) = *der Kobold*

Spritzer, der   A "splash" (of water, paint, etc.) or "dash" (of perfume, scent, etc.).

Spritzer (wine with soda) = *die Schorle, der Gespritzte*

Spur, die   1. Track, trail. *Wir fanden die Spur des angeschossenen Tieres.* We found the track of the wounded animal.   2. Trace, sign; also (pl.) "clues" left behind by criminal, or any "evidence" found on the scene of a crime. *Zu den Spuren gehörten ein Zigarettenstummel und eine leere Streichholzschachtel.* The clues included a cigarette butt and an empty matchbox.   3. Lane (on highway). *Zwei Spuren sind für eine solche Autobahn nicht genug.* Two lanes are not enough for a highway like this.   4. Gauge (of railroad); track (of car).   5. Small amount. *Das Wasser war eine Spur zu kalt.* The water was a shade too cold. *Von Taktgefühl keine Spur!* Not a trace of tact!

Spur (horse-riding) = *der Sporn* (pl.: *die Sporen*)

(fig., = incentive) = *der Ansporn*

spurten   1. To put on a spurt (in running). *Er spurtete in der letzten Runde.* He put on a spurt in the final lap.   2. (coll.) To run fast. *Wir mußten ganz* *schön spurten, um pünktlich anzukommen.* We really had to dash to arrive on time.

To spurt (blood, etc.) = *spritzen*

stabil "Stable" in many contexts (e.g., currency, prices, governments), but with reference to the strength or sturdiness of objects (e.g., houses, furniture, shoes), other words like "sturdy," "robust," or "solid" may be more appropriate. *stabile Schuhe* sturdy shoes; *eine stabile Gesundheit* a sound/robust constitution.

Stadium, das Stage (of development, etc.). *Die Planung des neuen Gebäudes tritt ins letzte Stadium.* The planning of the new building is now entering the final stage.

Stadium = *das Stadion*

Stall, der Denotes accommodation for various animals. The English word will depend on the animal: stable (horses), pen, sty (pigs), cowshed (cattle), hutch (rabbits). Sometimes used metaphorically. *Hier sieht's wie in einem Stall aus.* It's like a pigpen in here.

Stall (in market, etc.) = *der Stand*

Stalls (BrE, in theater = main floor) = *das Parkett*

Stand, der **1.** Stand (in a market, etc.). But there are many other uses: **2.** State (of affairs, etc.). *Beim jetzigen Stand der Dinge ist ein Krieg unvermeidlich.* In the present state of affairs a war is inevitable. **3.** Reading, level (with reference to meters, counters, etc.). *Hier sollen Sie den neuen Zählerstand eintragen.* You're supposed to enter the new meter reading here. **4.** Rank (for taxis). **5.** Status, station (in society, etc.). *Er hat unter seinem Stand geheiratet.* He married below his station. **6.** Standing position. *ein Sprung aus dem Stand* a standing jump.

Stand (point of view) = *der Standpunkt, die Einstellung*

(in sports stadium) = *die Tribüne*

To take a stand on a matter = *zu einer Sache Stellung beziehen*

To take a firm stand on a matter = *zu einer Sache einen festen Standpunkt vertreten*

Stapel, der **1.** Pile, stack. *Ein Stapel von Reiseprospekten lag auf dem Tisch.* A pile/stack of travel brochures was on the table. **2.** The "stocks" in shipbuilding, i.e., the timbers on which a ship stands during construction. Used in the nontechnical expressions *vom Stapel lassen* (to launch) and *vom Stapel laufen* (to be launched).

Staple = *die (Heft)klammer*

stapeln To pile up, stack. *Die Kisten wurden hinten im Laderaum gestapelt.* The crates were stacked at the back of the hold. *Auf seinem Schreibtisch stapelten sich die unbezahlten Rechnungen.* The unpaid bills were piling up on his desk.

To staple (papers, etc.) = *(zusammen)heften*

Stapler, der A short form for *Gabelstapler* = forklift truck.
Stapler = *die Heftmaschine*
Star, der There are three homonyms to be distinguished. **1.** Starling
(pl. *Stare*). **2.** A disease of the eye, in particular *grüner Star* (=
glaucoma), *grauer Star* (= cataract), and *schwarzer Star* (= am-
aurosis, i.e., pathological blindness) (pl. *Stare,* though pl. is rare).
3. Star (in films, pop music, etc.) (pl. *Stars*).
Star (astron.) = *der Stern*
stark Strong. The word has quite a wide range of uses and the context
may demand other translations. *starker Regen* heavy rain.
Stark = *nackt, kahl, schroff*
Stark naked = *splitternackt*
Start, der Start, in various contexts (esp. sport). But also "takeoff," of
an airplane, or launch (of a rocket). *Bei solchen Wetterverhältnissen ist
ein Start zu gefährlich.* A takeoff in such weather conditions is too dangerous. *Die neue Rakete hatte einen perfekten Start.* The new rocket had a
perfect launch.
Start (beginning) = *der Anfang, der Beginn*
starten. SEE START. *Das Flugzeug startet in fünf Minuten.* The plane will
take off in five minutes. *Das Raumschiff wird erst im Mai gestartet.* The
spaceship will not be launched until May. With reference to races *starten*
may mean literally "to start (running)," but may also mean "to take
part." *Der Favorit ist verletzt und wird im Finale doch nicht starten.* The
favorite is injured and will not take part in the final after all. *eine Kam-
pagne/Aktion starten* To launch a campaign.
To start (begin) = *anfangen, beginnen*
(with fright, etc.) = *aufschrecken*
Station, die **1.** Station, with reference to various establishments where
some kind of service is provided with the aid of complex technical
equipment. *Wetterstation* meteorological station; *Raumstation* space station. **2.** (Railroad) station, when the different points of arrival and
departure on a train journey are being considered. *Dieser Zug hält leider
an jeder Station.* This train unfortunately stops at every station.
Station and "station" are not equivalent in the following cases: **3.**
Hospital ward. *Er liegt auf Station C.* He's in ward C. *Intensivstation* intensive care unit. **4.** Stop (in bus or streetcar journeys). *Wie viele Stationen müssen wir noch fahren?* How many more stops do we have to go?
Station machen To break one's journey, stop off. *Der Präsident machte
in Athen zwei Tage Station.* The president stopped off in Athens for two
days. **5.** Stage, phase (in one's life, development, etc.). *Diese Stu-
dienzeit in den USA war eine äußerst wichtige Station in seinem Leben.*
This period of study in the U.S.A. was a crucial stage in his life.

Station (railroad) = *der Bahnhof*

(bus) = *der Busbahnhof*

stationär   **1.** Stationary, in a restricted number of formal contexts. *stationärer Planet* fixed, stationary planet.   **2.** Its commonest use is to refer to treatment requiring patients to stay in a hospital. *Zuerst konnte sie ambulant, jetzt muß sie aber stationär behandelt werden.* At first it was possible to treat her as an outpatient, but now she has to stay in the hospital.

Stationary = *stehend*, (car) *geparkt, parkend;* or paraphrase with a verb like *sich bewegen* = to move.

Stationery (noun) = *Schreibwaren* (pl.)

stattlich   Large (and impressive). The exact translation will vary according to context. Thus *eine stattliche Summe* is simply a "large" or "considerable" sum, while with reference to a building, a person or an animal, etc., other words like "splendid," "magnificent," "imposing" may be more suitable.

Stately (i.e., dignified) = *würdevoll*

steif   Stiff. Also "stiff" in the sense of "(excessively) formal." *Der Abend war etwas steif.* The evening was rather formal. *Sein Gruß wirkt immer sehr steif.* His greeting always seems very formal.

stemmen   **1.** To press (a part of one's body) hard against s.t. *Er stemmte den Rücken gegen die Tür.* He pressed his back against the door. *die Arme in die Hüften stemmen* to put one's hands on one's hips.   **2.** To lift up (s.t. heavy above one's head). *120 Kilo kann er inzwischen stemmen.* He can lift 120 kilograms (above his head) now.   **3.** To chisel, pry open (using a crowbar: *Stemmeisen*).

To stem (from s.t.) = *(von einer Sache) herrühren, (aus einer Sache) stammen*

(bleeding) = *stillen*

Step, der   Tap dance. *Der Step wird wieder beliebt.* Tap dancing is becoming popular again. The form *der Steptanz* is more usual, however.

Step (pace) = *der Schritt*

(measure, action) = *die Maßnahme*

steppen   Two homonyms. **1.** To stitch; to quilt.   **2.** To tap-dance, do tap dancing. *Sein Großvater konnte in seiner Jugend wunderbar steppen.* His grandfather was a wonderful tap dancer when he was young.

To step = *schreiten, treten*

sticken   To embroider. *Sie hat seinen Namen auf alle seine Taschentücher gestickt.* She's embroidered his name on all his handkerchiefs.

To stick (with glue, etc.) = *kleben*

stickig Stuffy, close, oppressive. *Die Luft ist immer so stickig, weil man die Fenster nicht aufmachen kann.* The air is always so stuffy because you can't open the windows.
Sticky (with glue, etc.) = *klebrig*

Stickstoff, der Not "sticky stuff," but "nitrogen." *Der Boden braucht mehr Stickstoff.* The soil needs more nitrogen.

still 1. Still, in the sense of "motionless." *Sie lag ganz still auf dem Bett.* She lay quite still on the bed. 2. Quiet, silent, sometimes with the sense of "secret." *Es war ganz still im Haus—fast zu still.* It was absolutely quiet in the house—almost too quiet. *Sie war schon immer ein stilles Mädchen.* She's always been a quiet sort of girl. *Er hatte die stille Hoffnung, daß er eines Tages Bürgermeister wird.* It was his secret hope to become mayor one day. *stiller Gesellschafter* sleeping partner/secret partner.

stillen 1. To still, satisfy (hunger, desire, etc.). 2. To breast-feed. *Ich habe nichts dagegen, daß eine Mutter ihr Baby in der Öffentlichkeit stillt.* I don't mind a mother breastfeeding her baby in public. 3. To stop, ease (pain, tears, etc.); to staunch (bleeding).

Stipendium, das A grant of money awarded to a student (normally a particularly deserving one) to help him/her pursue his/her studies. The vast majority of German institutions of higher education are state-run and charge no tuition fees as such, so that a *Stipendium* is usually meant to assist a student with his/her living expenses: the word thus corresponds to "stipend" in AmE but to "scholarship" in BrE. *Viktor erhielt ein Stipendium von 1.000 Mark monatlich, um seine Doktorarbeit zu schreiben.* Viktor received a scholarship of 1,000 marks a month to write his Ph.D.
Stipend (of clergyman) = *das Gehalt*

Stock, der 1. (Walking-)stick. *Großmutter kann ohne Stock nicht einmal bis zur Bushaltestelle gehen.* Grandmother can't even walk as far as the bus stop without a stick. 2. Floor, stor(e)y of building. *Er wohnt im dritten Stock.* He lives on the fourth floor.
Stock (supply) = *der Vorrat*

stocken The general sense is of an established rhythm being inter-rupted. 1. (elevated style) To miss a beat (heart, pulse); to catch (one's breath). *Ihr stockte das Herz/der Atem.* Her heart missed a beat/ She caught her breath. 2. To falter (in some activity). *Beim Vorlesen aus der Bibel stockte ich wiederholt.* I repeatedly faltered when reading aloud from the Bible. 3. To slacken, flag, stagnate. *Der frühe so rege Handel zwischen den beiden Ländern fängt zu stocken an.* The once so active trade between the two countries is beginning to fall off. *Die Ver-handlungen sind ins Stocken geraten.* The negotiations have gotten bogged down. 4. To set (of eggs, when being scrambled, etc.).
To stock (item in shop) = *führen*

Stoff, der **1.** Material, fabric (cloth). *Für mein neues Sommerkleid brauche ich drei Meter Stoff.* I need three meters of material for my new summer dress. **2.** Subject matter. *Der Professor ist zwar sehr nett, aber der Stoff seines Seminars ist unglaublich langweilig.* It's true that the professor is very nice, but the subject matter of his course is unbelievably boring. **3.** Substance. *Der Chemiker konnte diesen weißen Stoff nicht identifizieren.* The chemist was unable to identify this white substance.

Stuff = (in general sense) *das Zeug*

(person's things) = *Sachen* (pl.)

stoppen **1.** To stop, with the related uses: to freeze (wages, salary, prices, etc.); to trap (a ball, in soccer). **2.** To time, using a stopwatch. *Ich habe den Läufer gestoppt: 9,83 Sekunden.* I timed the runner: 9.83 seconds.

To stop (doing s.t.) = *aufhören (etwas zu tun)*

Stopper, der Various special uses: **1.** Curtain stop. *Ohne Stopper fällt die Gardine ständig runter.* The curtain keeps falling down without a stop/end piece. **2.** In soccer, a defender, usually a player who has to mark (i.e., stay close to and contain) an opposing striker (forward player) tightly. **3.** Timekeeper, i.e., s.o. using a stopwatch.

Stopper (of bottle) = *der Verschluß*

Store, der Usually plural: net curtain(s). *Meine Mutter hat neue Stores für das Wohnzimmer gekauft.* My mother has bought new net curtains for the living room.

Store (stock) = *der Vorrat*

(store-room) = *das Lager, der Lagerraum*

(shop) = *der Laden, das Geschäft*

(department store) = *das Kaufhaus, das Warenhaus*

strafen To punish. *Das ist kein Grund, die Kinder so schwer zu strafen.* That is no reason to punish the children so severely. The form *bestrafen* is more usual.

To strafe = *mit Bordwaffen (im Tiefflug) beschießen/bestreichen*

(Although English "strafe" is borrowed from German *strafen*, there is no succinct German phrase for the act of attacking troops from the air with machine-gun fire, etc.).

Strand, der The normal word for "beach," with none of the elevated or poetic connotations of English "strand." *Ich will nicht die ganzen zwei Wochen am Strand verbringen.* I don't want to spend the whole two weeks on the beach.

Strand (of hair) = *die Strähne*

Straps, der Garter belt, BrE suspender belt. Tends to have an erotic connotation (the world of "glamorous lingerie"). *Warum halten so viele Männer Strapse für sexy?* Why do so many men think garter/suspender belts are sexy?

Strap = *der Riemen*

streichen   **1.** To paint. *Wir müssen die Haustür noch streichen.* We've still got to paint the front door.   **2.** To cross out, delete, cancel. *Den dritten Absatz haben wir gestrichen.* We have deleted the third paragraph.   **3.** To stroke (in a smoothing fashion). *Sie strich dem Kind über den Kopf.* She stroked the child's head.   **4.** To apply, put on, spread (e.g., butter on bread).

    To strike (hit) = *schlagen*
             (withdraw labor) = *streiken*
             (seem) = *vorkommen* It struck me as strange. *Es kam mir seltsam vor.*

Streicher, die (pl.)   Strings (in orchestra).
    Striker (worker withdrawing labor) = *der (die) Streikende*

Streife, die   Patrol. *Eine Streife hat den Fahnenflüchtigen geschnappt.* A patrol picked up the deserter.
    Strife = *die Zwietracht*

streng   **1.** Strict. *Der Rektor ist sehr streng, und die Schüler haben alle Angst vor ihm.* The headmaster is very strict, and all the pupils are afraid of him. *Sie ist streng katholisch.* She's a strict Catholic.   **2.** Severe, intense (of cold, winter, etc.).
    Strong = *stark, kräftig*

Streß, der   Stress, but the German word is used more widely and does not always have the rather serious, often clinical, connotations of the English word. *Das ist vielleicht ein Streß!* Things are pretty hectic! *Als Journalist ist man dauernd im Streß.* As a journalist you're always under pressure.
    Stress (emphasis) = *die Betonung*

stricken   To knit.
    To strike (hit) = *schlagen*
             (withdraw labor) = *streiken*
             (seem) = *vorkommen* It struck me as strange. *Es kam mir seltsam vor.*

Strippe, die   Most commonly used as a colloquial term to refer to the telephone. *Seitdem Uschi einen neuen Freund hat, hängt sie dauernd an der Strippe.* Ever since Uschi's had a new boyfriend she's been on the telephone all the time.
    Strip (of cloth, etc.) = *der Streifen*

Strom, der   **1.** Electricity. *Sie würden billiger mit Gas als mit Strom heizen.* It'd be cheaper for you to heat with gas than electricity.   **2.** (Electric) current. *Wir haben den Strom gemessen: 3 Ampere.* We measured the current: 3 amps.   **3.** (Large) river. *Vor uns lag ein Strom, der nur der Mississippi sein konnte.* In front of us stretched a river that could only be the Mississippi. **4.** Stream (of people, visitors, etc.). *Der Strom von Touristen machte die Stimmung im Dorf etwas ungemütlich.* The stream of tourists made the atmosphere in the village rather unpleasant.

Stream (small river) = *der Bach*

Strömung, die   Current (of a river).

Stream (small river) = *der Bach*

Strudel, der   **1.** Strudel (as in "apple strudel" = *Apfelstrudel*). **2.** The primary meaning is "whirlpool," literally or figuratively. *Auch der beste Schwimmer ertrinkt, wenn er in diesen Strudel gerät.* Even the best swimmer will drown if he is caught up in this whirlpool. *Nach dem eintönigen Leben der Kleinstadt war dieser Strudel gesellschaftlicher Unternehmungen etwas ganz Neues für sie.* After the monotonous life of a small town this whirl of social activities was something quite new for her.

Stuhl, der   Chair. *Wir haben nicht genug Stühle für zwanzig Personen.* We don't have enough chairs for twenty people.

Stool = *der Hocker*

stupid(e)   May refer to a person in the sense of "stupid," "slow(-thinking)," but is used rather more often to refer to an activity in the sense of "dull," "monotonous," "mindless." *Die Arbeit am Fließband ist nach wie vor total stupide.* Assembly-line work is still totally mindless.

Stupid = *dumm, blöd*

Sturm, der   **1.** Storm (also figurative), though it refers primarily to high winds: gale. *Wir haben beim Sturm unser Dach verloren.* We lost our roof in the gale. **2.** Attack. *Die Türken bliesen zum Sturm.* The Turks sounded the attack. **3.** (sports) Forward line.

Storm (i.e., thunderstorm) = *das Gewitter*

subaltern   A formal word, normally pejorative, denoting: **1.** Of low rank, subordinate. *Ich weigere mich, mit solchen subalternen Beamten zu sprechen.* I refuse to speak to such low-ranking officials. **2.** Obsequious. *Das subalterne Verhalten der Diener widerte ihn an.* The obsequious behavior of the servants disgusted him.

Subaltern (esp. BrE: officer below rank of captain): No exact equivalent, but *der Leutnant* is close in meaning.

Subjekt, das   Subject, but also a colloquial pejorative expression for a person. *Er ist ein ganz übles Subjekt.* He's a really nasty customer.

Substanz, die   **1.** Substance. **2.** (fin.) Capital. *Keine Firma kann es sich langfristig leisten, von der Substanz zu leben.* No firm can afford in the long term to live on its capital. **3.** *Bausubstanz* Fabric (of a building). *Die Feuchtigkeit hat die Bausubstanz angegriffen.* Damp has attacked the fabric of the building. **4.** *an die Substanz gehen* (coll.) *Dieser ständige Lärm geht an die Substanz.* This neverending noise wears you down.

Substitut(in), der (die)   A term used in the retail trade, corresponding to assistant manager (of a department). *Noch zwei Jahre—dann bin ich Substitutin.* Another two years and I'll be assistant/deputy manager.

Substitute = *der Ersatz*

Subvention, die   Subsidy. This is the normal German word, whereas "subvention" is rarely used in English.

Sud, der   Stock (for soup, etc.).

Suds (lather from soap) = *der Seifenschaum*

(BrE soapy water) = *die Seifenlauge*

süffisant   Smug, self-satisfied, complacent. *Sein süffisantes Lächeln macht mich verrückt.* That smug smile of his drives me mad.

Sufficient = *genug, genügend, ausreichend*

suggerieren   Can sometimes be translated by "suggest," but the basic sense is of implanting an idea—usually one that is untrue or undesirable—in people's minds without their being consciously aware of this. *Durch solche Werbespots werden den Konsumenten Bedürfnisse suggeriert, die sie eigentlich gar nicht haben.* Such commercials make consumers believe that they have needs they do not in fact have. *Diese ganzen Doktortitel sollen Seriosität suggerieren.* All these Ph.D.s are supposed to give the impression of respectability.

Suggestiv-   Suggestive, but without any meaning of impropriety or indecency. SEE SUGGERIEREN. *Suggestivfrage* Leading question.

summen   1. To hum (a tune). *Er summte ein altes Volkslied.* He was humming an old folk song.   2. To hum, to buzz (of a machine, etc.).

To sum (add up) = *addieren*

(to sum up) = *zusammenfassen*

Suppe, die   Soup.

Supper = *das Abendessen, das Abendbrot*

surfen   For most Germans, Austrians, and Swiss this denotes the activity of windsurfing rather than California-style surfing, which is hardly possible in central Europe.

Surfer, der   Usually "windsurfer." SEE SURFEN.

Sykomore, die   Not a "sycamore," but the more exotic "mulberry fig" or "sycamore fig."

Sycamore = *der Bergahorn*

Sympathie, die   1. Sympathy, in the sense of agreement with or understanding of other people's views, feelings, etc. *Diese Politik genießt meine volle Sympathie.* I sympathize completely with this policy.   2. More frequently: liking, fondness, affection. *Er empfindet Sympathie für sie.* He has a liking for her.

Sympathy (compassion) = *das Mitgefühl, das Mitleid*

(condolence) = *das Beileid*

sympathisch   Nice, pleasant, likable. *Er ist zweifellos ein sympathischer Mensch.* He is without a doubt a likable person. *Elke war mir gleich sympathisch.* I took an instant liking to Elke.
   Sympathetic (compassionate) = *mitfühlend*
      (understanding) = *verständnisvoll*

Synchronisation, die   **1.** Synchronization.   **2.** Dubbing (film). SEE **SYN-CHRONISIEREN.**

synchronisieren   **1.** Synchronize, in the technical sense of causing s.t. to go at the same speed as s.t. else. *Die Stimmen der Schauspieler waren mit den Lippenbewegungen nicht synchronisiert.* The actors' voices weren't synchronized with their lip movements.   **2.** More commonly "to dub" (film). *Die meisten ausländischen Filme in Deutschland haben keine Untertitel: sie sind synchronisiert.* Most foreign films in Germany aren't subtitled: they're dubbed.
   To synchronize (watches): Let's synchronize watches *Uhrenvergleich!*

Syringe, die   Not a syringe, but a botanical term for "lilac" (everyday name: *der Flieder*).
   Syringe (med.) = *die Spritze*

Szene, die   Scene (also in the sense of a—public—argument). *die Szene* is also used to refer to the "alternative" subculture found in some big cities (e.g., Berlin), with rather more serious and intellectual connotations than English "the scene." *sich in Szene setzen* To draw attention to oneself, to play to the gallery, to put oneself in the limelight; *(Beifall) auf offener Szene* (Applause) during the game/performance.

T

Tablett, das   Tray. *Der Kellner brachte zwei Kännchen Kaffee auf einem silbernen Tablett.* The waiter brought two pots of coffee on a silver tray.
   Tablet (med.) = *die Tablette, die Pille*

Tachometer, der or **das**   **1.** The normal term for the speedometer in a car, truck, etc.   **2.** Tachometer.

Tafel, die   **1.** Can mean "table," but only in formal, ceremonial contexts. More usually: **2.** Blackboard. *Schreib' dieses Wort an die Tafel.* Write this word on the blackboard.   **3.** Bar (of chocolate). *Ich hätte gern eine Tafel Schokolade.* I'd like a bar of chocolate.
   Table (furniture) = *der Tisch*
      (of statistics, etc.) = *die Tabelle*

Takt, der 1. Tact. 2. Time, beat (in the context of rhythm). *Diesem Orchester gelingt es nie, im Takt zu bleiben.* This orchestra never manages to stay in time. 3. (mus.) Bar. 4. (prosody) Foot. 5. Stroke (engine). *der Zweitaktmotor* two-stroke engine.

Talk, der Not "talk," but "talc(um)." The English word "talk" has been adopted, however, in such compounds as *Talkshow,* to refer to TV talk shows.

Talk (conversation) = *das Gespräch*
 (idle talk) = *das Gerede*
 (lecture) = *der Vortrag*

Talkmaster, der A pseudo-anglicism: "talk show host." SEE **TALK**.

Tang, der Seaweed. *Hier könnte man wunderschön baden, wenn der ganze Tang nicht wäre.* This would be a wonderful place for swimming if it wasn't for all the seaweed.

Tang (smell) = *(scharfer) Geruch*
 (taste) = *(scharfer) Geschmack*

Tangente, die 1. Tangent. 2. Also a relatively recent term to denote a beltway, a sort of expressway built round a town or city to ease congestion (BrE ring-road): *Wenn du auf der Tangente fährst, sparst du mindestens zwanzig Minuten.* You save at least twenty minutes if you take the beltway (BrE ring-road).

tanken 1. To get, fill up with, gas (for a car); to refuel (racing car, airplane). *Wir müssen unbedingt tanken.* We really must get some gas. 2. To get, have (fig.)—in relation to fresh air, sunshine—and alcohol. *Wir haben eine lange Sitzung vor uns—wir sollten erst einmal frische Luft tanken.* We've got a long meeting in front of us—we ought to get some fresh air first. *Der Matrose da hat ganz schön getankt!* That sailor's really had a shotful (BrE is really tanked up)!

Tanne, die Fir(-tree). Species indicated by compounds with *-tanne* include, however, both firs and spruces: *Blautanne* Colorado spruce; *Rottanne* Norwegian spruce; *Weißtanne* silver fir.

Tan (suntan) = *die Bräune*

Tapete, die Not a tapestry, but "wallpaper." *Die alte Tapete können Sie einfach überstreichen.* You can simply paint over the old wallpaper. *der Tapetenwechsel* Change of scenery/surroundings.

Tapestry = *der Wandteppich, der Gobelin*

tappen 1. To grope (in order to find one's way): often used metaphorically. *Eine Lösung hat keiner—wir tappen alle im dunkeln.* No one has a solution—we are all groping in the dark. 2. To move, walk uncertainly, falteringly; to lumber (of a heavy animal, e.g., a bear). The verb *tapsen* is also used in this sense.

To tap (strike lightly) = *klopfen*
 (telephone) = *abhören, anzapfen*

Tarif, der 1. Tariff. 2. The German word is also applied to agreements and negotiations on wages, salaries, working conditions, etc., particularly in certain compounds: *Tarifverhandlungen* pay/wage/salary negotiations; *die Tarifpartner* management and labor; *der Tarifvertrag* pay/wage/salary agreement; *die Tarifautonomie* (free) collective bargaining, the right to undertake such bargaining.

Taste, die Key (on typewriter, computer, calculator, piano, etc.). *Bei diesem Taschenrechner sind die Tasten zu klein.* The keys are too small on this pocket calculator. In some contexts "button" may be a more suitable translation.

Taste = *der Geschmack*

tasten To grope, feel (for s.t.). *Es war stockdunkel: ich tastete nach dem Lichtschalter.* It was pitch-dark: I groped/felt for the light switch.

To taste = *schmecken*

(try food) = *probieren*

Tastorgan, das Organ of touch, tactile organ.

Organ of taste = *das Geschmacksorgan*

Taxe, die 1. Charge, or scale of charges; may also denote a (professionally produced) valuation or estimate. *Für unsere Sprachkurse mit sehr kleinen Gruppen gilt natürlich eine höhere Taxe.* Of course there is a higher charge for our language courses with very small groups. In the case of *Kurtaxe* the word does indicate a "tax," i.e., that levied on visitors to a spa town. 2. May also be found as a variant of *das Taxi* = taxi.

Tax = *die Steuer*

taxieren To estimate, value. *Auf wieviel würden Sie einen solchen Oldtimer taxieren?* What would you estimate the value of a vintage car like this to be?

To tax (econ.) = *besteuern*

Technik, die 1. May mean "technique." *Die Technik des Spinnens beherrscht sie noch nicht.* She hasn't yet mastered the technique of spinning. 2. More commonly, technology. *Er ist gegen alles, was mit Technik zusammenhängt.* He's against anything connected with technology. *Unser Sprachlabor ist mit der neuesten Technik ausgestattet.* Our language laboratory is equipped with the latest technology.

Techniker, der The German word is broader in application than "technician," and the context must decide whether it denotes someone with higher qualifications, in which case "engineer" is more appropriate. *Die neue Werkzeugmaschine haben unsere besten Techniker entworfen.* Our best engineers have designed the new machine tool. *Sind Sie mit dem neuen Labortechniker zufrieden?* Are you happy with the new lab technician?

technisch "Technical" or "technological," according to the context. SEE **TECHNIK.**

Teller, der   Plate (for food).
Teller (bank clerk) = *der Kassierer, die Kassiererin*
(of story) = *der Erzähler, die Erzählerin*

Temperament, das   Temperament, i.e., a person's essential personality or nature. But more commonly a particularly lively character, not always susceptible of self-control. *Seine Freundin hat vielleicht (ein) Temperament!* His girlfriend certainly has spirit. *Sie ist im Grunde genommen sehr nett, aber das Temperament geht manchmal mit ihr durch.* Basically she's very nice, but she sometimes loses her temper.

temperamentvoll   Denotes a lively, vivacious character. *Das Leben mit so einer temperamentvollen Frau ist nie langweilig.* Life with such a lively woman is never boring.
Temperamental (person) = *launisch, launenhaft*
(car, etc.) = *launisch*

temperieren   **1.** To temper (emotions, etc.), but this is elevated usage. **2.** The normal meaning is "to bring to the correct temperature." *Ein Pils muß unbedingt gut temperiert sein.* It's essential that a pilsener be served at the right temperature.
To temper (emotion) = *mäßigen*
(steel) = *tempern*

Tempo, das   (mus.) Tempo. But the German word is much wider in application and denotes speed generally. *Wir haben mit vollem Tempo gearbeitet.* We worked at top speed. *Bei Tempo 40 innerorts würde die Zahl der Unfälle bestimmt zurückgehen.* If the speed limit in built-up areas was 40, the number of accidents would certainly decrease. Frequently used in exhortations to hurry up. *Tempo! Tempo!* Hurry up/Get a move on!

Tendenz, die   Tendency. But the German word is occasionally used pejoratively in the context of influencing people or making propaganda. *Alle seine Erzählungen haben diese sozialistische Tendenz—für ihn war die Politik wichtiger als die Literatur.* All his stories have this socialist bias—politics was more important than literature for him.

terminieren   A formal word: to fix or limit, with regard to time. *Die Sitzung ist jetzt für den 20. Juli terminiert.* The meeting has now been arranged for 20 July. *Das Recht auf Einspruch ist natürlich terminiert.* The right to appeal is of course subject to a time limit.
To terminate = *beenden*

Terminus, der   A (technical or specialized) term. *Herr Jakob ist Rechtsanwalt—er müßte diesen Terminus kennen.* Herr Jakob is a lawyer—he ought to know this term. The longer expression *Terminus technicus* is used in the same sense.
Terminus = *die Endstation*

Terrasse, die 1. Terrace (e.g., for cultivation on slopes). 2. The normal word for a paved area between the back of a house and the garden, where English "patio" is perhaps the more normal term.

Terror, der Terror. Also used colloquially to denote a lot of (unnecessary) fuss and bother, esp. in the phrase *Terror machen. Ihre Kinder sind so verzogen, daß sie immer Terror machen, wenn sie ausnahmsweise ihren Willen nicht durchsetzen.* Their children are so spoiled that they always kick up a huge fuss if just once they don't get their way.

Testament, das 1. Testament (Bible). 2. Testament in the sense of the instructions a person leaves to be followed after death, but the German word is the normal one and corresponds really to English "will." *Es sieht aus, als ob dein Onkel doch kein Testament hinterlassen hat.* It looks as though your uncle didn't leave a will after all. 3. (fig.) Legacy. *Das dauerhafteste Testament dieses Politikers ist seine Bildungsreform.* The most durable legacy of this politician is his educational reform measures.

Text, der 1. Text, but certain specific uses require other translations: 2. Words, lyrics (of song, esp. pop song). *Die Melodie ist schön, aber der Text ist ziemlich blöd.* The tune's nice, but the lyrics are pretty stupid. 3. Libretto (of opera), though *das Libretto* is more usual. 4. Caption (of cartoon, etc.). 5. Script (of film, play, etc.).

Textbuch, das Most native speakers are hesitant about what this word means and it is felt to be unusual. It may be a book containing a script or a libretto, or an anthology or collection of texts for educational purposes. SEE TEXT.

Textbook = *das Lehrbuch*

Theater, das 1. Theater. 2. (fig.) (Making a) fuss, scene. *Mach' nicht so ein Theater!* Don't make such a fuss! 3. (fig.) Pretence, play-acting. *Laß dich nicht stören, wenn sie weint—es ist alles nur Theater.* Don't worry if she cries—it's all play-acting.

Thema, das Occasionally "theme," in the deeper sense of the English word (i.e., an underlying subject of s.t.), but more commonly simply "subject," "topic." *Alle diese Essay-Themen sind so abgedroschen.* All these essay topics are so trite.

Therme, die Thermal spring or, in historical contexts, baths. *die römischen Thermen zu Trier* the Roman baths at Trier.

Therm (calorie) = *die Kalorie*

(BrE = 100,000 thermal units) = *100.000 Wärmeeinheiten*

Tick, der (Muscular) tic. Also a strange obsession or interest that a person has. *Er hat einen Tick, immer nur den Dotter vom Ei zu essen.* He's got a thing about only eating the yolk of an egg.

Tick (of clock, etc.) = *das Ticken*

(insect) = *die Zecke*

ticken To tick. Note also the phrase *Du tickst nicht wohl (ganz) richtig/Bei dir tickt es wohl nicht (ganz) richtig.* You're crazy/out of your mind.

tingeln No succinct translation: the verb is applied to artistes who move around to earn their living, usually appearing in rather low-key and poorly paid entertainments. *Mit seiner kleinen Rockgruppe tingelte er durch ganz Amerika.* With his small rock group he worked his way (playing small dates) across the whole of America.

To tingle = *prickeln*

Tinte, die Ink. *in der Tinte sitzen* To be in a mess/in the soup.

Tint (shade of color) = *der (Farb)ton*

(dye for hair) = *das Tönungsmittel*

tippeln A colloquial verb, now rather dated, denoting movement, usually on foot over a long distance. *Ich zahle lieber für ein Taxi, als daß ich zwei Stunden durch die Stadt tipple.* I'd rather pay for a taxi than leg it across town for two hours. *der Tippelbruder* (hum.) Tramp, "gentleman of the road."

To tipple = *picheln*

tippen **1.** To bet; to guess (on the basis of appearances). *Ich tippe darauf, daß sie noch in diesem Jahr heiraten.* I bet they get married this year. *Ja, du hast richtig getippt—er ist Gebrauchtwagenhändler.* Yes, you guessed correctly—he is a secondhand car salesman. **2.** To bet in or play one of the national lotteries (or fill in the necessary coupon). *Ich habe noch nie in meinem Leben getippt.* I've never bet on the lottery in my life. **3.** To type. *Wie schnell kannst du tippen?* How quickly can you type? **4.** To touch lightly, tap. *Der Polizist tippte ihm auf die Schulter.* The policeman tapped him on the shoulder.

To tip (give gratuity) = *Trinkgeld geben*

(knock over) = *kippen*

Titan, das (chem.) Titanium.

Titan = *der Titan*

Ton, der **1.** Tone. **2.** (tech., mus.) Sound. *Bei diesen alten Filmen ist der Ton manchmal sehr schlecht.* The sound is sometimes very bad on these old films. **3.** Stress, accent. *Der Ton liegt auf der letzten Silbe.* The stress is on the last syllable. **4.** Word, utterance (usually in the negative). *Er hat den ganzen Abend keinen Ton gesagt.* He didn't say a word all evening.

There is also a homonym meaning "clay." *Alle Gefäße, die wir fanden, waren aus Ton.* All the vessels we found were made of clay.

Tonne, die **1.** (unit of weight) Ton or (metric) tonne. **2.** Any of various large, usually metal containers, in particular a barrel, cask, or drum, or (short for *Mülltonne*) a trashcan, garbage can, BrE dustbin. **3.** (naut.) A buoy.

Torf, der   Peat. *In Irland wird seit Jahrhunderten mit Torf geheizt.* The Irish have used peat as fuel for centuries.
Turf (lawn) = *der Rasen, das Gras*
    (piece of turf) = *die (Gras)sode*
    (horse racing) = *der Pferderennsport*

Torte, die   Though it cannot be said that a *Torte* is always a "cake" and never a "tart," it is true to say that the word usually denotes the sort of multilayer product that in the United States or England would normally be called a "cake" (or even BrE "gateau"). The *Obsttorte* may consist of simply a base covered with fruit, but the nature of the base would normally earn the designation "flan," rather than "tart," and corresponds to AmE "shortcake." The traditional translation of the famous *Schwarzwälder Kirschtorte* is "Black Forest Cake" (BrE: "Gateau"). The small, individual tarts so popular in American and British cooking are somewhat less familiar in Germany: *das Törtchen* will provide an adequate translation.

Tour, die   **1.** May denote a tour, but may also indicate s.t. shorter—a trip, drive, outing. *Gestern nachmittag haben wir eine Tour nach Köln gemacht.* We went on a trip to Cologne yesterday afternoon.   **2.** Rev(olution), of engine, etc. *Der Motor läuft auf vollen Touren.* The engine's running at full speed. *8000 Touren hält der Motor nicht aus.* The engine can't take 8,000 revs.   **3.** (coll.) A trick, ploy, or disingenuous plan of some sort. *Diese alte Tour zieht bei mir nicht.* That old trick won't work with me. *Komm' mir nicht mit der Tour.* Don't try that one on me.
Tour (as tourist) = *die Reise*
    (of musicians, actors, etc.) = *die Tournee*

Trafik, die   The normal Austrian term for a tobacconist's shop.
Traffic (movement of vehicles) = *der Verkehr*

trainieren   **1.** To train, coach (team, etc.).   **2.** To practice (a particular discipline). *Du mußt den Hochsprung noch trainieren, wenn du am Zehnkampf teilnehmen willst.* You'll have to practice the high jump if you want to take part in the decathlon.
To train (s.o. for a profession) = *ausbilden*
    (animal) = *abrichten, dressieren*

Trakt, der   **1.** Tract, in certain medical or anatomical contexts (e.g., digestive tract).   **2.** Wing, section (of a large building). *Im nördlichen Trakt ist das Dach noch leck.* The roof is still leaking in the north wing.
Tract (written work) = *das Traktat*

trampen   To hitchhike, go hitchhiking. *Nach Albanien trampen ist vielleicht nicht so romantisch, wie es sich anhört.* Hitchhiking to Albania may not be as romantic as it sounds.
To tramp = *stapfen, trampeln, marschieren*

trampeln   May mean "to trample," with its destructive connotation. But may simply mean "to tramp," "to stamp one's feet." *Die Häftlinge fingen an zu trampeln.* The prisoners started to stamp their feet.

transparent   Transparent, translucent, diaphanous. But often used metaphorically to denote clarity, lucidity. *Das neue System ist viel transparenter—jeder weiß, was er zu tun hat.* The new system is much clearer—everyone knows what his or her job is.

Transparent (literal meaning) = *durchsichtig, transparent*
(fig.: clear, obvious) = *eindeutig, offensichtlich, offenkundig*
(fig. of lies, dishonest intentions, etc.) = *durchschaubar*

Transparent, das   Banner. *Die Demonstranten wurden nicht festgenommen, aber ihre Transparente wurden beschlagnahmt.* The demonstrators were not arrested, but their banners were confiscated.

Transparent (adj.) (literal meaning) = *durchsichtig, transparent*
(fig.: clear, obvious) = *eindeutig, offensichtlich, offenkundig*
(fig. of lies, dishonest intentions, etc.) = *durchschaubar*

Transparenz, die   **1.** Transparency (i.e., quality of letting light through). **2.** Clarity, lucidity. SEE **TRANSPARENT.**

Transparency (for overhead projector) = *die Folie*
(slide, in photography) = *das Dia(positiv)*

transpirieren   **1.** To transpire (plants).   **2.** To perspire, of human beings. The word is formal and often affected in tone.

To transpire (become known) = *bekannt werden*
(turn out) = *sich ergeben*
(happen) = *passieren, geschehen*

Transport, der   **1.** Transport(ation), i.e., movement of s.t. (or s.o.) from one place to another.   **2.** The actual things being moved: here "consignment" and "shipment" are more appropriate translations. *Der Goldtransport ist nie angekommen.* The gold consignment never arrived.   **3.** With reference to sick or injured people a paraphrase with "move" usually provides the best translation. *Beim Transport verschlimmerte sich der Zustand des Patienten.* The patient's condition deteriorated while he was being moved.

Public transport(ation) = *öffentliche Verkehrsmittel* (pl.)

transportieren   **1.** To transport.   **2.** To move (sick or injured people). SEE **TRANSPORT.**   **3.** To wind on (film). *Der Film transportiert nicht—da stimmt irgendwas nicht.* The film won't wind on—there's something wrong.

Trapez, das **1.** Trapeze (circus, etc.). **2.** Also a geometrical term for a quadrilateral having two parallel sides of unequal length; trapezoid, BrE trapezium.

Trapezium (AmE) = *das Trapezoid*
(BrE) = *das Trapez*

Trapezoid, das Geometrical term for a quadrilateral having no parallel sides: trapezium, (BrE) trapezoid.

Trapezoid (AmE) = *das Trapez;* (BrE) = *das Trapezoid*

Trappe, die Bustard (bird).

Trap = *die Falle*

Traumtänzer, der Not a dancer who is so good that he or she can be called a "dream dancer," but a "dreamer" who has lost touch with reality and pursues unattainable ideals.

Trecker, der Another term for *Traktor:* tractor. *Erdklumpen fielen immer wieder vom Trecker herunter.* Clods of earth kept falling off the tractor. Trekker: No established German expression, but *das Expeditionsmitglied* expresses the general idea; the borrowed form *der Trekker* is also seen.

Tresor, der **1.** Safe, strongbox. *Wieviel haben Sie im Tresor gefunden?* How much did you find in the safe? **2.** Strongroom, (bank) vault.

Treasure = *der Schatz*

Tresse, die Usually found in the plural, this means (gold or silver) "braid" on uniforms, etc. *Wem sollen diese ganzen Tressen imponieren?* Who is supposed to be impressed by all this (gold) braid(ing)?

Tress = *die Locke*

treten **1.** To tread, step. **2.** To kick. *Ich habe gesehen, wie sie ihm gegen das Schienbein getreten hat.* I saw her kick him in the shins. **3.** To appear, come out, usually in certain fixed expressions. *über die Ufer treten* to burst its banks (river).

treu True, but only in the sense of "faithful," "loyal." *Zehn Jahre war er im Gefängnis, aber sie ist ihm trotzdem treu geblieben.* He was in prison for ten years, but she still remained faithful to him.

True (i.e., not false) = *wahr*

Tribüne, die **1.** A raised stand for spectators. *Auf der Tribüne prügelten sich die Zuschauer.* The spectators were fighting in the stands. **2.** Platform, rostrum for a speaker.

Tribune = *der (Volks)tribun*

Trickfilm, der Most commonly used to denote a cartoon, in the sense of a film made with animated drawings. May also mean "trick film" in the technical sense. *Als Kind habe ich am liebsten Trickfilme gesehen.* When I was a child I liked cartoons most of all.

trimmen 1. To trim, in certain technical senses (e.g., with reference to ships or aircraft). More commonly: 2. (coll.) To teach, train, esp. with reference to the inculcation of certain habits. *Den Otto hat sie wirklich auf Pünktlichkeit getrimmt.* She's certainly trained Otto to be punctual. 3. (coll.) To adapt the appearance of s.t. or s.o.: to do up. *Warum hat man bloß unser Stammlokal auf schottisch getrimmt?* Why on earth have they done up our local pub to look Scottish? 4. (reflexive) To do exercises to keep fit. *Mein Cousin hat sich jeden Tag getrimmt und hatte trotzdem mit 40 Jahren seinen ersten Herzinfarkt.* My cousin did exercises every day and still had his first heart attack when he was 40. To trim (cut) = *stutzen*

Tripper, der (med.) Gonorrhoea.
Tripper = *der Ausflügler*

Trivial- In such compounds as *Trivialliteratur* (which is the commonest) the first element does not have such a strongly pejorative sense as English "trivial." It refers to work that has no very high aspirations— "light fiction," perhaps, but not "trivial fiction."

Trott, der 1. Trot (of horses). 2. (Dull) routine. *Sie wußte nicht, wie sie aus diesem Trott herauskommen sollte.* She didn't know how to escape from this dull routine.

Trubel, der Denotes busy and possibly confusing activity, but with a suggestion of gaiety rather than trouble: bustle, hubbub, hurly-burly. *Dem Trubel einer großen Fete fühlte er sich noch nicht gewachsen.* He did not yet feel up to the bustle of a big party.
Trouble (bother, irritating) = *der Ärger*
    (bother, effort) = *die Mühe*
Troubles (serious) = *Sorgen, Probleme* (pl.)

Trupp, der 1. There is often a military element or connotation: troop, squad. *ein Trupp Bereitschaftspolizei* a squad of riot police. 2. In some cases the word may not mean much more than "group." *Ein Trupp Studenten verlangte, den Dekan zu sprechen.* A group of students demanded to see the dean.
Troops (mil.) = *die Truppen* (pl.)

Truppe, die 1. Troop. It is used in the singular as well as the plural to mean "troops" in the general military sense. *Diese Niederlage hat die Moral der Truppe/Truppen erheblich geschwächt.* This defeat has considerably weakened the morale of the troops. 2. Troupe, company (of entertainers).

Tube, die Tube. *auf die Tube drücken* (coll.) To step on the gas, to put one's foot down, to get a move on. This is applied to car travel, but also to other situations where more speed is required.

Tumult, der   Tumult, commotion. The German word may in some contexts, however, stress the idea of disorder and in this sense be used in the plural: disturbances. *Bei den Tumulten, die es zur Zeit gibt, ist es nicht sicher, auf die Straße zu gehen.* With the disturbances there are at the moment it is not safe to walk the streets.

turnen/Turnen, das   (To do) gymnastics; also, by colloquial extension, "to move (nimbly)" (over obstacles, etc.). *Ich habe mir beim Turnen den Knöchel verstaucht.* I sprained my ankle during gym(nastics). *Er ist mühelos über die Mauer geturnt.* He climbed over the wall without any trouble.

To turn = *(sich) drehen, (sich) wenden*

Turnus, der   Rotating schedule (BrE rota), most commonly used in the phrase *im Turnus. Das Abspülen machen wir im Turnus.* We have a schedule for doing the dishes. *Die Weltmeisterschaft findet in einem Turnus von vier Jahren statt.* The world championship takes place every four years.

Turn (movement) = *die (Um)drehung*
To make a right turn = *nach rechts abbiegen*
It's your turn = *Sie sind dran/Sie sind an der Reihe*

Tutor, der   This normally denotes an older student who gives classes to groups of younger students, often as a supplement to normal lectures and seminars given by academic staff. It may also denote a member of staff in a company who advises and supervises a student on placement with that company.

Tutor (private teacher) = *der Privatlehrer*
         (BrE, = college professor) = *der Dozent*

Twen, der   Pseudo-anglicism denoting a person who is in his or her twenties. *Solche Pauschalreisen sind bei Twens besonders beliebt.* Package tours of this sort are especially popular with people in their twenties.

Typ, der   1. Type, sort (esp. of person). *Er ist nicht mein Typ.* He's not my type.   2. Type, model (of machine, etc.). *Dieser Typ wird nicht mehr hergestellt.* This model is no longer manufactured.   3. (coll.) A very common expression for a usually young male person: guy, BrE bloke. *Kennst du den Typ mit der Sonnebrille?* Do you know the guy with the sunglasses?

Type (sort) = *die Sorte, die Art*

Type, die   1. Type, character (printing). *Diese zwei Typen sind falsch herum.* These two characters are the wrong way round.   2. (coll.) Eccentric person, character. *Der Helmut ist vielleicht eine Type!* Helmut is a real character/oddball.

Type (sort) = *die Sorte, die Art*

U

überall Everywhere.

Overall (adv.) (altogether) = *insgesamt*

(on the whole) = *im großen und ganzen*

überfliegen **1.** To overfly, fly over (territory, etc.). **2.** To scan, glance over (a document). *Ich weiß nicht genau, was im Vertrag steht—ich habe ihn nur ganz schnell überflogen.* I don't know exactly what the contract says—I just glanced through it very quickly. **3.** To flit across (a person's face: of a smile, blush, etc.).

Überhang, der **1.** Overhang (of rock, etc.). **2.** Surplus. *Zur Zeit gibt es einen Überhang an Wohnraum in dieser Stadt.* At the moment there is a surplus of accommodations in this city.

überholen **1.** To overhaul (machine, etc.). **2.** More frequently, to overtake (a vehicle). *Wegen der vielen Kurven konnte ich den Lkw nicht überholen.* I couldn't overtake the truck because of all the bends.

überhören **1.** Fail to hear. *Er hatte das Radio so laut gestellt, daß er das Klingeln des Telefons überhörte.* He had the radio on so loud that he didn't hear the telephone ringing. **2.** To pretend not to hear, esp. in the phrase *Das möchte ich überhört haben!* I'll pretend I didn't hear/I'll ignore that (comment). **3.** (as a separable verb) To be tired of s.t. because one has heard it too often. *Diese Kriegsgeschichten habe ich mir übergehört.* I'm sick and tired of hearing these war stories.

To overhear = *zufällig hören, zufällig mitbekommen*

überkochen To boil over. *Die Milch ist übergekocht.* The milk's boiled over.

To overcook = *verbraten, zu lange braten*

überkommen To come over (of a feeling). *Ein Gefühl des Ekels überkam ihn, als er zusah, wie die Schweine geschlachtet wurden.* A feeling of revulsion came over him as he watched the pigs being slaughtered.

To overcome (difficulties, etc.) = *überwinden, bewältigen*

übermannen A rather elevated expression for "to overcome" (of emotion). *Blinder Zorn übermannte ihn.* Blind anger overcame him.

To be overmanned (have too many staff): Both these industries suffer from overmanning. *Beide Industrien leiden darunter, daß sie zu große Belegschaften haben.*

Overmanning = *die Überbesetzung*

überreichen To hand over, present (ceremoniously). *Der Bürgermeister überreichte dem Sieger den Pokal.* The mayor presented the winner with the cup.

To overreach oneself = *sich übernehmen*

übersehen   **1.** To overlook, not see. *Wie hast du bloß diese ganzen Risse übersehen?* How on earth did you overlook all these cracks?   **2.** To pretend not to see. *Seine Tante übersah die Aktfotos an der Wand.* His aunt pretended not to see the nude photos on the wall.   **3.** To have a good view of (literally or metaphorically). *Vom Südturm kann man beide Täler übersehen.* You can have a view of both valleys from the south tower. *Anhand von diesem Computerprogramm kann man alle Kosten übersehen, die auf einen zukommen.* With the aid of this computer program you can get a clear view of all the costs that are in store for you.

To oversee (supervise) = *beaufsichtigen, überwachen*

Übersicht, die   **1.** Denotes that one can see the totality of s.t., not just the parts, but the whole. *In diesem Buch sind so viele überflüssige Details, daß man schnell die Übersicht verliert.* There is so much superfluous detail in this book that one soon loses the general picture. *Das Buch bietet eine Übersicht über 200 Jahre amerikanischer Geschichte.* The book gives an overview of 200 years of American history.   **2.** It may indicate an actual table, graph, list, etc., that gives one such an overview. *Anbei eine Übersicht der tatsächlichen Kosten.* Attached is a table of the actual costs.

Oversight = *das Versehen*

Uhr, die   **1.** Clock, watch. *Ich möchte eine neue Uhr für die Küche.* I'd like a new clock for the kitchen. *Ich habe vergessen, vor dem Schwimmen meine Uhr abzunehmen.* I forgot to take off my watch before swimming.   **2.** In certain compounds it may denote a meter or gauge. *die Gasuhr* gas meter.   **3.** Used in various time expressions. *zehn Uhr* ten o'clock; *Wieviel Uhr ist es?* What's the time?

Hour = *die Stunde*

Uhrglas, das   Clock glass, watch glass (i.e., the glass over the face of a clock or watch).

Hourglass = *die Sanduhr*

Umbra, die   **1.** (astron.) Umbra.   **2.** The color "umber."

ungraziös   Ungraceful. SEE GRAZIÖS.

Ungracious (impolite) = *unhöflich*

Union, die   Union, in the sense of parties, groups, countries, etc., coming together. But the word is perhaps most commonly used to refer to the political alliance between the two "Conservative" parties, the CSU (*Christlich-Soziale Union*) of Bavaria, and the CDU (*Christlich-Demokratische Union*) of the rest of Germany. *Die Union versucht, der Kostenexplosion im Gesundheitswesen Herr zu werden.* The CDU/CSU alliance is trying to get the explosive increase in health costs under control.

(Labor/trade) union = *die Gewerkschaft*

unkindlich   Unchildlike. SEE KINDLICH.

Unkindly (adj.) = *unfreundlich*

unseriös 1. Not respectable, untrustworthy. 2. Not serious in the sense of "frivolous." SEE SERIÖS.

Unserious (i.e., not serious) = *nicht ernst*

unsozial 1. Antisocial (of person disliking company). 2. Lacking social awareness, not public-spirited. *Das neue Steuergesetz, das die Höhe des Einkommens überhaupt nicht berücksichtigt, wird als unsozial empfunden.* The new tax law, which takes no account of income levels, is felt to be socially unjust. SEE SOZIAL.

To work unsocial hours = *außerhalb der normalen Arbeitszeit arbeiten*

unsympathisch Disagreeable, not likable, not nice. SEE SYMPATHISCH.

To be unsympathetic (lack compassion) = *wenig/kein Mitgefühl zeigen*

Unsympathetic (to a request, etc.) = *ablehnend*

unter It should be remembered that this can mean "among" as well as "under(neath)." *Unter den neuen Rekruten waren auch einige Frauen.* There were also some women among the new recruits. *unter anderem* Among other things, inter alia.

Unterarm, der Forearm (i.e., part of arm between hand and elbow).

Underarm (serve in tennis, etc.) = *(Aufschlag usw.) von unten*

(armpit) = *die Achselhöhle*

unterbieten 1. To underbid (e.g., in bridge). 2. To undercut (in price). *Wir müssen rücksichtslos alle Konkurrenten unterbieten.* We must ruthlessly undercut all our competitors. 3. (ironic) To be unbeatably poor, when referring to a particularly poor performance. *Ihre Übersetzung ist kaum noch zu unterbieten.* Your translation sets new standards of incompetence.

unterderhand/unter der Hand Does not have the clearly negative connotation of "underhanded" (i.e., "deceptively secretive"), but indicates rather the use of less public, less customary channels, and may mean not much more than "privately." *Das habe ich unterderhand erfahren.* I heard that on the grapevine. *Wir haben unser Haus unterderhand verkauft.* We sold our house privately.

Underhanded = *hinterhältig*

untergehen 1. To sink, be submerged. *Er zeigte uns die Stelle, wo das Schiff untergegangen war.* He showed us the place where the ship had sunk. *Seine Rede ging in Buhrufen unter.* His speech was drowned by booing. 2. To set (sun, etc.). 3. To be destroyed, come to an end (culture, etc.). *Davon geht die Welt nicht unter.* It's not the end of the world (i.e., it's not that bad).

To undergo (an operation) = *sich (einer Operation) unterziehen*

unterliegen **1.** To be defeated. *Bayern München unterlag dem HSV mit 1 : 2.* Bayern Munich lost to HSV 1–2. **2.** To succumb, give way to (temptation). **3.** To be subject to (conditions, etc.). *Die Herstellung dieser Chemikalien unterliegt den schärfsten Kontrollen.* The production of these chemicals is subject to the most stringent checks.

To underlie = *zugrundeliegen*

unternehmen Much wider in reference than English "undertake," and without the latter's connotation of difficulties to be overcome. It often means no more than "make," "do." *Heute abend müssen wir unbedingt was unternehmen—ich will nicht schon wieder fernsehen.* We really must do something this evening—I don't want to watch TV again. *Die Regierung hat fast nichts gegen die Umweltverschmutzung unternommen.* The government has done practically nothing about pollution.

To undertake (promise) = *sich verpflichten*

Unternehmen, das **1.** Undertaking, enterprise. **2.** Company, business, firm. *Das Unternehmen hat er seinem ältesten Sohn vermacht.* He bequeathed the business to his eldest son.

Unternehmer, der The owner of a company: employer, entrepreneur, big businessman. *Die Verhandlungen zwischen den Unternehmern und den Gewerkschaften sind gescheitert.* The negotiations between the employers and the unions have failed.

Undertaker (mortician) = *der Leichenbestatter*

unterwegs Denotes travel, movement. *Mein Bruder ist Vertreter und ist immer unterwegs.* My brother is a sales rep and is always on the move. *Das Päckchen mit den Kassetten ist unterwegs.* The parcel with the cassettes is on its way. *Insgesamt waren wir drei Wochen unterwegs.* Altogether we were away for three weeks. *Wir haben unterwegs gehalten und eine Tasse Kaffee getrunken.* We stopped on the way and had a cup of coffee. Also refers to babies that are "on the way." *Sie hat schon drei Kinder und jetzt ist das vierte unterwegs.* She already has three children and now a fourth is on the way.

To be under way (i.e., to have begun) = *im Gang/in vollem Gang sein* (naut.) = *in Fahrt/unterwegs sein*

untreu Untrue, but only in the sense of "unfaithful," "disloyal." SEE TREU.

Untrue (false) = *falsch, nicht wahr*

unverschämt Not "unashamed": it is applied to express indignation and outrage at other people's behavior. The meaning is sometimes akin to "shameless." *Vier Mark für eine Tasse Kaffee—das ist ja unverschämt!* Four marks for a cup of coffee—it's disgraceful/outrageous! *Es ist unverschämt, wie er die Leute ausbeutet.* It's disgraceful/disgusting the way he exploits people. *Seien Sie nicht unverschämt!* Don't be impertinent!

Unashamed = *schamlos*

unwillig This may mean "unwilling," "reluctant," but more usually means "indignant," "angry." *Er reagierte unwillig auf meine Frage.* He reacted indignantly/angrily to my question.

Unwilling (to do s.t.) = *nicht bereit (etwas zu tun)*

unwohl 1. Unwell (physically). 2. Uneasy (mental state). *Ich fühle mich immer unwohl, wenn er diese rassistischen Witze erzählt.* I always feel uncomfortable when he tells those racist jokes.

I feel unwell = *Es geht mir nicht gut/Ich fühle mich unwohl*

Urne, die 1. Urn (for ashes, etc.). 2. Ballot box (in elections). *Die Urnen wurden geleert und die Stimmzettel gezählt.* The ballot boxes were emptied and the ballot papers counted. *Am Sonntag geht das deutsche Volk zur Urne/zu den Urnen.* On Sunday the German people go to the polls. 3. May also refer to the box from which (winning) tickets are taken in a lottery or sweepstakes.

V

Vasektomie, die Like English "vasectomy," this may denote the specific operation to sterilize a man. But it is a far less familiar word than the English, and is often misunderstood by native speakers to mean something connected with the cardiovascular system. *Die Sterilisation des Mannes* is an unambiguous expression that will avoid any possible misunderstanding.

vegetativ A generally technical word, included here because of one use (which has nothing to do with vegetation) that has passed into the general language, namely that affliction of the *vegetatives Nervensystem* (autonomic nervous system) referred to as *vegetative Nervenstörungen* (pl.). This is something of a national disease in Germany (rather like low blood pressure) and is often blamed for various functional disorders involving, for example, the circulation and digestion. There is no obvious English translation.

Vehikel, das Vehicle, in the abstract sense (e.g., a vehicle for communication). But it is pejorative when applied to a car, etc.: jalopy, tin lizzy, BrE old banger.

Vehicle (car, truck, etc.) = *das Fahrzeug*

Ventil, das 1. Nothing to do with ventilation: a "valve" (in an engine, on a tire, on a trumpet, etc.). 2. (fig.) Outlet. *Sie braucht ein Ventil für diese überschüssige Energie.* She needs an outlet for this surplus energy.

Vers, der   May refer to a verse in the Bible, or in a hymn. But more commonly means a "line" of poetry. There is no single German word that can convey the negative, lowbrow connotation that English "verse" can have, in contrast to "poetry." *Angeblich brauchte Vergil manchmal einen ganzen Tag, um einen einzigen Vers zu schreiben.* It is said that it sometimes took Vergil a whole day to write a single line.

Verse (stanza) = *die Strophe*
　　(poetry) = *die (reimende) Dichtung*

Vesper, die   1. Vespers.   **2.** The word may also denote—esp. in South Germany—a short break for food. *Um drei Uhr haben wir Vesper gemacht.* We took a break at three o'clock. In this sense the word may also be neuter in gender.

Vikar, der   Usually denotes s.o. standing in for a permanently appointed clergyman: a curate. In Swiss German it denotes a substitute teacher (BrE: supply teacher).

Vicar = *der Pfarrer*

Viola, die   Two homonyms.   **1.** (mus.) Viola, though *die Bratsche* is the commoner term.   **2.** Violet (flower): *das Veilchen* is the everyday term.

virtuos   Displaying technical mastery: virtuoso, masterly. *Kein anderer Pianist konnte so virtuos spielen.* No other pianist could give such virtuoso performances/was such a virtuoso.

Virtuous = *tugendhaft*

Visage, die   The words in both languages refer to the human face, but, whereas English "visage" is poetical or archaic in style, the German word is colloquial and derogatory. *Dem werd' ich die Visage polieren, wenn ich ihn wiedersehe.* I'll smash his face/ugly mug in if I see him again.

Visage = *das Antlitz*

vis-à-vis/Visavis, das   As preposition, adverb, or noun this means "(situated, sitting, etc.) opposite" and does not have the most frequent sense of English "vis-à-vis," namely "with regard to." The forms *gegenüber* and *das Gegenüber* are generally preferred nowadays in Germany, though not in Switzerland.

Vis-à-vis (with regard to) = *in bezug auf, bezüglich, hinsichtlich*

Visier, das   1. Visor (of helmet).   **2.** Sight(s) (of a firearm). *Der Jäger hatte ein Wildschwein ins Visier genommen.* The huntsman had trained his sights on a wild boar. Also used metaphorically.

Visitation, die   Visitation, in the sense of an official visit in ecclesiastical contexts. But more commonly, in the compound *Leibesvisitation*, it denotes a body search. *An der Grenze gab es eine sehr gründliche Leibesvisitation.* At the border there was an extremely thorough body search.

Visitation (ghost) = *die Erscheinung*
　　(by disaster, etc.) = *die Heimsuchung*

Visite, die   Visit (dated). Now most commonly used on the "round" of a hospital doctor or "house-call" of a physician. *Herr Dr. Klemenz macht gerade Visite—er müßte in der Entbindungsstation sein.* Dr. Klemenz is making his rounds at the moment—he should be in the maternity ward. Visit = *der Besuch*

vital   Normally denotes energy and activity, esp. in older people. *Trotz ihres hohen Alters ist meine Großmutter immer noch recht vital.* Despite her great age my grandmother is still very energetic/lively/sprightly. Vital (essential) = *unerläßlich, unbedingt notwendig* (necessary for life) = *lebensnotwendig*

Vitamin B, das   **1.** Vitamin B.   **2.** (coll.) With the B standing for *Beziehungen* (= connections, contacts), denotes those useful contacts that can help one to get on or get what one wants. *Ohne Vitamin B kriegt man im Fernsehen keine Stelle.* You won't get a job in TV without contacts.

Vokal, der   Vowel. *Ist Y ein Vokal oder ein Konsonant im Englischen?* Is Y a vowel or a consonant in English?

Vocal(s): *der gesungene Teil eines Liedes/Schlagers* Ricky did the vocals. *Unser Sänger war Ricky.*

Volk, das   **1.** Nation, people. *das deutsche Volk* the German people, nation.   **2.** Crowd, people. *Auf dem Platz war viel Volk.* There were lots of people in the square.   **3.** (pej.) Rabble, crowd. *Mit diesem Volk will ich nichts zu tun haben.* I want nothing to do with that rabble.

Folk (people generally) = *Leute* (pl.)

Volontär, der   S.o. working for little or no pay in order to gain work experience. *Ich war drei Monate bei dieser Zeitung Volontär.* I was a trainee with this newspaper for three months.

Volunteer = *der Freiwillige*

volontieren   To work as a **VOLONTÄR** (Q.V.).

To volunteer (to do s.t.) = *sich freiwillig melden*

vorsehen   The underlying idea is that of "providing for." *Der Plan sieht vor, daß diese Straße in eine Einbahnstraße umgewandelt wird.* The plan provides for this street to be converted into a one-way street. *Weitere Zuschüsse sind nicht vorgesehen.* There is no provision for further subsidies. *Dieser Fonds ist für den neuen Kinderspielplatz vorgesehen.* This fund is earmarked for the new playground. *Daß es so lange nicht regnen würde, hatten wir nicht vorgesehen.* We hadn't allowed for such a long spell without rain. *sich vorsehen* To be careful. *Sieh dich vor!* Be careful/Beware/Take care!

To foresee = *vorhersehen, voraussehen*

Vorsehung, die   Not the act of foreseeing, but "Providence."

Vorsicht, die   Care, caution, prudence. *Als Ihr Anwalt würde ich Ihnen in dieser Situation zur Vorsicht raten.* As your attorney I would advise you to exercise caution in this situation. The single word *Vorsicht!* is commonly used to warn people of possible hazards (e.g., an oncoming car): Look out!/Mind (BrE out)!/Watch out!

Foresight = *der Weitblick*

Waage, die **1.** (Pair of) scales. *Diese billige Waage ist zu ungenau.* These cheap scales are too inaccurate. **2.** The astrological sign Libra (or a person born under this sign). *Meine Schwester ist Waage.* My sister's a Libra.

Wage(s) = *der Lohn*

Wagen, der **1.** Wag(g)on in horse-drawn contexts, but other uses are far more important: **2.** Car, automobile. *Mit dem Wagen brauche ich nur zehn Minuten.* It only takes me ten minutes by car. **3.** Car, coach, BrE carriage, with reference to trains and streetcars. *Der Zug hatte nur zwei Wagen und war hoffnungslos überfüllt.* The train had only two cars, and was hopelessly overcrowded. **4.** Carriage (of typewriter).

der Große Wagen = the Big Dipper/BrE the Plough.

Waggon, der A railroad term: freight car, BrE goods waggon.

Wall, der Earth, stones, etc., piled up, normally for protective purposes: rampart, embankment. *Rund um die Siedlung lag ein Wall aus Erde.* An earth rampart surrounded the settlement.

Wall (esp. internal) = *die Wand*
   (external) = *die Mauer*

walzen **1.** To roll (steel, etc., in a rolling mill; also lawn or other surface with a roller). **2.** (dated) To waltz.

To waltz = *Walzer tanzen*

wälzen **1.** To roll (move s.t. heavy but more or less round). *Wir wälzten das große Faß zur Seite.* We rolled the large barrel to one side. *sich im Bett wälzen* to toss and turn in bed. *sich vor Schmerzen wälzen* to writhe in pain. **2.** To shift (blame, responsibility, etc.). *Du kannst nicht dein Leben lang immer die Schuld auf andere wälzen.* You can't spend your whole life shifting the blame on to other people. **3.** To toss, coat (food in flour, etc.). **4.** (coll.) To study, pore over. *Du wälzt dieses Lexikon schon seit einer Stunde und weißt immer noch nicht, wie viele Einwohner Baden-Baden hat.* You've been poring over that encyclopedia for an hour now and you still don't know how many inhabitants Baden-Baden has. **5.** To think about, turn over in one's mind (a plan, etc.).

To waltz = *Walzer tanzen*

Wand, die   Wall (often internal).

Magic wand = *der Zauberstab*

wandern   1. May mean "to wander," with its connotation of aimlessness.   2. To go walking, hiking, i.e., as a hobby, activity. *Meine Eltern fahren jedes Jahr nach Österreich zum Wandern.* My parents go walking in Austria every year.   3. (coll.) To end up. *Die meisten Briefe wanderten in den Papierkorb.* Most letters ended up in the wastebasket.

To wander (aimlessly) = *umherirren, wandern*

(when shopping) = *bummeln*

Wanderung, die   1. A walk, ramble, hike. SEE **WANDERN**.   2. Migration (of birds, tribes, etc.).

Warenhaus, das   (Department) store. *Bei der Eröffnung des neuen Warenhauses wurden Luftballons an die Kinder verteilt.* When the new store opened balloons were distributed to the children.

Warehouse = *das Lagerhaus*

warm   1. Warm, though in several contexts (e.g., food) "hot" is the better translation. *Kann man abends im 'Waldhorn' warm essen?* Can you get a hot meal at the 'Waldhorn' in the evening?   2. In relation to rent it indicates that heating costs are included in the figure named. *Die Wohnung kostet 1.200 Mark warm.* The rent is 1,200 marks, including heating.

Warmblut, das   Type of horse: a crossbreed (between a thoroughbred, a *Vollblut,* and a carthorse, a *Kaltblut*).

Warm-blooded animal = *der Warmblüter*

Wäsche, die   1. Washing.   2. A collective term for "underwear." *Mir ist es egal, welche Farbe meine Wäsche hat!* I don't care what color my underwear is!

wassern   To land on water (aircraft), splash down (space capsule).

To water (houseplants, etc.) = *gießen*

wässern   1. To water (lawn, fields, etc.; also of eyes).   2. To soak (foodstuffs). *Diese Art Bohnen muß man über Nacht wässern.* You have to soak this sort of beans overnight.

To water (houseplants, etc.) = *gießen*

Watt, das   Watt (electrical unit): plural *Watt.*

There is a homonym (pl.: *Watten*) meaning "mud-flat," of the sort found, for example, on Germany's North Sea coast.

Weg, der   1. Way, in various contexts.   2. Path, track. *Es war leicht, dem Weg durch den Wald zu folgen.* It was easy to follow the path through the forest.

Weib, das   (Old) woman. *Auf dem Jahrmarkt sagte mir ein altes Weib, daß ich Zwillinge bekommen würde.* At the fair an old woman predicted that I would have twins. The word is often used in a pejorative manner. *Ich* *kann es nicht verstehen, daß er sich mit diesem Weib eingelassen hat.* I can't understand him getting involved with that woman.

Wife = *die (Ehe)frau*

weil   Because.

While (conj.) = *während*

Wein, der   **1.** Wine.   **2.** The plant or fruit from which it is derived: vines; grapes. *Das Gewitter hat den Wein stark beschädigt.* The storm has seriously damaged the vines. *Der Wein muß noch in dieser Woche geerntet werden.* The grapes must be harvested this week.

weinen   To cry, weep. *Sie weint immer, wenn sie dieses Lied hört.* She cries whenever she hears this song.

To whine (child) = *quengeln*

(dog) = *jaulen*

Welle, die   **1.** Wave (of sea; also radio, etc.).   **2.** (tech.) Shaft (for transmitting rotary motion). *Kardanwelle* drive shaft, of a car.

Well (for water) = *der Brunnen*

wellen   **1.** To wave (hair).   **2.** To corrugate (sheet metal). *das Wellblech* corrugated iron.

To well up (water) = *emporsteigen*

(emotion) = *aufsteigen*

(tears in eyes) = *in die Augen steigen*

welsch   **1.** A rather dated term to denote—usually pejoratively—"Latin," i.e., Southern European ways and manners.   **2.** (Sw.) The French-speaking part of Switzerland (without any value judgment). *die welsche Schweiz* French(-speaking) Switzerland.

Welsh (adj.) = *walisisch*

wenn   May mean "if" or "when(ever)," according to the context. *Wenn ich Zeit hätte, würde ich auf Urlaub fahren.* If I had time I'd take a vacation. *(Jedesmal) wenn ich sie besuchte, saß sie vor dem Fernseher.* When(ever) I visited her she was sitting in front of the TV.

When (referring to a single action in the past) = *als*

werken/Werken, das   (To do) handicrafts. *Werken gefällt mir nicht besonders.* I don't enjoy handicrafts particularly.

To work (person) = *arbeiten*

(machine) = *funktionieren*

Weste, die   Vest, BrE waistcoat: the sleeveless garment worn under the jacket of a suit. *kugelsichere Weste* Bullet-proof vest; *Schwimmweste* Life vest, life jacket; *Strickweste* sweater vest, BrE sleeveless cardigan.

BrE Vest (AmE undershirt) = *das Unterhemd*

Wicke, die   Vetch (bot.).

Wick = *der Docht*

wild   Wild. There are of course various collocations where other translations will be needed, e.g., *ein wilder Stamm* a savage tribe; *ein wilder Bart* an unkempt beard. One particular meaning foreign to English "wild" is that of illegality, lack of authorization: *wildes Parken* illegal parking; *wilder Streik* wildcat/unofficial strike; *in wilder Ehe leben* to live together without being married/"in sin." *halb so wild/nicht so wild* Not so bad/dreadful. *Zum Zahnarzt gehen—das ist doch heutzutage halb so wild.* Going to the dentist isn't so bad nowadays.

Wild, das   Game (animals, meat). *Ich esse nicht so gern Wild.* I'm not that keen on game. *der Wildpark* game park (or specifically, deer park).

In the wild = *in der Wildnis/in freier Wildbahn*

Wimpel, der   Small flag: pennant. *Wegen des Turniers waren alle Tennisplätze mit Wimpeln geschmückt.* Because of the tournament all the tennis courts were decorated with pennants/bunting.

Wimple (of nun) = *der (Nonnen)schleier*

(medieval) = *die Rise*

Wimper, die   (Eye)lash. *Sie hat so lange Wimpern—sind die echt?* She's got such long lashes—are they natural?

Whimper (dog) = *das Winseln*

(person) = *das Wimmern*

winden   To wind, bind, in the sense of coiling parts together. *sich winden* To writhe (in agony, etc.); to squirm (with embarrassment, etc.). *Eine halbe Stunde nachdem sie die Austern gegessen hatte, wand sie sich vor Schmerzen.* Half an hour after eating the oysters she was writhing in agony.

To wind (watch, etc.) = *aufziehen*

(tape on to reel) = *spulen*

windig   1. Windy.   2. (coll.) Not trustworthy, dubious. *Dieser windige Geschäftsmann ist wegen Betrugs schon zweimal vorbestraft.* This dubious businessman has two previous convictions for fraud.

Wink, der   1. A signal given by means of some sort of body language, a wave of the hand, nod of the head, etc. *Ein Wink (mit dem Kopf) genügte, um die Polizisten zu alarmieren.* A signal (nod) was enough to alert the policemen.   2. (fig.) Hint, tip. *Das Buch enthält allerlei nützliche Winke für den Heimwerker.* The book contains all sorts of useful tips for the do-it-yourself enthusiast. More common are *der Tip* and *der Hinweis.*

To give s.o. a wink = *jemandem zuzwinkern/zublinzeln*

Winkel, der   1. Corner (of room, etc.; also figuratively for a remote place). *In einem dunklen Winkel des Zimmers kauerten zwei kleine Kinder.* Two small children were crouching in a dark corner of the room.   2. Angle (geom.). *spitzer/stumpfer Winkel* acute/obtuse angle. *toter Winkel* Blind spot (e.g., in car mirror).

Winkle (shellfish) = *die Strandschnecke*

winken To signal, wave, beckon. SEE **WINK**. *Ich winkte dem Kellner.* I signaled/beckoned to the waiter.

To wink (at s.o.) = *(jdm.) zuzwinkern/zublinzeln*

Wippe, die Seesaw. *Auf dem Kinderspielplatz gibt es jetzt eine Wippe.* There's a seesaw in the playground now.

Whip = *die Peitsche*

wippen Movement to and fro is the basic idea: to rock/bob up and down, to seesaw, to sway—the exact translation will depend on the context. *Die Kinder benutzten das alte Brett zum Wippen.* The children used the old plank to seesaw on. *Der Junge hatte Langeweile und wippte auf den Füßen.* The boy was bored and rocked up and down on his feet. *Dieses Wippen mit den Hüften hält sie wohl für sexy.* I suppose she thinks that it's sexy to swing her hips like that.

To whip (horse, etc.) = *peitschen*
        (person) = *auspeitschen*
        (cream, etc.) = *schlagen*

wirken **1.** An unusual and formal expression for "to work" (in a profession). More usual meanings: **2.** To have an effect, be effective; work (of drugs, etc.). *Sein Lachen wirkte immer aufheiternd.* His laugh always had a cheerful effect. *Die neuesten Antibiotika wirken besonders schnell.* The latest antibiotics work especially quickly. **3.** To appear, seem. *Soviel ich weiß, hat er keine Probleme, aber er wirkt immer deprimiert.* As far as I know he hasn't got any problems, but he always seems depressed.

To work (person) = *arbeiten*
       (machine) = *funktionieren*

wischen To wipe.

To wish = *wünschen*

Witz, der **1.** Wit. **2.** Joke. *Hoffentlich fängt er nicht an, seine blöden Witze zu erzählen.* Let's hope he doesn't start telling his stupid jokes.

witzig According to the context this may mean "witty" or simply "funny." *Ich finde es nicht sehr witzig, daß ich eine Stunde im Regen auf dich warten mußte.* I don't think it's very funny that I had to wait an hour for you in the rain.

Witty (also) = *geistreich*

wobei When used as a conjunction, this often indicates a contrast between two statements. *In letzter Zeit arbeitet er in der Tat sehr schlecht, wobei man bedenken muß, daß seine Tochter vor einem Monat an Krebs gestorben ist.* It's true he's been doing bad work recently, though you have to remember that his daughter died of cancer a month ago.

Whereby = *wodurch/durch (den/die/das)* This is the policy whereby we shall achieve better results. *Das ist die Politik, durch die wir bessere Ergebnisse erzielen werden.*

wohl Only occasionally corresponds to "well," e.g., with reference to health (*ich fühle mich wohl*—though this is ambiguous: see 1 below). More typical are the following uses: **1.** Happy, at ease. *Ich habe mich in diesem Land nie wohl gefühlt.* I've never felt happy in this country. **2.** Probably. *Er wird wohl zurücktreten müssen.* He'll probably have to re-sign.

Wohl is a typical German particle whose precise meaning depends very much on the context and which in some cases may have no real English translation.

Well (in a good manner) = *gut* You've worked well. *Sie haben gut gearbeitet.*

Wolf, der **1.** Wolf. **2.** Short for *Fleischwolf* = grinder (BrE mincer) or *Reißwolf* = shredder. *So zähes Fleisch drehe ich immer durch den Wolf.* I always put meat as tough as this through the grinder. *Alle belastenden Akten wurden durch den Wolf gejagt.* All incriminating files were put through the shredder. **3.** (coll.) An inflammation of the skin between the buttocks (from cycling, etc.).

wollen The singular of the present tense (*will/willst/will*) is misleading: it normally means "want to," not "will" (as an indicator of the future in English). *Ich will diese Frau heiraten.* I want to marry this woman.

Will: The future in German is formed with *werden* (or the present tense is used if the future meaning is clear from the context).

wund Sore, of skin, through chafing, rubbing, etc. *Die wunden Stellen an den Füßen habe ich mit dieser Salbe eingerieben.* I rubbed this ointment on to the sore parts of my feet. Also used metaphorically to indicate great effort, activity, as in such phrases as *sich die Finger wund schreiben/ telefonieren. Ich habe mir die Finger wund telefoniert, bis ich alle Eltern erreicht habe.* I'd worn my fingers out telephoning by the time I'd reached all the parents.

Wounded = *verwundet*

Wunder, das **1.** Wonder, miracle, marvel, i.e., s.t. surprising. *Das ist ein Wunder, daß Otto auch mal geholfen hat.* It's a wonder/miracle that Otto helped for once. *Kein Wunder!* No wonder! *die sieben Weltwunder* the Seven Wonders of the World. **2.** Miracle (in the divine or supernatural sense). *Sie hält es für ein Wunder, daß ihr Sohn 100 Meter gestürzt ist und nicht getötet wurde.* She thinks it is a miracle that her son fell 100 meters and was not killed.

Wonder (sense of awe) = *die Verwunderung, das Staunen*

wunderbar/wunderlich/wundersam Of these three adjectives, only *wunderbar* means "wonderful." *Wunderlich* means "strange," "odd." *Wundersam* is hardly used in the standard language today and corresponds in meaning and stylistic register to "wondrous."

Wonderful = *wunderschön, wunderbar*

wundern To surprise; (impersonal, reflexive) to be surprised. *Es hat mich gewundert, daß du nicht angerufen hast.* I was surprised that you didn't ring. *Wundere dich nicht, wenn du im Examen durchfällst!* Don't be surprised if you fail the exam.

To wonder (ask oneself) = *sich fragen*

Z

Zelle, die Cell. Also short for *Telefonzelle:* phone booth/box.

zensieren **1.** To censor (book, film, etc.) **2.** To give a grade/mark for a piece of work. SEE **ZENSUR.** *Ich habe eure Hausaufgaben durchgesehen aber noch nicht zensiert.* I've looked through your homework, but I haven't graded it yet.

To censure = *tadeln*

Zensur, die **1.** Censorship. *Dieses Buch kommt nie durch die Zensur.* This book will never get past the censors. **2.** Grade, mark. *In der letzten Zeit bekommt Konrad bessere Zensuren in Englisch.* Konrad has been getting better English grades lately.

Censer (relig.) = *das (Weih)rauchfaß*

Censor = *der Zensor*

Censure = *der Tadel*

Zentrale, die **1.** Head office, headquarters (of firm, party, etc.; also the office from which a taxi service is run and directed). **2.** (Telephone) switchboard. *Ich verbinde Sie mit unserer Zentrale.* I'll put you through to our switchboard.

Center = *das Zentrum*

Central (adj.) = *zentral*

zimperlich **1.** Excessively sensitive, squeamish. *Sei nicht so zimperlich— es blutet ja fast gar nicht.* Don't be so squeamish—it's hardly bleeding at all. Often used in the negative when a tough attitude to s.t. is being proposed. *Mit diesen Rowdys darf man nicht zimperlich umgehen.* It's no good being soft with these hooligans. **2.** Prudish, prissy.

Simpering (coy, affected) = *geziert, affektiert*

To simper (smile affectedly) = *geziert lächeln*

Zinke, die Prong, tine (of fork); tooth (of comb).

Zinc = *das Zink*

zinken To mark (cards). *Diese Karten sind gezinkt!* These cards are marked! To zinc (i.e., cover with zinc, galvanize) = *verzinken*

Zinn, das 1. Tin (raw material). 2. The alloy known as pewter. *Er sammelt solche Trinkgefäße aus Zinn.* He collects this sort of pewter drinking vessel.
BrE Tin (container for food, etc.; AmE can) = *die Dose, die Büchse*

Zirkel, der 1. Circle (in particular of people with a shared interest). 2. (A pair of) compasses.
Circle (shape; also of people who meet) = *der Kreis*

Zirkus, der 1. Circus. 2. (fig.) Fuss. *So ein Zirkus wegen zehn Mark!* All this fuss about ten marks!

zitieren 1. To quote, cite. *Er zitiert dauernd aus der Bibel.* He's always quoting from the Bible. *Ich kann mehrere Beispiele zitieren.* I can cite several examples. 2. To summon (with the negative connotation of being called to account). *Er wurde vor Gericht zitiert.* He was summoned to appear before the court.
To cite (in divorce case) = *nennen*

zivil 1. Civil, in certain collocations. *ziviler Ungehorsam* civil disobedience; *ziviler Bevölkerungsschutz* civil defense. 2. Not military, civilian. *Die Rückkehr zum zivilen Leben fiel ihm schwer.* He found the return to civilian life difficult. 3. (coll.) Reasonable, acceptable, civilized. *Hier kann man gut essen und die Preise sind ganz zivil.* You can get a good meal here and the prices are perfectly reasonable.
Civil (polite) = *höflich*
Civil war = *der Bürgerkrieg*

Zivil, das Nonmilitary clothing: most commonly used in the phrase *in Zivil* = in civilian clothing (of soldiers)/in plain clothes (of police).
Civil (polite) = *höflich*
Civil war = *der Bürgerkrieg*

Zivilcourage, die Not "civil courage" or "civilian courage," but the courage s.o. displays when he or she stands up for (and speaks up for) his or her beliefs or principles, without fear of possible consequences: the "courage of one's convictions." *Er hat die Umweltpolitik der eigenen Firma gerügt—das zeugt von Zivilcourage.* He criticized the environmental policy of his own firm—that shows that he's not afraid to speak his mind/ stand up for what he believes in.

Zone, die Zone. Also used, esp. by older people, to refer to what used to be East Germany (i.e., the old Soviet zone: *sowjetische Besatzungszone*). *Einmal im Monat fuhr ich in die Zone, um meine Schwester zu besuchen.* Once a month I used to travel to the East/East Germany to visit my sister.

Zylinder, der 1. Cylinder. 2. In older or ceremonial contexts: a top hat, silk hat. *Aus Spaß habe ich einen Zylinder getragen.* I wore a top hat for the fun of it.

NTC'S LANGUAGE DICTIONARIES

The Best, By Definition

Spanish/English
Vox New College (Thumb-index & Plain-edge)
Vox Modern
Vox Compact
Vox Everyday
Vox Traveler's
Vox Super-Mini
Cervantes-Walls

Spanish/Spanish
Diccionario Básico Norteamericano
Vox Diccionario Escolar de la lengua española
El Diccionario del español chicano

French/English
NTC's New College French and English
NTC's Dictionary of *Faux Amis*
NTC's Dictionary of Canadian French

German/English
Schöffler-Weis
Klett's Modern (New Edition)
Klett's Super-Mini
NTC's Dictionary of German False Cognates

Italian/English
Zanichelli New College Italian and English
Zanichelli Super-Mini

Greek/English
NTC's New College Greek and English

Chinese/English
Easy Chinese Phrasebook and Dictionary

For Juveniles
Let's Learn English Picture Dictionary
Let's Learn French Picture Dictionary
Let's Learn German Picture Dictionary
Let's Learn Italian Picture Dictionary
Let's Learn Spanish Picture Dictionary
English Picture Dictionary
French Picture Dictionary
German Picture Dictionary
Spanish Picture Dictionary

English for Nonnative Speakers
Everyday American English Dictionary
Beginner's Dictionary of American English Usage

Electronic Dictionaries
Languages of the World on CD-ROM
NTC's Dictionary of American Idioms, Slang, and
  Colloquial Expressions (Electronic Book)

Other Reference Books
Robin Hyman's Dictionary of Quotations
British/American Language Dictionary
NTC's American Idioms Dictionary
NTC's Dictionary of American Slang and
  Colloquial Expressions
Forbidden American English
Essential American Idioms
Contemporary American Slang
NTC's Dictionary of Grammar Terminology
Complete Multilingual Dictionary of Computer
  Terminology
Complete Multilingual Dictionary of Aviation &
  Aeronautical Terminology
Complete Multilingual Dictionary of Advertising,
  Marketing & Communications
NTC's Dictionary of American Spelling
NTC's Classical Dictionary
NTC's Dictionary of Debate
NTC's Mass Media Dictionary
NTC's Dictionary of Word Origins
NTC's Dictionary of Literary Terms
Dictionary of Trade Name Origins
Dictionary of Advertising
Dictionary of Broadcast Communications
Dictionary of Changes in Meaning
Dictionary of Confusing Words and Meanings
NTC's Dictionary of English Idioms
NTC's Dictionary of Proverbs and Clichés
Dictionary of Acronyms and Abbreviations
NTC's Dictionary of American English
  Pronunciation
NTC's Dictionary of Phrasal Verbs and Other
  Idiomatic Verbal Phrases
Common American Phrases

Polish/English
The Wiedza Powszechna Compact Polish and
  English Dictionary

For further information or a current catalog, write:
National Textbook Company
a division of *NTC Publishing Group*
4255 West Touhy Avenue
Lincolnwood, Illinois 60646-1975 U.S.A.